PASSOVOTCHKA

BY THE SAME AUTHOR

The Devil's Virtuosos:
German Generals at War 1940–5

The Moscow Option:
An Alternative Second World War

An Atlas of Territorial Border Disputes

Russian Revolution 1985

Marlon Brando

The Red Eagles

A Dreamer of Pictures – Neil Young:
The Man and His Music

PASSOVOTCHKA

Moscow Dynamo in Britain, 1945

David Downing

BLOOMSBURY

First published 1999
This paperback edition published 2000

Bloomsbury Publishing Plc, 38 Soho Square, London W1V 5DF

A CIP catalogue record for this book is available from the British Library

ISBN 0 7475 4813 7

10 9 8 7 6 5 4 3 2 1

Typeset by Hewer Text Composition Services, Edinburgh
Printed in Great Britain by Clays Ltd, St Ives Plc

PICTURE SOURCES

Hulton Deutsch: pages 1 *top*, 2
Solo Syndication: pages 1 *bottom*, 3, 4, 5, 6, 7, 8 *top*
Topham Picturepoint: page 8 *bottom*

CONTENTS

Author's note

I came across the story of this tour, of which I had previously been in utter ignorance, while researching another subject. I found myself caught in its spell, and the more I delved, the more interested I became. This, it soon became clear, was more than a half-forgotten chapter of football history. It was fascinating from a purely footballing point of view, but it was other things as well: a mirror held up to the immediate post-war world in its entirety, a series of glimpses into the future.

Getting at the truth of the tour was easier imagined than done. The four matches which lay at its heart were not broadcast on the fledgling BBC Television service, and the surviving British News footage only covered a few minutes of the action from the Cardiff and Glasgow Rangers matches. The BBC Radio Home Service did broadcast live second-half coverage of the Chelsea, Arsenal and Rangers fixtures, but here again only a few minutes of commentary survived from each match.

Many of the participants later recorded their impressions for posterity, and others of course are still alive, but the objectivity of the former was all too often affected by the attitudes of the Cold War, and the memories of the latter, after more than half a century, are also apt to contradict each other. The newspaper reports of the day are still there to peruse, but there is no objective record by which to judge their accuracy, and when they disagree, as they often do, I have been obliged to fit the various pieces of the jigsaw together with an, I hope, judicious mix of common sense and educated guesswork.

In the matter of Russian names, I have simply stuck to the most common spellings used by the British press at the time of the tour. I have also remained faithful to 'Moscow Dynamo', even though 'Dinamo Moscow' would today be the preferred transliteration. Like the papers of the time I have used 'Soviet' and 'Russian' almost interchangeably; Moscow Dynamo is, after all, a Russian team in the same way that Arsenal is an English team, regardless of the various nationalities represented on the playing staff.

I would like to thank the staffs at the British Newspaper Library, the British Film Institute and the National Sound Archives, Jim Riordan at the University of Surrey, Iain Cooke at the Arsenal Museum, and Richard Shepherd, Cardiff City's unofficial historian, for their assistance. I would particularly like to express my gratitude to the three former Cardiff City players – Arthur 'Buller' Lever, Fred Stansfield and Ken Hollyman – who gave up their time to talk to me. They were not only mines of information, they were a real pleasure to meet.

April 1999
David Downing

1

The Russians are coming

In the autumn of 1945 it was not unusual to find groups of dark-suited and snap-brim-hatted Russians occupying large blocks of seats in London's premier football grounds. The war in Europe had been over for only six months, and requests for tickets from the Soviet Embassy were regularly acceded to in that spirit of friendship and gratitude which still typified the popular attitude towards Britain's wartime ally.

These groups of Russians, recognisable by their strange-smelling cigarettes and guttural accents, were usually made up of football-loving Soviet officials who just happened to be in Britain for one reason or another, but one Russian who attended the game between Chelsea and West Ham at Stamford Bridge on 13 October had more than just an afternoon's entertainment on his mind. His name was Revenko, he had recently arrived in London as an emissary of the Soviet Sports Minister, and on that particular afternoon he was sitting next to Football Association Secretary Stanley Rous in the Chelsea directors' box.

At some point during the game one or other of these two men suggested that the time might finally be ripe for the visit of a Soviet club team to Britain. If, as seems likely, it was Rous who took the initiative, then Revenko's response was certainly enthusiastic. After discussing the invitation with his superiors at the Embassy he dispatched a telegram to Moscow, and was soon reporting back to Rous that the Soviet capital's Dynamo club, which had recently won their league championship, was probably available for such a tour. The FA Secretary was sufficiently encouraged by this to book Chelsea provisionally for a match on 31 October, but no announcement was made to the press: experience had apparently taught Rous not to count on a fixture with a foreign club before formal agreement had been reached.

The news of a tour finally seeped out on 23 October. 'I learned yesterday,' the football correspondent of the *Daily Worker* proclaimed, 'that a Soviet soccer team – probably Moscow Dynamo – will arrive in Britain this weekend.' They would definitely play Chelsea, and probably Arsenal too. 'Last month,' the correspondent added, taking the first few steps along that epic trail of factual errors which would so characterise the tour, Dynamo had 'again run out champions of the USSR by winning the Soviet Cup Final'.

The first invitation to the Soviets had probably been issued as early as April. A London v. Moscow game at Wembley, with proceeds to the Aid to Russia Fund, was mooted, and the Prime Minister's wife, in Moscow on other business at the time, acted as an unofficial facilitator for the FA. That particular plan fell through, but the possibility of future matches was greatly enhanced, not least because the expressions of goodwill on both sides helped to erase the memory of Soviet visits banned by British governments in the 1930s.

With the European war over, and troops from East and West stationed in the German and Austrian capitals, representative games between the Allied armies became an obvious possibility, and on 30 September, two weeks before Comrade Revenko's visit to Chelsea, a Red Army team met a British Services XI in Berlin. The Russians won 2–0, and a re-match was scheduled for 7 October. Other significant victories followed for Red Army teams, against a French XI in Berlin and another British XI in Vienna: the Soviets were clearly interested in playing against foreigners in general and the British in particular. The latter's high standing in the football world owed more to memory than to present reality: the Russians, like many of their fellow Europeans, were still showing exaggerated respect for the originators of the organised game. One British officer tried for weeks to arrange a fixture with nearby Russian troops in occupied Germany, but was continually frustrated by postponements as the Russian corps commander sought to ensure his team was good enough. Satisfied at last, the latter warned his players how hard they would find the coming match. 'All Englishmen are born footballers,' he told them. 'For generations they have done nothing but practise sport.'

The re-match arranged for 7 October apparently fell victim to Russian nerves. The British had selected, among others, three famous Arsenal stars in Eddie Hapgood, Bernard Joy and Leslie Compton, and the Russians clearly took fright. They asked for a postponement until the 19th, claiming that they needed the extra time to gather a stronger side, but the rescheduled fixture was then cancelled in its turn. So many players had been demobilised, a Soviet official claimed, that he couldn't find a team.

This apparent Soviet reluctance to believe in the quality of their footballers was, at least in part, the product of thirty years spent in virtual sporting isolation. Those few outside observers who had seen Soviet teams in action over the previous couple of years had been more impressed. The word was that something might be brewing in football's eastern borderlands.

Ivan Montagu of the *Daily Worker*, who watched the Red Army's win over British opposition in Berlin, was struck by the Russians' clever positional play and individual skill. 'They are very fit and play in the classic Corinthian style,' he wrote, launching two refrains which would be much heard in the coming weeks. An NCO in the Royal Corps of Signals reported seeing Moscow Dynamo beat Iran's best club team 5–0 in Tehran. Home on leave, he told the *Evening Standard* that the Russians were 'magnificent footballers. If you did not know they were Russians,' he added, with an arrogance as breathtaking as it was unconscious, 'you would imagine you were watching an English or Scottish team.'

When it came to football, British delusions of grandeur were every bit as common as Soviet delusions of inferiority. And rather harder to justify, based as they were on little more than highly selective memory and abysmal ignorance. As the British press was to demonstrate amply during the build-up to the tour, its collective knowledge of Soviet football could be written on the back of a Fleet Street beer-mat.

On the day following the conversation between Rous and Revenko at Stamford Bridge, the Soviet Cup Final had been played in Moscow. The only British paper to mention the fact, Sunday's *Reynolds News*, merely noted that the game between Moscow Dynamo and Central House of the Red Army was expected to draw the biggest crowd in Soviet soccer history. The Dynamos were in London less than three weeks later, but that didn't stop a story later gaining currency that they had undergone a month of special training in the Caucasus mountains in preparation for their British tour.

In matter of fact, they had spent a couple of weeks in the Caucasian region of Abkhazia before the Soviet season began in late April. This fact, along with many others, could have been discovered by any British diplomat or journalist in Moscow, where the English-language *Moscow News* was easily available. A regular peruser of that bi-weekly paper could have followed the Soviet season in some detail. He would have seen Moscow Torpedo and Central House of the Red Army sharing the league lead for the first month or so, and then watched Moscow Dynamo gradually overhaul first the one and then the other. He would have known that between sixty and seventy thousand spectators were turning up to fairly humdrum games: football was clearly booming in the post-war Soviet Union, as it was in post-war Britain.

The *Moscow News* reader would not have noticed the names of many individual players – the cult of collectivism was still fairly strong in Soviet team sports – but there was one in particular that he could hardly have missed: Vsevolod Bobrov, already touted as one of the best young ice hockey players in the Soviet Union, had made his league début as a substitute in Central House's opening game against Moscow Lokomotiv, and scored a hat-trick in fifteen minutes. Throughout the season his successful striking partnership with Grigori Fedotov, then the Soviet Union's best-known player, had provided the main reason for Central House's excellent record – with thirty-nine points from twenty-two games, they finished only one point behind Dynamo – and by the end of the season he had established a new goal-scoring record for the Soviet league, scoring twenty-four times.

In the cup, Central House went one better, beating

Moscow Dynamo on a snow-cleared pitch before a packed Dynamo Stadium. With 80,000 inside and thousands more locked out, left-winger Sergei Soloviev scored an early goal for Dynamo, only for Bobrov to equalise on the stroke of half-time. In the second half Dynamo keeper Alexei Khomich made several wonderful saves to keep his side in the game, and when Vassili Kartsev was tripped in the area it looked as though a league–cup double was on. But Leonid Soloviev's penalty rebounded off a post and Vinogradov scored Central House's winner fifteen minutes from time. All those named – with the exception of Vinogradov – would figure prominently in the coming tour: Bobrov would score crucial goals, Leonid Soloviev would miss another crucial penalty and Khomich would make many astonishing saves.

One thing unfortunately missing from the *Moscow News* report of the final was a listing of the Dynamo team. Their victorious opponents were listed, and the fact that only Bobrov of the Central House team would appear in Britain gave a lie to the notion that the touring Dynamos were a Soviet Union XI in disguise, but the actual make-up of the Dynamo team that played through the 1945 Soviet season was and would remain a matter of surmise and guesswork for their British hosts.

For the British press and the British football authorities none of this seemed to matter. There is no indication that any of the nation's football journalists thought to tap their Moscow-based foreign correspondent colleagues for information, and the latter doubtless considered such proletarian matters too far beneath them to volunteer any. In any case, most of them were far too busy misunderstanding what was happening in their own supposed areas of expertise. The newspapers of late 1945, as is now almost comically evident, were not noted for the depth of their insights into the way the Soviet Union worked.

So, deprived of any real information about the Soviet season which had just finished, yet facing the imminent arrival of the Soviet league champions, Britain's football journalists were reduced to waffling and mostly inaccurate guesswork. The day before the Dynamos arrived the *Evening Standard* produced an 'information box', which tied together a few disconnected facts and a few bland generalisations. It claimed, quite wrongly, that British sailors had introduced soccer to Russia in 1902, and then offered readers two meaningless statistics: in 1935 there had been 6 million footballers in the USSR, and a year later 2 million citizens had applied for tickets to an international match. As for the Soviets' footballing pedigree . . . well, in 1935 a touring Ukrainian side had beaten Paris Red Star 6–1 in France. In the USSR they played football all year round except when the grounds were frozen, and Soviet youth had 'gone so crazy about it that they took very little interest in anything else'.

There wasn't much here on what to expect from Moscow Dynamo. What style of football did they play? The Red Army team Montagu had watched in Berlin had not employed a third back, but according to the *Evening News* the Dynamos did, with the two wing-halves playing well up with the forwards. The *Standard* agreed but the *Star* went one further, claiming that Dynamo played four at the back and two centre-forwards. The *Star* even named names: leading scorer Kartsev was the nominal inside-right and *de facto* second centre-forward, Blinkov the nominal right-half who covered the centre of the field in front of the back four. This sounded like a 4–2–4 formation, unheard of at the time, but the *Star* made nothing of it. The Russians might prove either naive or eccentric, but no one was expecting a tactical revolution.

The *Daily Worker*, on Tuesday 30 October, was the first paper to give a rundown of the team as a whole, under the headline 'Moscow Dynamo's Team of Stars'. The mood of the piece was relentlessly chatty, as if the writer was doing his best to convince his readership that this was just another bunch of lads, no different in essence from any British football team. 'At least half the side are especially beloved in the Soviet Union,' the writer claimed, 'and rank in public esteem as highly as Stanley Matthews, Tommy Lawton and Frank Swift do over here. As over here, the fans love to find a good nickname for their particular favourites, and three of the Dynamo side sport names which will without doubt catch on over here.' Goalkeeper Alexei Khomich had apparently been dubbed 'Tiger' by Red Army men in Iran for his springy leaps, left-half Leonid Soloviev was 'Snowy' for his pale blond hair, and Konstantin Beskov was 'the Bombardier' for his all-out assaults on goal. Leonid Soloviev was also known as Russia's 'penalty king', or at least he had been until his catastrophic miss in the Soviet Cup Final. At least none of them was called 'Psycho'.

The two full-backs, Vsevolod Radikorsky and Ivan Stankevich, were said to be great friends on and off the pitch. Both were 'very correct players', whatever that meant, but Stankevich was faster. Mikhail Semichastny was introduced as 'Russia's Stan Cullis' – a reference to the Wolves and England stopper centre-half – but right-half Blinkov didn't even get a mention. Both inside-forwards were 'pretty well ideal . . . great schemers and powerful shots'. Vassili Kartsev was considered a 'virtuoso of the game', Nikolai Dementiev a 'master of the game', a 'wee slight lad' with great stamina. Sergei Soloviev, the faster of two fast wingers, liked wandering infield for a shot, while 'short, thickset' Vassili Trofimov was hard to dispossess and had once, on a particularly cold day, played with a nightcap on his head. What a scamp! the writer seemed to be saying. What a bunch of lads!

Investigative journalism doesn't seem to have played much part in this piece, which probably originated in the Soviet Embassy. Nine days later the London-published *Soviet Weekly* would run a slightly expanded version of the same article, in which the full-backs were both handsome and veteran internationals, Semichastny the oldest man in the team, and Dementiev possessed of a boyish figure. Blinkov managed to get a line to himself – 'the right-half is a player whose outstanding quality is his uncanny knack of getting in his opponent's way and staying there' – without actually being named.

While the British football press was displaying its ignorance of Soviet football, the football-going public waited patiently for the Russians to arrive. Two days after the initial announcement, on Thursday 25 October, the *Daily Mail* noted that a 'puzzling silence' now surrounded the expected tour, and over the following ten days rumours and counter-rumours took the place of hard news. Tottenham had invited the Russians to watch them play Swansea on Saturday 27 October, and had joined Chelsea in expressing a willingness to play against them. On the Friday, 'official Soviet circles' were telling the *Mirror* that Dynamo – the 'runners-up in the USSR football championship' – though definitely coming, would not be in England until the following week. Stanley Rous chimed in with the news that the invitation had been extended to any Russian team, and that the Soviet Embassy had no idea if anyone had left for London. That evening the London

Evening News confidently claimed that it was Moscow Torpedo who were the likely visitors, not Moscow Dynamo.

There was still no solid news on the Saturday; in the *Daily Sketch* L. V. Manning now believed that the Russians were only coming to watch and learn, as part of their preparations for a full international between England and the Soviet Union in the coming spring. Alluding to the very real possibility of industrial action, he added, 'Tough if they arrive with a players' strike on. Meantime, if you see any Russians stamping the snow off their football boots, ring up Paddington 0377.' Other papers erroneously and variously reported that Dynamo were arriving in a few hours, were coming on Monday as part of a Soviet delegation to the World Youth Conference, were not coming at all. Central House were coming instead, according to the Soviet Tass news agency, who should have known better.

By Monday Reuters were claiming the trip was imminent, but by Wednesday it had been postponed until the following week. According to the *Mirror* the delay in Dynamo's departure was 'due to the difficulty in obtaining the release of players from factories where some hold high executive positions'. The *Daily Worker* concurred; the delay had been 'occasioned because of the nature of the jobs the members of the team have in the Soviet Union. Some of them are key men in important industrial undertakings and there has been a little difficulty in securing their release.' This was about as credible as the notion of Tottenham postponing a game on account of David Ginola's modelling commitments, but British ignorance of how football was run in the Soviet Union was even more complete than British ignorance of how the Soviets played the game, and such statements were simply taken at face value.

Later that same day the *Evening News* passed on Moscow Radio's announcement that Dynamo had left for England and would arrive on the following day, 1 November. They would probably stay in the UK for two weeks. The Central House team, meanwhile, was on its way to Yugoslavia.

Thursday came and went with no sign of Russian footballers. According to some works of football reference, Moscow Dynamo stopped off *en route* to England for the purpose of playing the Swedish side FC Norrköping; according to others, they broke the return journey for the same reason. All are agreed on the score – Dynamo are said to have won 5–0, which in itself would have represented a considerable achievement. Norrköping dominated Swedish football at that time, and were soon to sell several of their players to top Italian clubs.

If the game did take place in 1945 then it seems more likely that such a comprehensive victory would have been won before the Russians added an exhausting British tour to an exhausting Soviet season, but it seems even more probable that football historians have simply got their tours mixed up – Dynamo definitely toured Sweden and played Norrköping in 1947 – and have collectively contrived to create a false memory. The Swedish FA has no record of such a match in 1945, and there was no mention of it in any of the then-current British daily or Sunday newspapers.

If they weren't in Sweden, warming up for the English, where were they? Probably still in Moscow, waiting for the weather to clear, as several papers claimed on the Friday. There seemed no doubt that they were coming: on the previous day a Moscow radio station had spent £92 on a phone call to Chelsea – Fulham 3321 had been engaged for twenty-three minutes as some eager scribe in the Soviet capital jotted down Chelsea club history and player biographies.

At Stamford Bridge they were certainly assuming the tour was on: office staff were working overtime on preparations for a game on the 7th. A place to stand on the terraces would cost 1/6, a seat in the grandstand either 5/6 or 10/-, and since there wasn't enough time for application and distribution by post everyone would have to queue. Other clubs thought likely to host the Russians at this stage were all from the Third Division South: Bournemouth or Port Vale on the 10th and Cardiff on the 17th.

Despite hopeful headlines – 'Soviet Soccer Aces Fly Here Today' in the *Mirror*, 'Dynamo will arrive at Croydon at 3 p.m. today' in the *News Chronicle* – there was no arrival on the Friday, just more titbits of information about the putative tourists. The party would be led by trainer Mikhail Yakushin, and would include sixteen players, a masseur and a doctor. Saturday brought more bad-weather excuses and news that the game against Chelsea on the 7th had been postponed. The *Star*, for lack of anything better to say, decided that there was 'Danger Of Dynamo Tour Losing Interest'. It had been 'in the air for weeks', the paper lamented. It was becoming 'like a much publicised and much postponed heavyweight fight'.

On Sunday 4 November they finally arrived. FA Secretary Rous had only a few hours' notice of the event, and spent them scurrying round London organising transport from Northolt and trying to book satisfactory accommodation in a city desperately short of hotel beds. The welcoming party, which included Rous, several blue-overcoated and star-adorned representatives from the Soviet Embassy, and a phalanx of pressmen, still contrived to reach Northolt aerodrome with time to spare, only to discover that the Dynamos were flying into Croydon. The convoy of vehicles hurriedly set off southwards.

It had still not arrived when two lend-lease Dakotas, their wing-tips emblazoned with red stars, touched down in the south London sunshine. First off the plane, according to the party's radio commentator Vadim Sinyavsky, was a fly which had travelled all the way from Moscow to escape the ten-below-freezing weather. Second down the steps was Mikhail Yakushin, 'merited master of sports of the USSR', the tall, lithe and fair-haired head coach. Filing down the stairway behind him there followed thirty-seven men and one woman, most of whom were wearing dark blue overcoats and velour hats.

They had only a few moments to wonder why there was no one to meet them before the welcome party arrived, fresh from their race across London. Hands were shaken and the Russians were led across the tarmac to an admin building for the immigration formalities. According to one source, there were eleven first-team players and seven reserves; according to another, two players for each position. Konstantin Andreanov, the Chairman of the Ministry of Physical Culture, was in overall charge of the party, which also included club officials, coaches and trainers, radio commentator Sinyavsky and at least one print journalist from a Moscow daily, cine-cameraman Yashurin and three photographers, a doctor, a masseur and a female interpreter named Alexandra Elliseyeva. And hidden among the thirty-nine there was bound to have been a contingent from the Soviet security apparatus, the NKVD. The great purges, after all, were less than ten years in the past, the gulags still a prospering concern.

Once the Russians were through the formalities the press corps was allowed its opening salvo of questions.

The Dakotas had apparently left Moscow at 6.15 that morning, and the two-hop flight via Berlin had taken eleven hours. Asked to explain the long delay in the team's departure, the travelling officials claimed, somewhat suspiciously, that it had been caused by problems in obtaining exit visas. No one asked them about Sweden, but then there was no reason to. And if the Dynamos had stopped off *en route* to play Norrköping, what possible reason could they have had for trying to hide the fact?

When the questions turned to football, it was clear that Yakushin was the boss, and a popular one at that. The head coach and former Dynamo star was still only thirty-four, but by Soviet standards he had a wealth of international experience, having played representative games in both Eastern Europe and France before the war. The players 'nod their heads in agreement when he speaks', the *News Chronicle* observed, 'and smile delightedly at his sallies.'

Others also took their turn at talking through the interpreter. It was team captain Mikhail Semichastny, three years older than Yakushin, who set in motion the diplomatic offensive, announcing that they had come as 'ambassadors of sport', that 'by clean sport we can strengthen our wartime friendships better than politicians can'. Goalkeeper Alexei Khomich chipped in with: 'Football makes friends. We hope to make friends with you.' Another player took this generosity of spirit rather too far, claiming that they weren't out to beat their English opponents. If they had some good games, he said, then they didn't care who won. Perhaps realising that this sounded too good to be true, he hastened to add that of course they would be doing their best to win.

The Soviets' immediate aim was obviously to endear themselves. Semichastny made the point that Russian football rules – particularly when it came to charging – were different from British ones, but seemed almost eager to play it the hosts' way. One player, Vladimir Subdunin – his name was spelt a different way in almost all the following morning's papers – was presented as a Red Army soldier thrice decorated for bravery and, given that he didn't play in any of the tour games, a cynic could have been forgiven for wondering whether his presence in the party was simply to remind the British public of Soviet sacrifices in a common cause. The cynic would have been wrong: Subdunin, who alone survived to play against Arsenal in the 1954 re-match in Moscow, must have been one of the youngest and least experienced members of the Dynamo squad.

Like the rest he had apparently met his match in the milky English tea. The Dynamo players, who had each been presented with this brimming symbol of English culture, sat gingerly holding their still-full cups, probably wondering why there were no convenient receptacles for a surreptitious dumping of the evil brew. They must have wondered how alien a land Britain was going to prove, and felt grateful that at least they'd brought a plane-load of proper food with them.

The welcome ceremony over, they were driven off towards the centre of London, pursued by their food in an extra motor-coach, still blissfully unaware of the accommodation that awaited them. Through the windows they saw big buildings which reminded them of Leningrad, narrow streets which made them think of Moscow – a bizarre and alien blend. Even the weather was wrong: they had expected the traditional fog, not this strangely damp and sunny day.

On what sort of planet had they landed? What other surprises were waiting for them in the home of football?

2

Snow on their studs

It might be a statement of the obvious, but it's worth saying anyway: Great Britain in the late autumn of 1945 was a very different place from Great Britain around the cusp of the millennium. Walk down any street and you would smell coal smoke rather than car exhaust, hear police bells rather than sirens, see as many lamps lit by gas as by electricity. The street itself would probably feel decidedly empty, but if by chance it was blocked then a tram would be the most likely culprit. The skies above would be innocent of jets and helicopters, the railway stations still cathedrals of steam, the faces of your fellow citizens overwhelmingly white. Enter a shop and there would be no chance of serving yourself; enter a house and you would be lucky to find a fridge or a vacuum cleaner, let alone a television. Pick up an object or run a hand along a surface and you would most likely find your skin in contact with wood or metal – plastics and other synthetics were still rare.

Most of the above reflected contemporary levels of technological and industrial progress, but there were also particular legacies of the war which, only three months earlier, had come to a cataclysmic close with the atomic obliteration of two Japanese cities. The post-war world was not really in black and white, but in Britain it was giving a damn good impression: clothing was generally utilitarian and drab; most essentials, including petrol, would be rationed for several more years yet. The war might have been won, but sometimes it was hard to appreciate that fact. For a victor, Britain was in very poor shape.

At the level of state there was a new government, the first-ever majority Labour Government. Its victory in the summer over Churchill's Conservatives had been a clear sign of the public desire for a radical renewal, and blueprints for the transformation of the country's health and welfare regimes were in various stages of completion on Whitehall's drawing-boards. This British hunger for change, however, did not extend to the world of overseas empires, whose rebellious citizens were making the Fleet Street front pages more often than the Government. India, Palestine, Egypt, the East Indies, China . . . the conflagration just seemed to keep on spreading, a consequence of the war as unwelcome as it was unexpected. In 1945 most of the British wanted to have their cake and eat it: socialism at home and empire abroad.

At the level of the individual it was a time of great uncertainty, obviously more so for some than for others. Many had lost loved ones on the battlefield and in the urban bombing, many had been traumatised by what they had seen of what humans can do to each other. Jobs and wives might still be waiting for the returning soldiers, but neither had been preserved in mothballs during their absence, and in any case they themselves were no longer the same. Wars change the people who survive them, just as they change the societies those survivors return to. And this one had lasted longer, been more all-embracing, than any British involvement since the Civil War 300 years before. There were the usual cries of 'never again', the usual demand for a fairer redistribution of the economic spoils, but in the autumn of 1945 even the dourest pessimist could hardly have expected such a short interlude of openness and uncertainty between Hitler's demise and the onset of the Cold War. The ideological blinkers would be back on before anyone had time to miss them.

People might hunger for the world they had lost – the world as it had been in 1939 – but there was no going back; only an unknowable future was on offer, full of promises and terrors. The youth of sixty-four nations who rallied at the Albert Hall to outlaw war were clearly a part of it, but so were the two Hollywood-influenced young men, vicious and inept in turn, who held up a Mrs Conyers at gunpoint as she lay ill in her bed at Makepeace Avenue, Highgate. 'Stay where you are,' said one, 'if you make a move you know what's coming to you.' Having remembered their lines correctly they then, in the words of a *Daily Express* correspondent, 'ransacked her room in an obviously inexpert way'.

Of course most people were neither rallying for peace nor holding up bedridden ladies, just struggling to get by in situations that might be difficult but were still a lot better than they might have been. Shortages were irritating, frustrating and time-consuming, but there were no V-2s whistling overhead and few now had to face the fear of the letter informing them that a son or husband had been killed in action. The Government had been in office for only a few months, and hadn't yet done anything to undermine seriously the hopes for a fairer society with which it had been entrusted. Every day the papers seemed to announce that something or other was becoming available again after a long absence – the first boat cargo of bananas for five years was apparently being loaded in the distant tropics – and the range of popular entertainment was steadily expanding as war damage was put right and restrictions receded.

Cinema-going had of course continued through the war – albeit with many an impromptu interlude while the bombs rained down – and it would retain its primary role in the entertainment industry through the early years of peace. The theatre was popular too, along with the dance halls which had been revolutionised by the huge American presence in Britain during 1941–4. Like the pubs, these shrines to the jitterbug were suffering from a shortage of beer in the autumn of 1945.

Among the outdoor sports both speedway and greyhound racing were popular, but there was no doubting which sport was booming in the post-war climate. The Dynamos' visit was well timed in more ways than one, for association football in Britain was enjoying a major revival, and the chance to see the possible future of football, 'socialist' trimmings and all, in the ultimate psychological comfort of a familiar terrace spot or grandstand seat, offered as fine a chance to have your cake and eat it as anything in the post-war world.

When war was declared on 3 September 1939 the Football League had lost no time in suspending the 1939–40 season, but only a few weeks later the teams were playing once more, albeit in a restricted format. The leagues were regionalised to take account of the War Office regulation that no side could travel more than fifty miles, crowds were initially limited to 8,000 and entry was by ticket only. Of course many of the players enlisted immediately, some joining the regular Army, Navy or Air Force, others the legion of PT instructors that was now required to keep the troops fighting fit. Within a year many of the nation's footballers were stationed abroad, mostly in Africa and India, playing in their bare feet and using palm trees for goalposts.

Those still left in Britain found that their wages had been cut, bonuses outlawed and contracts suspended for the indefinite future. On the positive side, they could turn out for any club in the various leagues, in Britain that wanted them and for more than one club in the same cup competition. This 'guest player' system, which was necessitated by the fact that many players were stationed too far from their own clubs to make weekend return journeys on the overcrowded and unreliable wartime railways feasible, was still in operation when Dynamo arrived.

The uncertainty wasn't confined to the railways. Managers and coaches – themselves often part-time – could never be certain how many players and officials would put in an appearance, and appeals to the crowd for stand-ins were far from rare. There were many instances of young men with false names and histories – playing for a club at the other end of the country was the favourite story – inveigling themselves into starting line-ups. A lack of skill usually found them out, but crowds often derived considerable amusement from watching them make fools of themselves.

The quality of football at club level suffered from the endless chopping and changing of line-ups, and of course devalued the various cups and championships – Chelsea, for example, won the League South Cup in 1945 with eight guests in their team – but the home international teams – or at least the English – benefited from the increasing frequency with which they played together during the war in the various representative teams. Many long-time observers reckoned that the team that played Wales once and Scotland twice in a six-month period – winning 8–3, 8–0 and 6–2 respectively – was one of England's best ever. A different goalkeeper played in each game – Swift (Manchester City), Roxburgh (Blackpool) and Ditchburn (Tottenham Hotspur) – but only thirteen outfield players in all three: Scott (Arsenal), Hardwick (Middlesbrough), Britton (Everton), Cullis (Wolverhampton Wanderers), Mercer (Manchester City), Matthews (Stoke City), Carter (Sunderland), Lawton (Everton), Hagan (Sheffield United), Dennis Compton (Arsenal), Soo (Stoke City), Welsh (Charlton Athletic) and Smith (Brentford). Many of these would play a starring role in domestic football's post-war years, and three of them would face Moscow Dynamo.

The end of the war raised hopes that football would soon be back to normal, but the various legacies of the conflict made for a slow process. Since D-Day Europe had been added to the list of continents playing host to the far-flung legion of professional footballers, and it would be some time before they were all home: it is often forgotten that it took the better part of two years to complete the demobilisation of the forces.

Many of the stadiums were in need of significant repair. Highbury, for example, had been requisitioned back in 1939 and utilised in turn as a clearing house for refugees, a storage depot for air-raid shelter materials, a gas-decontamination centre and an air-raid shelter. A thousand-pound bomb had demolished half the south terrace during the Blitz and most of the covered North Stand had been burned out by a shower of incendiaries. In November 1945 the club still had no idea of when they would be able to reopen for business.

Chelsea, where Dynamo were due to play their first game, had been luckier. Two bombs had fallen on Stamford Bridge, one on the vast popular terrace which faced the grandstand, the other in front of the unfinished new stand which stood in the northern corner. Neither bomb had caused serious damage, and the ground had remained in use throughout the war. So had White Hart Lane, which played host to both Tottenham and Arsenal for the duration, but even here the war had staked a claim: the upper tier of the East Stand had been pressed into use as a mortuary for victims of the bombing.

There were also shortages to deal with. It took 158 clothing coupons to outfit a team – five per pair of boots, four per shirt, three per pair of shorts, two per pair of socks, eight for the goalkeeper's jersey – and most of the smaller clubs found it hard to raise the necessary numbers. Footballs had been hard to come by since the fall of Singapore in 1942 cut off the rubber supplies required for making the bladders, and when deliveries were resumed in 1945 there was still a leather shortage to contend with. For the foreseeable future clubs would have to get used to darning socks and using balls for more than one game.

Given all these problems the FA and Football League decided that the 1945–6 season would be a transitional one. Eighty-six of the eighty-eight teams who had begun the 1939–40 season would begin this one – Hull City (temporarily) and New Brighton (permanently) having fallen by the wayside – but all divisions would continue in their regionalised form and guest players would still be allowed. The FA Cup would be national once more, the first six rounds all being two-leg affairs, and in this competition the clubs would be forced to rely on their own players.

The season started promisingly enough in August, the rising gates reflecting public enthusiasm, but relations between the players and their clubs, now freed from the moral restraints of wartime, soon began to sour. Wages were still below pre-war levels and many of the older players, whose careers had been effectively cut in half by the war, felt that their time was now running out. The best full-time civilian players were earning a maximum of £8 a week, but the vast majority were getting closer to the £4 minimum. The union wanted significant rises in both, not to mention greatly improved benefits, particularly adequate compensation for injuries and life pensions for permanent incapacity. The necessary money, they claimed, could be found by levying compulsory annual payments from the pools companies.

In 1945 neither the FA nor the League was prepared to touch pools money, which, in true Victorian style, they considered tainted by its source in the gambling habits of the proletariat. But despite rising gates the clubs were all pleading poverty, so where was a decent wage to come from? Several weeks of threats and bluffs finally came to a head on 5 November; on the afternoon of the Dynamos' first full day in Britain the Players Union provisionally called a strike for two weeks hence. There were plans to exempt the Russian tour matches from any industrial action, but the Dynamo party must have felt like visitors arriving in the middle of a heated family argument.

Over the last couple of centuries the British and Russian peoples have fought three major wars as allies, several minor wars as adversaries, and tirelessly played the so-called 'Great Game' with each other in central Asia. There has been almost continual awareness of the other, but this has not led to any depth of mutual understanding. The mention of Russia has always conjured up a series of images for the average Briton, not real knowledge.

A classic example came early in the First World War. Towards the end of August 1914, with the German advance in France looking virtually unstoppable, a seventeen-hour delay in the London–Liverpool train service was attributed by rumour to Russian troop movements in Britain. A huge force, it was claimed, had recently landed in eastern Scotland, and was now being transported south in a fleet of trains for shipment to Belgium. The source of the rumour was never discovered, but it soon acquired a life of its own, as people fell over themselves in the rush to offer evidence that it was true. Stationmen had swept snow off Scottish platforms where the milling Russians had stamped their boots; trains full of strange-uniformed men had been seen; an Oxford professor told of the colleague who'd been taken away by the army to act as an interpreter. Ten thousand men had been seen marching along the Thames Embankment after midnight, while a Scottish laird wrote to a relation in America that 125,000 Cossacks had marched across his estate. Having conquered Britain the rumour finally swept across the Channel, and as the Battle of the Marne neared its climax Parisians gathered at railway stations in the hope of welcoming their Russian saviours.

It was all nonsense, but it rang true, it fitted the way people thought of the Russians: faceless and numberless, snow on their boots, a remorseless horde from the back of beyond who seemed more machine than human. The Russian Army was nicknamed 'the Russian Steamroller', and that said it all – the parts didn't matter, only the weight of the whole.

In the twenties and thirties nothing much happened to undermine this composite image; on the contrary, the Revolution and the massive mobilisations of labour under the Five-Year Plans produced reinforcing images of Russia as a land of beavering ants. Add to that the fact that the Soviet Union represented something completely new in the matter of social and economic organisation, and it's easy to see how this huge country at the other end of Europe became even less understandable to the average Briton.

When Churchill made his famous statement in 1939 that Russia was 'a riddle wrapped in a mystery inside an enigma', few would have disagreed with him.

Most people, of course, couldn't have cared less. Few people travelled to the Soviet Union before the cheap Intourist package-holiday era of the seventies and eighties, and most of those who did were motivated by a mixture of curiosity and political sympathy. Even today, with the Soviet Union a memory, most of the same images hold sway – the Russian people are still trudging round in huge numbers with snow on their boots making a mess of things. No one in the West seems really interested, or at least not until the disintegrating Russian economy begins to look as it it might take a few others down with it. Post-Soviet Russia has become a lot like Africa: it doesn't have enough things that other people want, and if it disappeared tomorrow not many people would be unduly inconvenienced.

That wasn't the case in 1945. The British didn't know much about Russia or the Soviet Union, but for a brief few years a lot of them were interested. The country's enormous contribution to the Allied victory over Nazi Germany had created a corresponding fund of goodwill, and the fact and the manner of that victory had won both people and regime a great deal of respect. It was not widely known that a mere tenth of the *Wehrmacht*'s divisions had faced the Western Allies in France and Italy, but everyone knew that the Russian sacrifice had been both enormous and crucial.

The nature of the Soviet regime wasn't really appreciated; the scale of the holocausts which had accompanied collectivisation and the purges was still unknown, but at least some attempt was now being made to understand the country and its people, to seek out what was positive as well as the traditional negatives. On 14 September A. J. Cummings took note in the *Daily Mirror* of the general British goodwill towards the Soviets and the desire to learn more about Britain's erstwhile allies. He hoped that the Soviets would let down their guard a bit and let this happen, but was honest enough to add that Anglo-American secrecy *vis-à-vis* the atom bomb was not setting a very good example. Three days later the Moscow correspondent of *The Times* detected hopeful signs of a more democratic Soviet Union: anti-red-tape measures, criticism of stereotyped teaching methods and frequent press attacks on heartless bureaucracy. 'It is is interesting to note that this prodding comes from above as well as from below,' he added.

Looking on the bright side where the Russians were concerned was an almost universal habit among the British press during early autumn. Some, like the Right Hon. Walter Elliot in the *Daily Express*, took it rather too far: 'Stalin is sardonic, direct,' he began. 'He has a cutting edge, like the steel from which he takes his *nom de guerre* – for Stalin simply means "steel man". He sat among the others with that air of fanged benevolence with which a collie lies panting and eyeing its sheep . . . Stalin's mind is a literal mind. He sees life in the clear lines of steel. Either a thing is so or it is not so.'

The same paper's staff reporter in Moscow, Alaric Jacob, made the same wishful thinking sound more reasonable: the Soviet Union had 'become the most stable society in the world'; Stalin's successors would be 'a group of middle-aged Men of Good Will'. More perceptively, he noted that the democracy missing from Soviet politics did exist, at least in embryo, in the Soviet workplace, and drew an interesting parallel between Stalin and Oliver Cromwell. 'If you believe that the Commonwealth was a great period in British history,' he argued, 'you may agree that the Stalinist period is also great in Russian history.'

Few were denying that the Soviets were behaving badly in parts of Eastern Europe, but most were bending over backwards to provide excuses for them. Alexander Werth, then the *Sunday Times* representative in Moscow, observed how the Swedish press had 'hooted with joy' when the announcement of America's atom bomb had seemed to offer the Soviets instant relegation in the league table of world powers. 'It was rubbed in that Victorious Russia, with all her bemedalled Marshals, could now be "kept in order" . . .' Their pride had been injured, and they now had good reason to distrust the capitalist world, good reason to feel insecure.

J. B. Priestley, the prominent novelist, playwright and commentator, returned home from the Soviet Union a few days after Moscow Dynamo arrived, and in a series of articles for the *Sunday Express* painted quite an upbeat picture of life in the East. He and his wife had flown to Moscow in a Red Army Dakota, 'piloted by a cheerful young woman and crammed with Red Army officers and shifting mounds of luggage. Everybody smoked; piano accordions were brought out and played and sung to; bottles circulated; and there was a birthday-party atmosphere, very Russian and very genial . . .' Mrs Priestley spoke reasonable Russian, and her husband made it clear that they had not spent 'their time hedged around by interpreters, detectives and dictaphones'; they had seen what they wanted to see and 'often made last-minute choices and so paid unexpected visits'.

And what had they found? 'Ivan and Natasha and their like' had made great sacrifices in the thirties to build up Soviet industry, only to have all their hard work destroyed by the Germans. Now they had to start all over again. 'No doubt they look shabby, have to make the best of inadequate transport, and live in crowded discomfort. But there is plenty of useful work for them to do, with never a shadow of unemployment; and if they have any special talent or skill, they will be eagerly encouraged to make full use of it.'

But there was more than vocational opportunity and material progress on offer. Priestley's Ivan and Natasha had 'grown up free from the pressure of commercial interests which too often vulgarises life and fosters a triviality of the mind. (There is none of that overstimulation of sex which is all too common elsewhere.) They like football, volleyball and all the fun of the fair in the park; but they also have a passionate desire to learn, to read and discuss, to enjoy great drama and music.' Not only were they ordinary people wanting ordinary things, but in some ways they were better off than the British.

This series of articles – and the many like them which appeared in the war's aftermath – must have been music to Soviet ears after the harsh propagandist truths of the interwar years. Priestley had not only missed, or skated over, most of what was bad about Soviet life; he'd also found a great deal that was actually admirable. He might be unconsciously turning Western minuses into Soviet pluses, but that didn't make security of employment, freedom from commercial pressures or respect for high culture any less valuable. There were positive things to say about the old Soviet Union, and in the afterglow of a shared triumph it was possible for a man of Priestley's intellect to believe that the pluses at least balanced the minuses, to convince oneself that Uncle Joe's Russia was not beyond the pale, as Nazi Germany had so clearly been. Better to see Soviet Russia as a long-estranged member of the family, brought home by the need to fight a common enemy, and now invited to share in the building of a joint future.

Unfortunately this leaning together, this popular desire in both countries for more understanding, less suspicion and a growing friendship, was finding few echoes in the councils of the powers-that-were. There had as yet been no public intimations that a complete crack-up was inevitable, but by September 1945 the wartime alliance was obviously under considerable strain, and the way certain issues were handled during the next couple of months would probably prove decisive in determining just how bad relations were going to get. Each of the so-called Big Three – the USA, Britain and the Soviet Union – had a lot to play for, a lot to lose.

Three important negotiations were taking place at this time, two of them between governments, one between factions inside the American Government. The first, which involved only the British and the Americans, was concerned with the world economy in general, and the Americans' price for rescuing the British economy in particular. The British might have been among the war's victors, but in the process of victory they had almost bankrupted themselves. Lend-lease had abruptly been cancelled in August, and a few weeks later Lords Halifax and Keynes had arrived in Washington to start bargaining for the enormous loan required to set the UK back on its feet.

At around the same time the Big Three's Foreign Ministers had gathered in London to continue their resolution of the many post-war political disputes. Here the British tended to side with the Americans, who didn't like the way the Soviets were behaving in occupied Eastern Europe. The Soviets politely pointed out that they were doing no more in, say, Hungary than the Americans were doing in

Italy or Japan; the disputes might be real, but the mood was not yet confrontational. When the conference ended in deadlock at the beginning of October it was with regrets rather than anger and recrimination. There still seemed everything to play for at this stage, particularly if the third negotiation went the way of conciliation.

The subject under discussion in Washington was the atom bomb, a weapon that had been designed and built by an international team of scientists, under Anglo-American auspices, and mostly with American money. The question was whether to share its remaining secrets – much of the science was already well known – with the rest of mankind. Half a century later the idea of simply giving Stalin's Soviet Union the scientific and industrial knowledge required to build a bomb might sound unthinkable, but it certainly wasn't at the time, and on 11 September soon-to-be-retiring US Secretary of War Stimson sent a memo to President Truman recommending just that. His argument was simple. The Soviets were bound to get the bomb eventually in any case, so why risk the embitterment of relations by a refusal to share its secrets now? If the two powers trusted each other, then it might be possible effectively to outlaw the bomb's use and make the most of atomic energy for peaceful purposes.

The Soviets may not have been aware of Stimson's memorandum, but the views it expressed were not hard to find in the published utterances of British and American mainstream opinion. A *Times* editorial on 9 October suggested entrusting the UN with the secrets of the bomb; five days later the Association of Los Alamos Scientists advised that an attempt to keep these secrets would lead 'to an unending war more savage than the last'. They not only recommended international control but considered that 'the abolition of secrecy in national and international relations may be necessary', providing free access to 'all laboratories, industries and military installations'.

Here was a chance for the Americans to test the Soviets' trustworthiness, but Truman was having none of it. Towards the end of the month he gave an aggressive keynote speech, outlining what he considered the twelve essential aims of American foreign policy, one of which – the demand for full economic collaboration between nations – was clearly impossible for the Russians to accept without dismantling their entire socio-economic system. On the question of atomic weapons the American President announced upcoming discussions with Britain and Canada, but emphasised that 'these discussions will not be concerned with the processes of manufacturing the atomic bomb'. In America's possession of the weapon there was 'no threat to any nation'.

The British press disagreed. *The Times* argued that the 'sacred trust' which Truman claimed for the US should rest with the UN Security Council. The *Daily Express* went further. 'World peace,' it editorialised on 31 October, 'depends absolutely on the collaboration of Britain, the United States and Russia. There is no other way. How can there be collaboration without trust? Take off the blinkers. Mutual trust does not yet exist. It has still to be created. Create faith! Create conditions in which each great nation believes in the desire of the others for world peace. Give the secrets of the atomic bomb to Russia.'

On the same day US Secretary of State Byrne offered a much more conciliatory line than that taken by the President. The US, he said, would never join any European group hostile to Russia.

Perhaps hoping beyond hope that all was not yet lost, Soviet Foreign Minister Molotov replied in a similar tone on 3 November. The Soviet Union's sacrifices in the war entitled them to share in the bomb, he said, and in any case sharing the bomb was the best way to preserve the peace. Maybe Prime Minister Attlee, who had recently arrived in Washington to discuss this very question with Truman, could persuade the American President to think again.

Attlee, of course, was also in Washington to discuss the US loan. An important couple of weeks lay ahead for both Britain and the Soviets, and during that time the latter's most visible presence in the Western world would be a party of footballers. Rarely, it seemed, had a sporting event reverberated with such wider significance.

3

Fourteen points, six balls

The sun was sinking beneath the skyline when the coach drove into the Wellington Barracks adjoining St James's Park, and the long shadows must have helped foster the atmosphere of intimidation which confronted the new arrivals. A sergeant-major of the Coldstream Guards was putting a group of defaulters through their punishment paces, doubling them around the parade ground with the usual ghastly shrieks of authority. According to FA Secretary Rous, the Russians at first refused to get out of the coach, fearing that it had all been some horrible trick to land them in a British gulag.

Whether they asked why they were surrounded by foreign troops is not recorded. In fact the FA, finally despairing of ever getting a definite date for their arrival, had given up on hotels and simply requisitioned a room in a barracks.

It was not a popular decision with their guests. Even Rous admitted that the room itself was decidedly spartan; Sinyavsky, six months later, remembered that the decoration consisted of mould on the walls and cobwebs. The beds were like stone blocks; there were no sheets or pillows, only hard bolsters. There was not even a ready supply of hot water for showers or baths, which must have made the Russians wonder about the personal cleanliness of the Coldstream Guards.

The Dynamo officials presumably mentioned at this point that they were less than happy with the arrangements. Rous claims he then phoned the Arsenal Chairman, Sir Guy Bracewell Smith, who happened to own the Park Lane Hotel. It was agreed that beds could be set out in the hotel's ballroom.

Whether they ever were remains a moot point. Rous says that this new arrangement 'saved the day', but according to the following evening's papers most of the players endured at least one night in the barracks – 'making friends with the Coldstreamers', according to one optimistic scribe – while the other members of the party, split into two groups, stayed at the Rubens Hotel in South Kensington and the King George Officers' Club in Piccadilly. Perhaps the temporary dorm in the Park Lane ballroom came into use on the Monday night; it was certainly not until Tuesday that the FA finally got the whole party booked into one place, the Imperial Hotel on the eastern side of Russell Square.

Rous meanwhile was doing his best to defend the FA's preparations – or lack of them. The Russians, he said, had refused to accept accommodation until they had inspected 'everything from the kitchen upwards' and had failed to give any advance warning of their arrival. Hotels refused to take vague bookings ahead of time, so what else could he have done? There had been four days of inconclusive conferences between FA and Embassy officials, and one hotel had actually been booked, only for the booking to be cancelled when the party failed to arrive. Rous claimed that he had rung up 114 hotels and received only two responses. He had also enlisted the help of, among others, the Director-General of Army Quartering, the Trades Union Congress, the Government Hospitality Committee, the American Red Cross and Scotland Yard, all to no avail. 'All the arrangements have fallen on me,' he claimed somewhat pathetically. But that didn't mean he was taking any of the blame. 'No fault lies with the British side for the apparent failure to accommodate them,' he insisted.

Through all this the Soviets managed to keep their tempers remarkably well. They were said to be 'disgruntled', and on Monday the *Evening News* quoted a Soviet official who considered Wellington Barracks 'a slight', but on the same day Mikhail Yakushin told reporters that the Dynamos understood the accommodation shortage – it was 'like that too in Stalingrad and Kiev'. Radio commentator Sinyavsky also accepted that housing conditions in London were difficult, but couldn't resist mentioning that it took an hour for their coach to pick everyone up in the morning. 'The last one to be collected is quite happy about it. But what about the first one?'

The party's officials made no bones about the need for a hasty solution to the problem. On the Monday the FA was bluntly told that football would not be discussed until proper sleeping arrangements had been finalised. 'First things first is our motto,' one Embassy official added somewhat tendentiously. He had his wish. By Tuesday evening the Russians were happily ensconced in the Imperial, where they were said to be enjoying the hotel's Turkish baths, and by Wednesday tour manager Konstantin Andreanov was blithely denying that they had any complaints, and insisting that any misunderstandings had occurred only at the beginning of the tour.

But if the tourists were no longer feeling slighted, the British were still feeling slighted on their behalf. The *News Chronicle* had kicked things off on Tuesday, deciding that there was 'something seriously lacking in British hospitality'. If a team of British footballing stars was in Moscow 'it would be provided with the best accommodation in the capital, shown around the city and made to feel at home'. In Thursday's *Daily Worker* letter-writer E. H. Wharton professed to be 'disgusted'. 'If it had been Hess, our enemy, he would have been found a castle. It makes me wonder if we will ever realise how much we owe to the Russians – the people who, to quote Mr Churchill's words, "tore the guts out of the German Army".'

On the same day Bob Crisp in the *Daily Express* agreed that 'we have made a bad start with the Russians', and went on to share some embarrassing new information. The duty officer at Wellington Barracks, given an hour's notice of the Dynamos' arrival, had 'phoned a person who-shall-be-nameless' – Rous seems a good candidate – 'and asked if he should put sheets on the beds'. He had been told that they wouldn't be necessary.

A remarkable column in the *Evening Standard* took a broader view. While lambasting the FA for a 'lamentable display of bad management and manners', the paper cast the net wider in its search for responsibility. Pointing out that the FA was not financed by the taxpayer, and therefore severely bound by financial constraints, the writer noted that 'no portion of the British Council's £3,500,000 grant was available for Operation Dynamo, not one tittle of its authority exerted on our Russian visitors' behalf.' Of course the British Council was concerned with culture,

> not the common enjoyments of the common man . . . a mere football club is beneath its dignity. And yet, of all the many things Britain has given to the world, sport is the most renowned and universal of them all. It is an English word, yet there is no language in which it is not spoken. Soccer is an English pastime, yet it has taken firm root in the hearts and limbs of men throughout the world. The truth is that the propaganda efforts of the

> amateurs have obscured Britain's real fame in the eyes of the nations of the world, and the acts of the bureaucrats made private hospitality impossible. They infest our hotels, squander our resources, and prevent that healthy commerce between the ordinary citizens of the nations on which world peace must be founded. Our Russian guests must accept our apologies. They can rest assured that there is no home in Britain but would be honoured to receive them.

If the Russians' accommodation problems had placed world peace in jeopardy, more than a few people must have been wondering what global disasters the football would unleash.

While this war of words was flying over their heads, representatives of Moscow Dynamo and the FA set about the none-too-simple task of organising the footballing side of the tour. The Soviets wanted to observe their first opponents in action before taking them on, so the opening game against Chelsea would not be played until the following Tuesday, 13 November. In the meantime, rather like diplomatic delegations gathered to settle a series of political disputes, Dynamo and FA officials held daily conferences on the where, when and how of the footballing conflicts to come.

Dynamo had come prepared, producing, like President Wilson before them, a charter of fourteen points. According to the FA these were presented for acceptance, not negotiation. The points were:

1. As they were a club side they only wished to play other clubs.
2. They didn't want to play more than once a week.

3. They wanted to play on the day that was normally a football day in England.
4. They hoped one of their opponents would be Arsenal.
5. They were unable to number their players.
6. They wanted the referee they'd brought with them to have control of at least one game.
7. They wanted substitutes to be permitted.
8. They wanted an assurance that their opponents' teams would be chosen only from a list of players submitted several days in advance.
9. They agreed to the financial arrangements suggested by the FA.
10. They wanted to practise before the match on the pitch to be used.
11. They wanted to see their prospective opponents in action in normal league matches.
12. They would take all their meals at the Embassy.
13. They wanted 600 tickets made available for the Russian colony in London.
14. They aimed to give a good exhibition of football and didn't want much social entertainment arranged for them.

Brian Glanville later described this list as 'formidable', but with half a century's hindsight it seems likely that what irritated the British most was the Russians' temerity in presenting a list at all. Under close examination the demands they made hardly warranted the sort of spluttering indignation with which they were received.

The first four points concerned the drawing up of a fixture list, and as joint delegations took up the task it soon became apparent that the visitors were suffering from several misapprehensions. Firstly, they were under the impression that they could simply approach whichever clubs they fancied, who in turn could choose whether or not to give up a league game for a crack at the tourists. This fallacy had led to another, that the FA and Football League would allow Saturday league games to be postponed in their favour. The British authorities were not having their precious schedules tampered with; they insisted on the Dynamos' playing most of their games in midweek.

The Dynamo officials were not happy. On which day are the big matches played, the ones that all the people go to watch, they asked Rous. On Saturdays, he reluctantly admitted. So why couldn't they play on Saturdays, the Dynamo officials asked. Because such a game would affect other London attendances, the FA officials replied. But if a British team came to Moscow all other games would be stopped, the Russians said.

They were perhaps being naive, but the FA were just being bloody-minded. 'Rous would have a hard job telling me why they can't play on a Saturday against a top-line team,' Bob Crisp mused in the *Express*. 'Is it any wonder the Russians can't quite understand it? The league programme this season is not really of any great consequence. Certainly not as important as dissipating any misunderstanding or ill-feeling which our Russian guests may be harbouring.'

So Point 3 was history from day one of the negotiations, and Point 2 didn't last much longer. The Russians were offered one Saturday date, against Third Division Cardiff City, who had only a friendly against Chester planned for the 17th, but this fixture would necessarily be sandwiched between two midweek games. Point 1 was also under threat from the word go, with a continuously rising clamour in favour of a match between Dynamo and an

FA XI, but Point 4 was agreed almost immediately. Arsenal were more than eager to take on the Russians at their temporary White Hart Lane home, even though many of their star players were still stationed abroad.

Looking back, it's easy to criticise the choice of opponents who were to play Dynamo – indeed, the choice was coming under considerable criticism before the tour ended – but the first three fixtures practically chose themselves, Chelsea by virtue of their original invitation, Cardiff by virtue of their availability on a Saturday, and Arsenal at the tourists' own request. The fact that none of these three clubs could offer the best of British football at this time was unfortunate, but it's hard to believe that it was deliberate, either on the FA's part or the Russians'. And in any case, at this stage there were still many other possibilities. No one seemed to know how long the tour was going to last – the tourists least of all – and thirty-four invitations had already arrived from British clubs eager to stage a game.

So by Wednesday the first three games were fixed: Chelsea on Tuesday 13 November, Cardiff on Saturday 17 November, Arsenal on Wednesday 21 November. After the third game there would be a conference to consider other invitations, particularly those from Portsmouth, Glasgow Rangers, Birmingham City, Bournemouth, Nottingham Forest and Sheffield Wednesday. From the FA's point of view a lot would depend on how well the visitors acquitted themselves: if they struggled as badly as many expected, then it would be cruel to expose them to further humiliation by one of the stronger British teams. And those in charge of the Dynamo party were probably making similar calculations, though in their case a real confidence in the team's ability seems to have been doing battle with atavistic fears of British superiority.

Points 5–7 in the Russian list were, on the surface at least, more controversial than Points 1–4. But once again the initial British reluctance to concede these points was based at least as much on British self-importance – and the insularity which allowed it to flourish – as on any reasoned objection. The Dynamo reluctance to number their shirts was unfortunate in that it denied spectators easy identification of individuals, but it was hardly a matter for reproach. The *Daily Mail* claimed that the visitors had initially agreed to wear numbers, but then changed their minds for fear that the sewn-on numerals would spoil their new shirts. This sounded like nonsense, but then the tour was fast acquiring a reputation for throwing up truths that looked anything but. An alternative theory held that Dynamo, as representatives of an aggressively collectivist culture, didn't like bringing attention to individual players. Either way, it was a bit rich for their hosts to complain – compulsory numbering of shirts had been introduced in Britain only in the summer of 1939.

In the matter of substitutes, it was agreed that a maximum of three would be allowed, and then only for injured players. The British authorities seemed to think they were doing the Dynamos a favour here, but as L. V. Manning pointed out in the *Daily Sketch*, this was in fact international law, 'though not many people here seem to be aware of it'. The UK's four football nations – like the Soviets, but for rather different reasons – were still trying to ignore the existence of FIFA. It would be twenty years and many ruined Cup Finals before the FA finally sanctioned one substitute per team in English competitions.

Manning was rather less understanding when it came to Point 6. 'I have no doubt that this unusual request will, like everything else they have asked, also be conceded,' he began quite erroneously, 'but it would not surprise me if, when the Russians have seen an English referee operating, they will be quite happy to leave it to Lancaster Gate to appoint the official for the big representative match with which it is proposed to wind up the tour.' Who could argue with such hubris? At the tour's end this point was still rankling with those who thought Britain's honour had been unjustly impugned. Gerard Walter in the *News Chronicle*, after steeling himself to admit that British pre-eminence in world sport was a thing of the past, refused to agree with 'anyone who denies us our pre-eminence as sportsmen in the truest sense of that over-worked word . . . the idea that a British referee or umpire would dream for one moment of discriminating against competitors of another country is preposterous . . . When we go abroad we unhesitatingly accept the decisions and adjudications of the officials of the country of which we are the guests . . . they should do the same.'

The FA's concession on this one point, and the placing of the Arsenal game under Nikolai Latyshev's control as a consequence, would certainly prove momentous, but it would also prove instructive, pointing up those differences in rule interpretation between the two footballing cultures that had been passed over in relative silence during the first two games. These differences were also under discussion at Lancaster Gate; but without any actual play to go on, it was rather like watching the sparring of two blind pugilists.

At Croydon the Dynamos had announced themselves anxious to play the British way, and FA textbooks had been translated into Russian so that players and officials could look for differences in the laws. These were hard to find – as ever, it was the customary interpretation of the laws that tended to vary from culture to culture, not the laws themselves. The Russians knew that British goalkeepers enjoyed considerably less protection than their own – in 1945 both charging the goalkeeper and kicking the ball out of his hands were still permitted in British football – and that the parameters of the physical shoulder-charge were much wider in Britain than elsewhere. Their hosts, more accustomed to seeing their way of doing things as the right way – who had invented the game, after all? – were also inclined to consider offences like obstruction and shirt-pulling more heinous than straightforward brutality. There was much room for conflict here, but no way of sorting it out in theory – such sorting would have to be done on the pitches by the chosen referees.

Point 8 on the Russians' list – their need to be assured that opponents' teams would be selected from a list submitted in advance – would eventually cause more ill-feeling than any of the others, but during these initial meetings the FA clearly accepted it. Point 9 simply meant that gate receipts would be divided on the usual cup-tie principle: once ground expenses and entertainment tax had been deducted the balance would be equally divided between the two teams. Dynamo's share would go to the FA for deduction of tour expenses and then returned to a charity of their choice. They chose the Stalingrad Fund, which besides making perfect sense in its own right also served to remind the British public once again of the Soviet contribution to Germany's defeat.

The final five points seemed uncontroversial, and in theory they were. The problems came with the application, undertaken in that spirit of repressed irritation which hung like a cloud over the first few days of the tour. Basically, both sides were afraid they were being taken advantage of. The British didn't take to a bunch of foreigners telling them how to run the game they'd invented, particularly when those same foreigners spent the rest of the time being stand-offish. The Russians, dumped in a barracks and told they couldn't play on Saturdays, felt they were being treated less than royally; a feeling guaranteed to feed the suspicion and paranoia which they'd brought from home.

For all the non-stop conferencing there was a definite failure to communicate, as the bungling of the Dynamo training arrangements made amply clear. On the Monday they turned up at Stamford Bridge as agreed, and everything seemed to be going smoothly, but on the following morning they simply dropped in to collect their footballs – of which, more later – and, in Charles Buchan's words, 'drove away in their coach without warning', destination White City. Chelsea lamented the fact that they'd heated up their boilers specially for Russian baths, and the world was presented with an image of unpredictable and ungrateful tourists. It was then reported in one paper that Chelsea had forbidden the Dynamos to train on the Stamford Bridge pitch in their heavy boots, and though no one said so at the time, it's hard to imagine the Russians sequestrating – or even knowing about – the White City without help from either the FA or Chelsea. In retrospect it looks like a classic piece of FA incompetence, but the impression bequeathed to most newspaper readers was of Soviet rudeness, an impression reinforced the following day by the news that the Russians had left White City without eating the afternoon tea which had been prepared for them. 'Though informed that they were ready', the *Manchester Guardian* wrote accusingly, the visitors callously ignored several plates of chicken sandwiches and chocolate meringues.

It was hard to say who was most to blame for the communication breakdown, but most of the accusing fingers seemed to be pointing at the party's interpreter,

Alexandra Elliseyeva. No one questioned the technical skills of this English teacher from a Moscow University; it wasn't so much the way she said things as the fact that she hardly said anything at all. It took only a few days for her to acquire the nickname 'Alexandra the Silent', hardly a plus on an interpreter's CV.

Reporters quickly discovered that she had two sons: Gyorgi, aged eighteen, who was a keen Dynamo fan, and Mikhail, fifteen, who was just getting interested. She herself was not. She admitted to liking Dickens, but found London still a little too redolent of his novels. 'There is no modern spirit in it. All those little cottages I saw on the way from Croydon aerodrome – quaint, yes, but not modern. Now Moscow – ah! There is much life there, and brightness and spirit! London is so solemn.'

Beyond that – nothing. The press was left with not much more than her appearance, which of course they found fascinating. Having already described her as 'a slim little woman in a blue serge suit and a little black hat with two tassels at the back', one journalist interrupted his own question on the Dynamo diet to notice 'how piquant was her small face, and how pretty her dark brown hair'.

The fact that her gender prevented her accompanying Britain's male football journalists into the Russian dressing room was obviously unfortunate, but no one wondered out loud if that was one of the reasons she'd been chosen, as a deliberate means of limiting journalistic access to the Dynamo players. Some light was inadvertently thrown on this subject when a second interpreter was lent to the Soviet party by the War Office on the Monday evening. Russian-born Briton Alex Marcovich (or Makaroff, depending on which newspaper you read – 'If you've heard one Russian name you've heard them all' seemed to be the motto of the British press corps in 1945), when asked if the Dynamos enjoyed playing, replied that he had no idea – they didn't talk to him.

Tabloids, like nature, abhor a vacuum, and the unwillingness to provide them with usable copy was obviously going to rebound on the visitors. Denied information about the Dynamos' lives, loves and hobbies – even the players' heights and weights were on the restricted list – British journalists settled for making the mundane more interesting by playing up the 'Russianness' of the tourists, portraying them according to time-honoured stereotype as awkward, silent, humourless and mysterious in all the wrong ways.

The *Daily Mail* account of their arrival at Stamford Bridge on the Monday morning has a 'silent' Yakushin 'silently' signalling the 'silent figures' of his players on to a 'grey-misted pitch'. They have already run into Chelsea manager Birrell and club trainer Stolley: 'the meeting was wordless'. After the training session nothing avails 'to loosen their tongues'. The players are 'marched' into the dressing room, leaving a 'tall, lean, intense' Yakushin with Alexandra the Silent. She 'flashes' him a look of understanding, 'frowns a little', picks up a football, and then 'demands' of the Chelsea trainer, 'How much does this ball weigh?'

It sounds like a bad spy novel.

'Er, pardon,' says Stolley.

The frown deepens. 'How many grams?'

'Well, the usual weight, you know . . .'

'Hmmm,' she says, bouncing the ball and handing it back to Yakushin. He also bounces it, 'purses his lips doubtfully, and shrugs'.

A nice touch that – first the peasant's archetypically suspicious nature, then the peasant's traditional surrender to fate.

But it wasn't just the weight of the balls, it was also the number. In Britain the emphasis in training was still all on legwork and general physical fitness, but the Dynamos had arrived with the revolutionary notion of using footballs. One per man, to be precise – a notion that seemed radical beyond belief to the FA officials. According to the *Daily Mirror*: 'Tall, immovably serious, dressed in a pale blue siren suit, Yakushin stood with arms folded on the field while it was explained to him that footballs were very difficult to come by.' He had five already, the officials told him, as if that should be enough for any team. But they could manage three more, news that was dutifully passed on to Yakushin by 'greying, slim, taciturn Alexandra Elliseyeva'. '*Tree miachi*,' she murmured – 'three balls.'

Yakushin never moved a muscle. 'Six balls.'

'But that would make one new ball for every member of the team,' pleaded the officials.

'Six balls,' said the immovable Mr Yakushin.

'We'll try and borrow another three from Fulham tomorrow,' sighed the officials.

Once again we have what was probably a straightforward conversation, albeit mediated through an interpreter, transformed into something that sounds like a tense negotiation between Mafia clans. If the balls hadn't been delivered as promised, *Mirror* readers might have expected to hear that Rous had woken up with a dead horse's head on his pillow.

None of which helped the cause of the Dynamo tour. No matter how aggrieved or suspicious or stressed out the members of the Soviet party might be feeling – and they had good reasons to be less than happy with their official welcome – by the middle of the first week it was becoming distressingly apparent that their current *modus operandi* was neither winning friends nor influencing people in the intended manner. All the evidence suggested that there was still a huge reservoir of goodwill out there waiting to be tapped, but the tapping wouldn't happen of its own accord. If the Dynamo tour was to achieve a significant proportion of its several goals then the party would have to get its PR act together without much further delay.

4

'So slow you can almost hear them think'

In 1923 the young Soviet Union sent a representative team from the Russian State Republic on a tour of Sweden. There were footballing reasons for the tour, most notably an eagerness on the part of Soviet coaches and players to test their progress against foreign opposition, but the main motivation was political. The country was still emerging from the dislocation of civil war, the New Economic Policy had recently been instituted, and the Government was eager for a resumption of economic links with the outside world.

Sweden seemed like a good bet. A debate was already under way in Stockholm about the possible resumption of trade with Red Russia, and it was hoped that the goodwill engendered by a successful football tour would tip the balance in the Soviets' favour.

At the same time, the Soviet Government had by no means given up on its vocation to revolutionise the world, and to this end was also hoping that the tour might both increase the prestige of the first workers' state and further the cause of so-called worker sports – sporting activities organised by and for workers independently of the local upper classes. At first sight it might appear that firing up the local proletariat was bound to antagonise the very people whom the Soviets needed to help resolve the trade issue, but happily for them things were not that simple.

The Swedish bourgeoisie might well feel more than a little annoyed by such interference, but in the short run they were more likely to be swayed by the potential profits of renewed trade with the Soviet Union. As long as the Soviets coated their revolutionary pills with enough honey they could be everyone's flavour of the month.

As it turned out, the tour was a huge success. The mere presence in Sweden of 'these nice, good-looking young men', as one Swedish paper called them, helped to un-demonise the revolutionary state from which they came. 'They could just as well have been from Copenhagen,' the paper announced obligingly.

The Russians also proved stylish and sporting winners, and made a favourable impression on Swedish bourgeoisie and proletariat alike. The latter demonstrated their solidarity by singing the 'Internationale' at games, the former, despite occasional outbursts from the right-wing press, were reassured by the sheer ordinariness of the visitors. The tour was marred only in its final days by the Swedes' desperate desire for a win, and the public squabbles over team selection which arose as a consequence. These aspects – and the Soviet players' penchant for acquiring Western fashions in their off-duty shopping hours – would be echoed in Britain twenty-two years later.

In their ground-breaking book on the subject, Jim Riordan and V. Peppard consider the Swedish trip the first major Soviet exercise in 'sports diplomacy'. This, like war in Clausewitz's famous definition, is a continuation of policy by other means. Engaging in such an exercise doesn't turn the sportsmen into something else, or imply that the sport in question is no longer enjoyed or important as sport, but it does mean that other, often hidden, processes are also at work; sports diplomacy doesn't so much interfere with sport *per se* as consciously seek to manipulate the context and consequences of sporting encounters. It is usually a highly complex business, and more of an art than a science, for the simple reason that most of the many variables are human.

In Sweden in 1923 there were many messages, many messengers and many audiences, and it would be the same with the Dynamo tour. This exercise in sports diplomacy was aimed at the Soviet and British peoples, and as much of the rest of the world as was watching. Those with parts to play and axes to grind – some consciously, some less so – would include managers, coaches, journalists, politicians, spectators and players, the latter in different guises on and off the pitch. The messages would of necessity be many and often contradictory.

One of the most important things at issue in the autumn of 1945 was the continuance or otherwise of the war-generated friendship between Britain and the Soviet Union. In this context the mere fact of the tour was significant, and the Russians' frequent statements that they were here to learn offered further symbolic extensions of the hand of friendship. Stressing, as they tried to do in myriad ways, that they were just ordinary people offered reinforcement of this message, whereas showing up the differences – as they had allowed themselves and the British press to do in the tour's opening days – clearly weakened it.

All this could be got across without lacing a single boot. The games themselves offered the chance of winning or losing, gracefully or not, stylishly or not, and here the Dynamos had the opportunity to speak not just for themselves or Soviet sport but for their country as a whole. If the team didn't make a fool of itself, if it actually held its own against the British, then the message would be clear: we're as good as you, we've caught up, with the added implication that this applied both on the pitch and off. Not being considered weak was important, particularly after a war, and at the very least the Dynamo team was expected to show a level of vigour which would supposedly reflect a revitalised Soviet Union, not one cowering at the threat of the West's atomic bomb.

If the team proved victorious then the sky was the limit. In that case the message could be: we're better than you, and that should make you wonder about the way you organise your society. Perhaps we in the Soviet Union represent the future in more than football.

Such a triumphant outcome was the stuff of dreams. For the moment the Soviet organisers of the tour must have been more nervous than anything else – sports diplomacy was not an easy trick to pull off. Events off the pitch were already becoming hard to control, and that placed an even greater onus on the football itself. The Dynamos might prove fair-minded, efficient and wonderfully entertaining winners, the best advert for Soviet socialism imaginable. Or they might lose their matches and their tempers, and leave a lasting impression of the Soviet Union as a land of graceless losers.

The first Briton to be quoted on the Dynamos' footballing prowess was the manager of their first opponents, Billy Birrell. He was impressed. 'They are fast, with and without the ball, and they can shoot both accurately and hard, in contrast to most Continental sides.' He wished he had twenty-five men on the Chelsea staff who were 'so thoroughly fit', and thought 'Tiger' Khomich earned his nickname: 'He's always on the move, is very agile and, will, I think, be hard to beat.' Birrell's only caveat was that he hadn't seen much evidence of heading ability.

The capital's football journalists were denied the chance

to watch the Dynamos train at Stamford Bridge, but they had several opportunities to observe them at White City over the next few days. The verdict on the visitors, as delivered by first the dailies and then the Sundays, was strangely mixed, as if each journalist had watched a different squad in training. Some seemed reluctant to pass overall judgement: ex-Sunderland and Arsenal star Charles Buchan praised the visitors' close passing but thought they seemed troubled by the soft turf; an unnamed colleague merely declared the Russians 'adept at fancy work', which in 1945 was tantamount to accusing them of unnatural sexual preferences.

After witnessing one practice game the *Daily Mail* reporter announced that the Dynamos' style of play and team formation – 'whether or not they favour a close passing game' – remained a mystery, but J. G. Orange of the *Evening News* was way ahead of him. When the opposition had the ball the Russian wing-halves and inside-forwards would all fall back to join the defence, and when Dynamo were in possession they would all move swiftly forward to join the attack. According to Orange these were the same tactics that the Austrian national team had used to such great effect at Stamford Bridge in December 1932. The visitors had lost 4–3 on the day, but most thoughtful observers had agreed that victory – a first on English soil for a foreign national team – would hardly have flattered them.

This perceptive note of caution found no echoes in the columns of the *Evening Standard*, where football writer Harold Palmer predicted probable humiliation for the Dynamos. They were 'thoughtful but slow', and didn't tackle. Though he liked Semichastny and Bobrov – the latter's first name-check – he thought the visitors would be 'swept off their feet'.

The *Daily Worker* took an extra couple of days to make up its mind, and came up with a more balanced judgement. Their reporter also thought the Dynamo players reluctant to tackle, weak in the air and, somewhat incredibly, poor trappers of the ball. The defence generally preferred covering, re-covering and waiting for opponents' mistakes to getting physical, either in the tackle or through the charge, and the lack of power in Khomich's kicks would make it harder for the Russian defenders to get a breather. But that said, it was the visitors' attacking skills that left the most vivid impression. 'Once they get the ball moving along the carpet they are one of the finest club combinations I have seen for many a day. Make no mistake about it, they know football and their style makes you think: "These lads play chess a lot." Their play is really scientific, really football. Positioning, passing and first-time shooting – these are their best accomplishments'.

On Sunday, with the game just two days away, only Raymond Glendenning, BBC Radio commentator and *Sunday Graphic* sports columnist, was expecting much from the Russians. In the *People* Tom Morgan predicted that Chelsea would 'uphold the football supremacy of the fatherland of football with a ringing victory and ninety minutes of liberal education for their opponents'. He thought the Dynamos 'too slow-motion for the top drawer', a view that found echoes elsewhere, particularly in the *Sunday Express*. Having watched them in training at the White City, that paper's Paul Irwin found them 'an ordinary lot'. They had 'a fairly good idea of passing, but nearly all their work is done standing still. And they are so slow that you can almost hear them think.' Chelsea would expose a defence that could neither tackle nor shoulder-charge, and Tommy Lawton would probably bag a hatful. Irwin was not 'trying to take a crack at the Russians – far from it'. On the contrary, he obviously felt sorry for them, urging the spectators at Stamford Bridge not to expect too much from these out-of-their-depth foreigners, 'factory workers who train at night and go through the motions on their off-duty day'.

Just as mistakenly, but rather more entertainingly, Stanley Walton in the *Sunday Dispatch* noted that 'every child in Russia kicks a football in the long summer evenings and graduates steppe by steppe to factory teams and the pleasant vista of Moscow's spires . . . Most of the players are thick-set, broad in the shoulder, with slightly inturning toes – which in my younger days in Scotland was usually the hallmark of a useful shot.'

Back in the real world, the one scribe who would soon be finding out at first hand just how good the Russians were – Chelsea centre-half and *Reynolds News* columnist John Harris – knew only too well how hard it was to judge sides by their performance on the practice field. They might not have impressed many of his fellow journalists, but they had certainly given his manager Billy Birrell pause for thought.

It didn't take the Russians long to settle into a routine. Each morning they were picked up from their hotel in Bloomsbury and driven in the shiny maroon coach to the Soviet Embassy in Kensington's Palace Gate for breakfast. A small group of officials would then make the short journey north to Lancaster Gate for another round of the seemingly endless negotiations that surrounded the practicalities of the forthcoming fixture programme. The players' training was confined to the afternoons, leaving them free in the mornings and evenings, but for the first few days they kept a low profile.

On Tuesday they reportedly searched in vain for the

British Museum, driving round and round central London in their coach, faces pressed prisoner-like to the windows. Wednesday morning brought more of the same, and that evening they joined hundreds of others as guests of Ambassador Gusev and his wife at the Embassy bash to celebrate the twenty-eighth anniversary of the Revolution. The British Prime Minister and half his Cabinet were there, along with members of the diplomatic community and assorted celebrities from the arts and sciences; the Dynamos must have felt as if they were swimming round in a huge goldfish bowl. They had now been in Britain for four days, and their lack of any real contact with the country they were visiting must have been as frustrating to them as it was to the British press corps. Strangers in a strange land would have been a definite step up from footballers trapped in a bubble.

Fortunately for them, things had already begun to change. At some point on the Wednesday those in charge of the Soviet party, with or without express sanction from Moscow, must have decided on a change of policy. They seem to have realised that keeping the team effectively sequestered behind the language barrier simply wasn't working, and they decided to opt for a more media-friendly approach.

It's also possible that the Russians' reception in England had been more friendly than anticipated, and that the change of tack reflected this fact. In the first few days of the tour radio commentator Vadim Sinyavsky and one of the cine-cameramen, realising that they'd lost their way, headed down into the first available tube station in search of directions. According to Sinyavsky they were saved by a stout Englishman, who, noticing the enamel Dynamo badges in their lapels, approached them, shook hands, and said something in English which included the two words 'Russian football'. The two Russians responded with 'Soviet Embassy', which did the trick. 'The polite gentleman led us into the carriage, stayed with us all the way, and then escorted us to the door of the Embassy. His was a courtesy we shall remember.'

Of course, Sinyavsky may have simply concocted this story – published a fortnight later in *Soviet Weekly* – as evidence of how many friends the Soviet Union had, even in the land of the enemy. Or perhaps a portly Samaritan really did offer these Soviet babes in the wood some much-needed proof that capitalist England wasn't all darkness and hostility.

The trip to Gillingham on the Wednesday afternoon was undoubtedly real. The Russians had been invited by Captain R. E. East, the Royal Engineers Football Secretary, to watch a game between District and All-England Engineers' XIs, and an FA car was placed at their disposal, presumably with a driver. According to the *Daily Sketch* six of the team made the trip, but the *Mail* had Alexandra the Silent along for the ride – she had forsaken dark colours for a light-brown ensemble – so the car must have been pretty full. What tasks the driver did perform on arrival remains an open question, but helping the Russians find their hosts was clearly not one of them. Seats had been reserved for them in the stand, but with half-time approaching they still hadn't appeared, and it took a thorough search of the terraces before they were found standing together in a remote corner of the ground. The officials offered to take the visitors to their seats, but Elliseyeva 'silenced them with a look' before saying, 'Please do not disturb. It is the game that is important.'

At half-time they allowed themselves to be shifted, and through the opening exchanges of the second half trainer Yakushin and captain Semichastny 'sat as though carved in stone – only their keen eyes moved'. But then, wonder of wonders, an easy chance was missed, the 4,000-strong crowd erupted in jeers, and the Dynamos were seen to laugh – 'for the first time in public in this country', as the *Daily Mail* portentously proclaimed. And as the game went on the visitors clearly got into the spirit of the thing, 'mingling their loud Russian exclamations with the English shouts'.

They had been out and about, they had shared a terrace and a stand with ordinary Britons, and the tour hadn't blown up in their faces. They had answered a couple of questions from the press, offered the opinion that the tackling was 'some very good hard, some very hard', and no one had asked them about Trotsky or the missing Polish officer corps. The next morning Konstantin Andreanov addressed the problem of his players' aloofness and secretiveness by claiming it had all been a misunderstanding. 'I don't think there is any secrecy,' he said. 'Indeed, it is the contrary. Sometimes the questions which have been asked were strange. The difficulty of interpretation is, no doubt, the cause of any misunderstandings.'

It was all down to language. Or not quite. When one journalist asked how linguistic difficulties had prevented the players from answering simple questions about football which had been put to them in Russian, Andreanov was forced to grope for another reason. 'The players are modest,' he decided on, 'and, as you say, shy. And as it is their first visit to England they try to make friends first.'

This was mostly nonsense, of course, but it did signal the beginning of a significant opening up on the Soviets' part. By getting out and about more, and by making themselves marginally more accessible when it came to direct questioning, they hoped to offer the press corps fewer obvious opportunities to conjure up its anti-Soviet lexicon. No one expected British journalists to abandon such colourfully biased populist imagery, and no one would be disappointed – at Andreanov's press conference he was described as 'laughing softly' and 'blowing smoke-rings' like any half-decent head of 007's arch-enemy Smersh. But the more they got out among the people, the more they showed the British that they were ordinary people who enjoyed ordinary things, the more those images would be subverted.

On Thursday evening most of the players turned up at White City for the greyhound racing, and in the first event they backed Wings for Victory, a 5–1 shot. It nearly won too, but after consulting the Magic-Eye photo, the stewards announced that Jubilee Don had come home by a short head. The sports headline in the morning's *Sketch* – 'Russians See The Dogs – And Lose Their Roubles' – was a definite improvement on accusations of obsessive secretiveness.

On the same morning the *Mail* noted that the Russians had 'thawed' considerably, and the process was taken a step further that evening when the tourists visited the Cambridge Theatre to see *A Night in Venice*, then considered the best musical in London. They had been invited by Jay Pomeroy, the show's Russian-born producer, and before it began he delivered a welcoming speech in Russian and introduced them to the rest of the audience. They went backstage between acts, posed for photographs with the stars, and generally behaved like people who wanted to make friends, autographing newspapers and programmes brought to them by members of the audience 'with the charm and poise of veteran film stars'. They also talked and talked, 'trying to see who could get out the most words in English', according to the *Sketch*. So much for silence. The Dynamos, suddenly, seemed eager to please.

And they were obviously succeeding. Most of them were at Stamford Bridge the following afternoon to see Chelsea take on Birmingham in a Division South match, and they were given an ovation as they took their seats. There was still some reticence in evidence, however, and the Dynamo players refused to comment on the football they had seen, other than to say that a lot of the charging on display would have been illegal on a Soviet football pitch. Chelsea lost 3–2, and played quite abysmally, but the Russians must have been impressed with Lawton, who scored twice on his début for the London club. Their cine-cameras were rolling throughout the ninety minutes, so the performance of their first opponents could be reviewed in the comfort of the Embassy's screening room.

As if to remind everyone how badly organised the tour's first few days had been, the Russians sent in a request to meet with the Chelsea team after the game, waited an hour, and were then told that the players had gone home. 'The Soviet bus,' the *Mirror* reported almost wistfully, 'slipped disappointedly into the mist.'

Earlier in the week one reporter had announced that the Dynamos were in for a shock at Stamford Bridge that Saturday, but if the Russians did come away feeling surprised it was not by the high quality of football they had just witnessed. No great tactical innovations were noticed by any of the match reporters; this Chelsea–Birmingham game had been played in much the same way as any league game that day. The pace was similar, as were the formations, the levels of physicality and technical skill. British football had been in a rut for the better part of twenty years.

Both sides played with a back three, the full-backs marking the wingers and the 'stopper' centre-half patrolling the middle, the whole swinging as a unit to cover the direction of the threat. In front of them the two wing-halves and two inside-forwards played in a rough square, the former moving forward to assist their own side's attacks, the latter retreating to help defend against the opposition's. The wingers, whose primary job was to get crosses into the penalty area, stayed wide and much further forward than their modern counterparts. The centre-forwards, traditionally strong and good in the air, pushed up on the opposing centre-backs and challenged for the long balls forward and crosses that were aimed in their general direction.

Though dribbling with the ball was still considered the highest of the footballing arts, the overall level of ball control would not have been considered high by the standards of today's Third Division. A heavier ball and inferior pitches had something to do with that, but so did the low priority accorded to ball skills in training. And because players needed those crucial extra seconds to control the ball, a close-passing game was hard to sustain. Long balls and crosses gave players more chance to bring their physicality to bear, with juddering charges and tackles from behind that took ball, player and several cubic feet of earth and turf.

It was a game tailor-made for the fast and the strong, for players like Lawton who were majestic in the air, who could use speed of thought, physical power and fearlessness to compensate for any clumsiness on the ground. But it was a game that also had room for the likes of Stanley Matthews, Raich Carter and Alex James, players whose magical skills on the ball could be used to set up the Lawtons. It was not a football that encouraged finesse, it was neither smooth nor flowing. It was kick and rush, all-action, spasmodic and violent. At its best it was exciting to watch, exhilarating to play.

It was also, or so most Britons believed, the best in the world.

This was not the case, and probably hadn't been for a couple of decades. True, no English or Scottish international team had been beaten at home in that period, but there had been several close-run things, most notably the above-mentioned match against Austria in December 1932. More significantly there had been several calamitous defeats on foreign soil, including a 5–2 thrashing by the French, but in those days the bad news didn't travel quite so fast or so fully. There was no television, let alone an information superhighway, and somehow defeats you couldn't see never seemed quite as real as the victories you could. The three pre-war World Cups might have given the British public a clue as to the relative merits of the football they were watching at home, but the four home countries had declined to take part.

Still, for anyone who cared enough to look, the symptoms of Britain's relative decline weren't that hard to notice. So why were they ignored? Simple denial is the obvious answer – how else to explain the English player in the Wembley tunnel in 1953 who pointed out the 'fat little chap' and deduced that 'we won't have any trouble with this lot'? With hindsight it's not the misjudgement of Puskas that's so telling, it's the fact that this English international footballer either was unaware of the Hungarians' stunning recent record or considered it irrelevant. In either case, he was demonstrating an insularity of mind-boggling proportions.

Fathers unable to accept defeat at the hands of their children have become a cliché, and the British were similarly incapable of accepting that their erstwhile pupils – those to whom they had so generously bequeathed the gift of football – were now at least their equals. The knife was twisted further by the fact that Britain's decline as a footballing power mirrored its decline as a nation. The country's claim to membership of the so-called 'Big Three', like its claim to footballing superiority, was based on little more than past glories. For the moment the nation's illusory status could be sustained: Britain was still a military power, and both Americans and Soviets, for reasons of their own, were temporarily unwilling to burst the bubble. The Empire was still there, colouring a quarter of the world pink, though both the imperial tariff preferences which made it pay and the will to sustain a global presence were about to be swept away, the one by intense American pressure, the other by that worldwide resistance to overt colonialism which would come to dominate the next twenty years.

But for a few months in 1945 the illusions could still be maintained. The British had enjoyed their finest hour, won the war, and were even now deciding the shape of the post-war world as equal partners with the United States and the Soviet Union. The English football team still hadn't been beaten by foreign visitors, so English football was obviously still the best. The strength of such illusions was perhaps best illustrated by the fact that others shared them, even – perhaps especially – those who came to puncture them. The Hungarians later admitted to being nervous wrecks before the game at Wembley in 1953, and on the eve of the Chelsea game the Dynamo tourists took their maroon coach in search of Highbury, home of the glory that once was Arsenal. The Russians too were living in England's footballing past.

A better team than Chelsea might have been chosen to lead off the defence of this golden heritage, but the Stamford Bridge club's location and influential support saw it – not for the first or last time – reaping rewards, both financial and in terms of prestige, that its playing strength hardly credited. On the day the Dynamos arrived in England the team occupied a respectable-looking eleventh position in the twenty-two-team Division South (see Appendix 1), but given the relative strength of the two regional first divisions, this was probably equivalent to nothing more than a top-six berth in an imaginary second division.

The club's history was hardly littered with glory. Founded in 1905 and attaining league status only two months later, the team see-sawed between Divisions One and Two until the First World War. Having finished nineteenth in the spring of 1915 they should have resumed business in the Second Division when football restarted in the autumn of 1919, but were saved by the two-club enlargement of the First. It was only a temporary reprieve, though, and in 1924 the club began a six-year stint in the lower league. Promoted once again in 1930, they clung to First Division status throughout the decade, only twice finishing in the top half of the table. This despite the presence, early in the decade, of three of the so-called 'Wembley Wizards' – members of the Scotland team who had thrashed England at Wembley in 1928. Hughie Gallacher, Alec Jackson and Tommy Law were brought to Stamford Bridge for a combined total of almost £25,000, an absolute fortune by the standards of the time, but besides helping the club reach one FA Cup semi-final the threesome only added to Chelsea's reputation for maddening inconsistency.

Billy Birrell inherited quite an old side when he took over as manager in the spring of 1939, and only Woodley, Spence, Buchanan, Argue, Foss and Tennant were still on the books in 1945. The last two usually occupied the left-half and right-back positions, and both played against

Birmingham in the match viewed by the Dynamos, but Foss, suffering from water on the knee, would miss the game against the Russians. Neither Spence nor Argue was a regular first-teamer, but Peter Buchanan and Vic Woodley were both internationals, the former a winger who had played once for Scotland, the latter an excellent goalkeeper, now nearing the end of his career, who had appeared nineteen times for pre-war England. Buchanan didn't play against Birmingham, but Dolding, who had been preferred to him, picked up a knock which made him doubtful for the Dynamo game.

Several new players had become semi-regulars during the war – wing half Bobby Russell, forwards Reg Williams and Jimmy Bain – but with the post-war restart looming Birrell had dusted off the Chelsea cheque book and written out some large numbers. Two frequent wartime guests – England international inside-forward Len Goulden and centre-half John Harris – had been persuaded to make permanent moves from West Ham and Wolves respectively, and most dramatically of all, England's regular centre-forward Tommy Lawton had just been acquired from Everton for £14,000. He had been happy at the Merseyside club, but doctors had told him that his wife Rosaleen's health would benefit from a move to the south. Unlike the thirty-three-year-old Goulden, who was past his brilliant peak, the twenty-six-year-old Lawton was at the height of his powers, and he at least was guaranteed to give the Dynamos a stern test.

Watching his two-goal performance against Birmingham, first at Stamford Bridge and then in the privacy of the Embassy screening room, the Soviets knew this only too well. Doubtless Yakushin and the players discussed how they would deal with this threat and others as they watched and re-watched their film in the days that followed. By the time the two teams filed out on the Tuesday afternoon the Dynamos must have had a very good idea of their opponents' strengths and weaknesses.

Chelsea, by contrast, had very little notion of who and what they were up against. British ignorance of the Russian game was almost total – the only fact every Briton knew was that 'we' had introduced the game to 'them'. Given that, not much else seemed to matter.

5

From Blackburn with love

The first British sporting export to the Russia of the Tsars was rugby football. A Scottish resident by the name of Hopper introduced it in the early 1880s, but his success was short-lived. The Tsarist authorities decided that such a violent game could only encourage the population's regrettable tendency to riot, and banned it in 1886.

The following year Clement Charnock, another British long-standing resident, tried the more civilised association variant. He was the eldest son of William Charnock, one of three Lancastrian brothers who had played a key role in the creation of the Russian textile industry in mid-century. Now his generation – himself, his three brothers and one cousin – ran the huge mill complexes at Serpukhov, some sixty miles to the south of Moscow, and Orekhovo-Zuyevo, a similar distance to the east. Clement was manager of the latter Morozov mills, and it was here in 1887 that he began seriously pursuing the Charnock family's other vocation, as missionaries of football.

The whole family seem to have been daft about the game, but there were also practical reasons for their proselytising zeal. The Charnocks were highly paternalistic employers who believed in giving their workers the best of everything, from free flats with hot and cold running water through classes in music and painting to a factory theatre. They were also keen to rid the Russian workers of their appalling habit of spending the weekly day off in a vodka-induced stupor. A countervailing passion for football would provide them with a good reason to stay conscious.

There were teething troubles. According to Robert Bruce Lockhart, the Foreign Office agent who spent considerable time in Russia both before and during the Bolshevik Revolution, Clement Charnock first inflated a football before a curious crowd of workers and peasants and then kicked it high in the air. 'When it came down with a thud and bounced high again, the workers ran away.' Natives will be natives.

Apparently undeterred by this precipitate – and probably fictional – flight, Charnock persevered. A pitch was laid and marked out, posts raised. Shirts, shorts and socks were imported from England, all in the blue and white of the Charnocks' beloved Blackburn Rovers, but boots proved too expensive, so studs were fitted to the players' shoes instead. The only thing missing was local enthusiasm, and after a year or so of exhortation Clement Charnock finally accepted defeat. The team that would one day bear the name of Moscow Dynamo appeared stillborn.

In the capital, St Petersburg, football was doing rather better. The first recorded match between Russians was played at the Semyonov Hippodrome in 1892, but no one was too sure of the rules, and this referee-less encounter bore as much resemblance to village kickabouts in medieval England as it did to that country's recently founded Football League. The city's British and German communities formed the first club in 1894, but it was another two years before a Frenchman's translation of the rules into Russian allowed for the first properly policed game between locals. In 1897 the first Russian club, Sport, was formed.

Meanwhile, back in the Moscow area, Clement

Charnock's younger brother Harry was revitalising the dormant Morozovtsi. An advertisement in *The Times* sought out British 'engineers, mechanics, and clerks capable of playing football well', and several other clubs were organised in nearby towns. For three or four years it seemed as if this time the game would stick, but increasing opposition to the sport on religious grounds proved hard to overcome. The district was home to a large number of Old Believers, a dissenting and extremely conservative sect of the Russian Orthodox Church who believed games to be sinful, and naked knees especially so. Once again the Charnocks' missionary dreams had to be put on hold.

St Petersburg was more cosmopolitan, and as the century turned there was a big expansion in the number of teams, both Russian and foreign. A league was formed by the foreigners in 1901, and the Russian team Sport gained entry a year later, although not without some opposition. Indeed, the next few years were marked by growing local resentment of foreign meddling in all things Russian, and football was among the lesser battlefields. Jim Riordan recounts one series of incidents which took place in 1903, beginning with the sending-off of a Russian player, Chirtsov, for fouling an English player, Sharples, in a Sport v. Nevsky game refereed by another Englishman, V. S. Martin. Chirtsov was banned for a year, although according to the Russian magazine *Sport* he had simply put in 'a hard but quite legitimate tackle'. Sharples, who had retaliated by knocking the Russian to the snow and 'almost throttling' him, was let off with a caution. 'Will this gladden the hearts of Russian sportsmen?' the magazine asked sarcastically. 'I don't think so. The English, in their typically high-handed way, with their large voting majority, are banning a Russian who is completely guiltless and exonerating a man who is obviously dangerous but is one of their own! Let Russian clubs band together and form their own league.'

In Moscow any sort of league was still several years away, but at last the Morozovtsi, now bearing the name Sports Club, Orekhovo (OKS), were up and properly running. Harry Charnock had finally gone right to the top in his efforts to gain official sanction for the club, travelling to the local provincial capital, Vladimir, for tea with the Governor. While His Excellency's good lady presided over the samovar, Harry answered the Governor's probing questions.

'What is football?' he was asked.

'A game played by twenty-two players, divided equally, to obtain possession of an inflated rubber and leather sphere, and each striving to drive it through posts fixed at the ends of a playing field,' he explained.

'And do people gather to watch this?' His Excellency asked. 'What stupidity!'

Harry assured him that it was no more stupid than horse racing, and that football's political pedigree was just as pure. Pulling a handy German periodical out of his pocket, he showed the Governor a photograph of the German Crown Prince taking part in a game on Berlin's Tempelhof field. 'And Your Excellency knows that he is a cousin of our gracious ruler the Tsar,' he added somewhat superfluously.

At which point His Excellency's good lady interrupted with the suggestion that her twenty-stone husband should try the game himself. 'Yes,' he agreed, adding that he greatly admired the English, even if they did beat their wives. Charnock could have his football club.

And so the future Dynamo was finally set in motion by a minion of the Tsar, just before the latter's moribund regime suffered its first major intimation of mortality – the revolutionary upsurge of 1905–6. This, as it turned out, was mostly good news for Russian football fans, for in its aftermath the regime set out to encourage team sports in the hope that they might soak up some of the passion that was fuelling the demands for revolutionary change. In practical terms this meant the Tsarist state getting much more involved in the organisation of Russian sport, which had, like Russian industry, been left largely in the hands of foreigners. As a consequence sport in Russia, even before the Revolution, was leaning towards the Mediterranean and Latin American model of state-sponsored multi-sport clubs, not the Anglo-American model of self-financed bodies for separate sports. When the Bolsheviks finally triumphed over their enemies in 1921 they would need only to pick up the cast-off reins of an already centralised organisation.

In the immediate aftermath of 1905–6, however, the Russians were still seeing off the foreign challenge, and a significant landmark was reached in 1908 when Sport became the first Russian team to win the St Petersburg league. There was another sending-off in a Nevsky match, only this time it was an Englishman who received his marching orders. He left the field to a 'terrible din' of complaint from the English section of the crowd and loud hissing from the Russian, and no doubt found little comfort in any realisation that his expulsion was an obvious sign of the times.

More were to follow. The illustrated magazine *Russian Sport* commenced publication in 1908, and during the following two years leagues in Moscow and many other provincial centres were formed in imitation of the capital's. Foreign influence lasted longer in Moscow, where the Charnocks' OKS won the league in five consecutive seasons with a team split roughly fifty-fifty between Russians and Brits. Bruce Lockhart played for them throughout the 1912 season, and had happy memories of the experience. 'The ground,' he reported, 'was dead-level and had a good covering of grass. There was an excellent pavilion with an enclosure of seats in front . . . it had dressing rooms, baths, a dining room, a large hall for social gatherings and a cinema theatre.' Crowds of more than 10,000 were commonplace.

The team itself, which in 1912 usually contained six Britons and five Russians, 'always turned out in a beautifully clean kit provided by the firm, and was played on to the field by the factory band'. It was still dominated by Charnocks, three of whom – William's younger sons Ted and Billy and their cousin Jim – played left-half, centre-forward and centre-half respectively. Jim captained the team, while Billy was probably the best player in Russia, having played for Bishop Auckland and been coveted by Manchester City.

The team's style of play would not have seemed out of place in the Charnocks' Blackburn; it was based, according to Bruce Lockhart, on the old 'Newcastle and Scottish scientific game of ball control' which the English league had later 'scrapped for speed'. More noteworthy was a 'complete absence of dirty and rough play'. In three years of playing and watching he claimed to have seen only two instances of bad sportsmanship, both the work of non-Russians.

The crowds were well-behaved too, especially at Orekhovo-Zuyevo, where there was no roar or booing, and goals were greeted with polite applause. This said much for the workers' training, Bruce Lockhart added paternalistically, 'for the refereeing was far from good, partly because referees operated from the touchline and rarely moved from the centre of the ground'.

The game was now firmly implanted in the big cities and spreading swiftly through the rest of the Tsar's empire. In 1912 came the establishment of the All-Russia Football Union, whose remit was to unify the various football organisations, make sure everyone was playing to the same rules, and affiliate itself to the international governing body FIFA. An all-Russia championship followed that autumn, involving five representative teams from St Petersburg, Moscow, Kiev, Kharkov and Odessa. No team was allowed to field more than three Englishmen.

The first international contacts had already been made. Sport travelled to Stockholm in 1907, and Corinthians of Prague were the first foreign side to visit Russia, playing three matches there in 1910. An *ad hoc* team of British professionals calling themselves the Wanderers arrived the following year, winning their three games 14–0, 7–0 and 10–0. Clearly the Russians had some catching up to do.

Undaunted, they sent a team to Stockholm for the 1912 Olympics; it lost narrowly to the Finns and then calamitously to the Germans by sixteen goals to nil. Later that year the Hungarians came to Moscow and scored twenty-one times in two matches against an unofficial Russian national XI. In 1913 things got marginally better: the Swedes scored only four and the Norwegians were actually held to a draw. Reruns in Oslo and Stockholm during the pregnant summer of 1914 saw steady improvement: the same Russian XI secured two hard-fought draws.

In that same summer a London University XI played four games in Russia – the first against the Morozovtsi, the last against an all-Moscow side – winning three and drawing the other. This humbling of the best the Russians could offer by a bunch of British amateurs was the last British experience of Russian football before war, revolution and Stalin dropped a curtain round the country, and not surprisingly it lingered longer in the British memory than it should have. Admittedly thirty years had now passed since then, but how much more could they have learned on their own?

During the first week of the tour there had been few mentions of individual Dynamos. Trainer Yakushin had borne most of the media brunt on his own, with occasional help from team captain Mikhail Semichastny and goalkeeper Alexei Khomich; the rest of the players remained almost as anonymous as the day they arrived. No one had yet questioned anyone's bona fides as a regular Moscow Dynamo player, and whichever team was named to play against Chelsea would be accepted in blissful ignorance by FA, opponents and press.

The *Daily Worker* article on Tuesday 30 October had named ten members of a team: Khomich, Radikorsky, Stankevich, Semichastny, L. Soloviev, Trofimov, Kartsev, Beskov, Dementiev and S. Soloviev. The right-half's characteristics were described but his name omitted, probably by accident. There seems no reason to doubt that it was Blinkov.

Two days later, and still three days shy of the tourists' arrival in Britain, the *Evening News* came out with a slight variation on the same theme, listing an eleven that comprised Fomich, Valikovski, Ankevich, Blinkov, Semichatny, Soloviev, Sbloviev, Trofimov, Kartsbv, Bobkov and Mariakin. Someone on the copy-desk had obviously had a bad day, even given the traditional difficulties encountered in transliterating from the Cyrillic. Blinkov, Soloviev and Trofimov were correct; Fomich for Khomich, Semichatny for Semichastny and Mariakin for Mariavkin seemed close enough. Ankevich for Stankevich was only a slight stretch, as was Kartsbv for Kartsev. Sbloviev merely suggested the writer couldn't cope with two Solovievs, but Valikovski was a long way from Radikorsky, who was one of Dynamo's longest-serving players. Bobkov could have been either Beskov or Bobrov, both of whom played on the tour, but was probably Beskov, who along with Semichastny was one of the team's better-known stars.

Assuming that this team, which the *Evening News* had conjured up from sources unmentioned and unknown, comprised Khomich, Radikorsky, Stankevich, Blinkov, Semichastny, L. Soloviev, S. Soloviev, Trofimov, Kartsev, Beskov and Mariavkin, then it differed in only one player from the *Daily Worker* XI, with Mariavkin substituting for Dementiev.

All twelve players mentioned in these two teams would apparently play in every tour game for which they were passed fit. Eight of them – Khomich, Radikorsky, Stankevich, Blinkov, Semichastny, Sergei Soloviev, Kartsev and Beskov – would start every game, and the remaining four would all be ruled out through apparent injury or illness. Dementiev, according to a fellow player on the eve of the fourth game at Ibrox, pulled a muscle in the team's first practice match at the White City. Trofimov strained ligaments in an early training session, and would not last the distance in the one game he started. Mariavkin was hospitalised with jaundice in the first few days of the tour, though the fact of his illness would become widely known only after the Chelsea game. Leonid Soloviev would be injured and substituted in the Arsenal match.

Of the twelve, only Nikolai Dementiev's status as a bona fide Moscow Dynamo player has been subsequently called into question. Jack Rollin, in his *Soccer at War*, states that Dementiev was a Moscow Spartak player in 1945, but the credibility of this claim is weakened by another: his unlikely assertion that Bobrov, who was only around twenty-three in 1945, played for Leningrad Dynamo from 1939 to 1941.

There is no doubt that Dementiev was playing for Moscow Spartak in 1947, and this, together with his omission from the team printed in the *Evening News*, adds credence to the suggestion that he was not a Dynamo player. On the other hand, he was, unlike proven ringers Bobrov and Archangelski, mentioned in the *Daily Worker/Soviet News* piece, and given a star build-up to boot. On the Saturday before the Chelsea game he was even singled out for praise: he would soon be 'a firm favourite', George Sinfield wrote. He was the 'image of Alex James in craft and stature', with 'an unruly tuft of hair, cheeky face and twinkling feet'. He even wore 'knee-length pants as baggy as any worn by the famous Scot in the heyday of his career'.

The fact that Dementiev merited such publicity, especially when set against the fact that neither Bobrov nor Archangelski received a single Soviet mention until their names suddenly appeared on the revised team-sheet for the game against Chelsea, suggests that he may have been a regular Dynamo player at this time. If so, then the twelve players listed in the *Daily Worker* and *Evening News* bore a very close resemblance to the team that had just won the championship. And the fact that each of the twelve played in every game for which he was passed fit makes it seem at least possible that the Soviets intended fielding the regular Moscow Dynamo first team if and when they could.

The early removal of Trofimov, Dementiev and Mariavkin denied them this choice, and led to the drafting in of

Vsevolod Bobrov and Evgeny Archangelski, both of whom were undoubtedly guest players. Inside-forward Bobrov had just played a starring role in Central House of the Red Army's season, and, according to the *Moscow News*, winger Archangelski didn't join Moscow Dynamo until the beginning of the 1947 season. Who he played for in 1945 remains a moot point. He may have been one of the mystery Leningrad Dynamo players, but one slim piece of circumstantial evidence suggests that he was on Spartak's books. When that club's famous Starostin brothers were arrested in 1942 there was an Evgeny Archangelski among the team-mates who were taken in for questioning.

Both Bobrov and Archangelski were clearly excellent players, and their inclusion in the team as replacements for the highly-rated Dementiev and Trofimov seems – at first glance, anyway – to have made little difference to the strength of the original team. But the evidence, fragmentary as it is, suggests that using guests to strengthen the team was not the deliberate intention, that their last-minute inclusion constituted Plan B rather than Plan A. They had been added to the party not so much to allow for the fielding of a stronger Dynamo as to mitigate against the possibility of fielding a weaker one.

6

Passovotchka

For those moving hell and high water to get tickets for the first game, one list of tongue-twisting Russian names was doubtless as good as another. There were no famous players whose inclusion or otherwise would cause comment, no TV clips of the Russians playing either at home or abroad. The only thing anyone knew about the individual players was what the newspapers had told them, and that was precious little. Moscow Dynamo, whether by design or by accident, remained a credit to its collective origins.

The lack of proven stars was no hindrance at the ticket office. Stamford Bridge opened its sales windows at 9.30 on the day before the game, but by then people had already been queuing in the bitter cold since before seven, many of them women standing in for their husbands. Eight hundred of the 10/- seats went in two hours, which exhausted the number Chelsea had ready. It was decided that names would be taken for a further 300 tickets, to be printed up later that day, but once the queues had shortened by that number thousands remained unsatisfied, and it took two appeals from Chelsea manager Birrell to disperse the angry crowd.

In its coverage of these scenes on the following morning the *Daily Mirror* concluded that Moscow Dynamo's 'Garbo act' was going to pay 'a rich dividend', but as yet the only people who realised just how rich were the touts, who had been happily selling 10/- tickets for three times that amount in the West End. British football fans, starved of anything out of the ordinary for six years, imaginations now gripped by this exotic invasion of football-booted mutes from the mysterious East, wanted to see this match. And some of them, it turned out, would willingly risk both life and limb to do so.

It was around 8 a.m. that the first would-be spectators arrived at Stamford Bridge; these included both British and foreign servicemen, one of whom was carrying a large red banner. The gates were not scheduled to open until 1p.m. for the 2.30 kick-off, but these early birds obviously knew something, because in next to no time the trickle of arrivals was turning into a flood. Prominent among the first wave were several hundred members of London's Russian community, who could be seen and heard excitedly discussing the match prospects in groups strung out along the Fulham Road.

The British, reading their newspapers in the queue, discovered that the dates had been fixed for the demobilisation of the country's 55,000 Land Girls: those with four years' service would be out in December, the rest by March. There was no fresh news from Washington, where Prime Minister Attlee was holding talks with President Truman about the atom bomb in particular and the state of the post-war world in general. According to the previous day's *Express* the PM was still opposing the American assumption of an atomic monopoly, arguing instead for a handover to the Security Council.

Nor was there any news of a breakthrough in the 'clippie' row, and London's aggrieved bus conductors were still refusing to take standing passengers. On

Remembrance Sunday several heated rows between conductors and passengers had been broken off at 11 a.m. for observation of the two minutes' silence, and resumed with gusto at 11.02.

The threatened industrial action on the football field, by contrast, had finally been called off. The League had agreed to a new £9 maximum weekly wage, £5 match fees for servicemen, the reintroduction of pre-war win and draw bonuses, and improved compensation for injuries. All this was for one season only, and everything would be up for renegotiation in the spring. L. V. Manning reckoned the Players Union would double its membership in the intervening months.

On the back page of the *News Chronicle* Charles Buchan delivered his pre-match verdict. The Russians would 'have no excuses to offer if defeated, as I anticipate they will be. They are, after all, only a strong club side playing in strange conditions and cannot be expected to hold a strong First Division side just strengthened by the transfer of Tommy Lawton.'

It was a cold and overcast autumn day, but the morning mood was good, with each new arrival quick to appreciate the lengthening queues behind him, and congratulate himself on his perspicacity in getting there so early. The locals were soon doing a roaring trade in hiring out their gardens for bicycle storage at threepence a bike, and anything up to 2/6 for helping drivers find a side-street space for their cars. Hawkers were getting inflated prices for toffee apples and oranges, pickpockets cheerfully waiting for the crowd to get denser. Competing sellers dispensed the official match programme, whose blue-printed pages welcomed the Dynamos in English and Russian, and a pirate version printed in red. A few cheerful bus conductors were even breaking ranks for the day and allowing a limited number of standing passengers.

But as the morning drew on this carnivalesque atmosphere slowly faded. The numbers intent on reaching Stamford Bridge were packing the District Line trains to suffocation point, and there were still plenty of conductors ready to enforce the no-standing rule and frustrate the beseeching groups which surrounded their buses. When they did finally arrive, these second- and third-wavers found swollen queues inching their way forward along the Fulham Road towards the now-open gates, a dense pack of bodies pressing dangerously hard against the glass shop-fronts. Most of the newcomers simply took their places at the end of a line, but some, emboldened by the obvious shortage of police, created more ill-feeling by jumping the queue. The pickpockets were now doing brisk business: one man, noticing a prominent warning sign, instinctively felt for his wallet. It was gone.

At 2.10, with a mass of seething fans some 20,000 strong – many of them ticket-holders – still trying to gain entrance, the gates were closed. Mounted police were already arriving to combat the expected trouble, but mounted police were not what the situation required. 'The most exciting battle since the Cup Final of 1923', as the *Daily Mail* somewhat irresponsibly tagged the events of the next forty minutes, would be fought on walls and in gardens, along railway lines and on roofs, none of which offered much room for a cavalry charge.

Confronted by the clang of the closing gates, a few people decided to give it all up as a bad job and go home. A few more walked off down the road in the hope of selling their tickets to people who didn't yet know that the gates were closed. The rest set about finding some illegitimate way of seeing the match.

Then as now, Stamford Bridge occupied the centre of a

rough triangle drawn by the Fulham Road, the electrified London Transport District Line north of Fulham Broadway station, and a section of the cross-river West London Extension Line between Kensington Olympia and Clapham Junction, then closed to passenger traffic. Some of the buildings on the Fulham Road had windows and roofs high enough to allow a view into the ground, and these were an early target, groups of fans tackling them from both within and without. Gardens were trampled, windowsills mounted, pipes clambered up. Residents who answered their front doors were shoved aside, the intruders rushing upstairs in search of suitable vantage points. Many who made it on to the roofs, clinging to chimneys, even balanced precariously on top of the stacks, were left to their own devices, but the invaders of homes were eventually cleared out by the police. One group rampaged through a block of flats, broke down a woman's door, and pushed through to her kitchen window, from which at least part of the pitch was visible. She calmly called the police, who arrived a while later to eject them.

Other residents were luckier, in that the invaders came through one door or window, went straight through their flats, and disappeared out of another into the gardens behind, where low palings offered a way into the ground. There were at least 15,000 people intent on breaking into Stamford Bridge at this point, and most of them were to be successful.

The problem was attacked with varying degrees of subtlety. One man realised the possibilities inherent in the twenty-foot wall which flanked the main entrance, and a few moments later a long column of fans was silhouetted against the grey sky as they threaded their way along the narrow rim and into the back of the stand. On the Fulham Road two further means of admission were discovered: an unmanned staff entrance which needed some physical persuasion and a 'Ticket Holders Only' gate which was happily found to be unlocked. Hundreds poured through both these holes in the Chelsea defences, while the police made largely ineffectual attempts to stop them.

Even more direct methods were being used elsewhere on the Fulham Road, with men tearing down gates to use as battering-rams against the various fences and railings in their way. A more lateral approach was taken by a group of several hundred fans, who found their way into the disused Chelsea station on the south side of Fulham Road, walked north up the West London Extension tracks, and emerged from the tunnel under the road directly behind the main stand. After scrambling up the embankment they began climbing the back of the stand towards the roof.

Another even more intrepid bunch made the long trek round to the western side of the ground, where they stormed the high wrought-iron gates of the Oswald Stoll Foundation for Disabled Soldiers, rushed through the institute grounds, scaled another wall and picked their way across the electric Underground tracks, only to find themselves defeated by the stadium wall.

Those who had succeeded in breaking into the ground were now busily searching for a place from which they could actually see the action. Some 75,000 spectators had been allowed admission before the gates were closed, and space inside was definitely at a premium, so climbing was the only solution. A few people worked their way up inside the greyhound-racing tote box, removed clusters of light bulbs, and settled down to watch through the holes, but most aimed higher, clambering through girders or perching precipitously on roofs. The stand roof was mostly glass, and several people fell through it, the first, aptly enough, a man wearing the uniform of the Parachute Regiment. He landed in an empty seat, grinned widely at his new neighbours and settled down to enjoy the match. His successor was not so lucky, crash-landing on a ticket-holder who punched him violently on the nose.

This was not the only injury suffered. Several people were cut by falling glass, and one man had his face quite badly lacerated. As pressure built up on the terraces a few barriers buckled, and several bones were broken in the crushes. The unlucky ones, together with a number of women who had fainted, were manhandled down over the heads of the crowd to the waiting St John's Ambulancemen. Fourteen people were taken to the nearby St Stephen's Hospital, five detained, all with fractures. Given the scale of the 'battle', not to mention the mass dicing with electrocution on the District Line tracks, it was a miracle nobody was killed.

Eventually the crush on the terraces proved too much, and the crowd spilled over, across first the outer perimeter of the greyhound track and then the inner, right up to the edge of the pitch. This of course left thousands trying to see through a solid wall of human bodies, and the consequent frustration soon produced a hail of assorted missiles from those in the rear.

There had already been much in the way of pre-match entertainment. At around 1.45, to a surprised roar from the crowd, a large posse of Dynamos emerged from the tunnel. Three in sweatsuits stayed on the touchline, but the rest raced out on to the pitch, all but one of them wearing darkish blue shirts with a scrolled white 'D' on the left breast, long, slightly lighter blue shorts with circling white rings just above the hem, and white-ringed bottle-green socks. The odd man out, a coat over his kit, was Khomich the goalkeeper; he took photographs as his fellow players – much to the crowd's amazement – made good use of the balls Yakushin had insisted on in a fifteen-minute warm-up training session. Such a strange ritual had never previously been witnessed in the home of football.

Soon after two, the Dynamos retreated down the tunnel, only to emerge again a few minutes later behind Yakushin, as the coach led them out alongside the red-shirted Chelsea. The two teams had only been finalised in the hours before kick-off, Dynamo bringing in, without any explanation, Archangelski and Bobrov at outside-right and inside-left respectively. Chelsea had also drafted in two 'foreign' guests from Fulham to replace the injured White and Foss: Jim Taylor, an England international left-half, and Joe Bacuzzi, the popular left-back.

The teams lined up facing each other, and it slowly dawned on the huge crowd that each Russian was armed with a bouquet of red and white flowers. As the band of the Royal Marines launched into the Soviet national anthem, many in the crowd waved the small red flags they had purchased from hawkers in the Fulham Road, a scene proudly described by Vadim Sinyavsky to millions of radio listeners in the Soviet Union. The Russian cine-cameras were whirring to record everything for later broadcasting back home, their British Army equivalents for the future benefit of the forces away in Germany. The press box overflowed with journalists, most of whom would soon be eating their words. Raymond Glendenning waited behind a dead BBC microphone: live commentary was scheduled only for the second half.

The two anthems over, an extraordinary thing happened. In Tommy Lawton's words: 'Suddenly, at a word of command from their trainer, they stepped smartly forward and with a bow – but without the flicker of a smile on their faces – they handed each of us a bouquet.'

Photographs of the immediate aftermath are telling. The Chelsea players stand there holding their bouquets, their faces offering numerous variations on the universal theme of embarrassment. John Harris and Billy Birrell are sharing an 'Oh my God, look what just happened' smile, goalkeeper Vic Woodley stares straight at the photographer wishing the pitch would swallow him up. Others giggle nervously or stare open-mouthed in disbelief. You can almost feel them shuffling their feet. This, the faces seem to say, is what comes of inviting foreigners to play football.

Few in the crowd could see the expressions on the home team's faces, but most could imagine them, and a huge roar of laughter echoed round Stamford Bridge, swiftly followed by a prolonged roar of approval. 'What's this then – Chelsea's funeral?' one wag shouted. The crowd could see the funny side, but they also appreciated the gesture, evoking as it did the emotional bond between the two countries which lay at the heart of the tour. In that moment more than a few minds must have gone back to the summer and autumn of 1941, when only Britain and Russia had stood between Nazi Germany and victory.

In the absence of royalty the teams were presented to some less exalted dignitaries, which gave Lawton time to take a good look at the opposition. He decided 'they looked a young, beautifully-built team, rather exotically dressed . . . When they stood still it looked for all the world as if they were wearing old-fashioned bathing costumes.' He made no mention of their looking nervous, but it would have been surprising if they hadn't been. The Russians were a long way from home, and they were about to play a crucial game in front of the largest crowd they'd ever seen, a crowd, moreover, that seemed with every passing moment to be encroaching further on to the playing area. Looking up at the lines of silhouetted figures clinging to the various roofs they must have wondered if this was the way the British usually did things.

Introductions over, the teams took to their respective halves. The two captains joined referee Lieutenant-Commander G. Clark, RN, in the centre circle, where it soon became apparent that Semichastny had no idea what was meant by heads and tails. A Russian-speaking referee could have explained, but of course one hadn't been chosen. Had the Dynamo captain spoken English he might have explained to Clark and John Harris that in the Soviet Union there were no heads on coins, and that referees offered the captains a choice of two slips of paper, one bearing the words 'choice of ends', the other 'kick off'. But of course he didn't.

Eventually a mixture of mime and hand signals succeeded where language had been found wanting. The coin was tossed, the call made, the teams lined up in formation. Lieutenant-Commander Clark took one last look round, checked that there were only twenty-two players on the pitch, picked out the bright-coloured flags of his linesmen against the dark wall of the encroaching crowd. After weeks of waiting for their arrival, and ten speculation-filled days waiting for this particular moment, the British were about to see the Dynamos play football.

The start could hardly have been more dramatic. The Dynamos, 'so slow you could almost hear them think', immediately mounted a series of fast-moving attacks on the Chelsea goal, drawing gasps from the crowd with their skill on the ball. Before two minutes had passed Woodley had saved one shot, been hit by another, and punched a third away for a corner. Chelsea were under the cosh.

Right – **CHELSEA** – Left

WOODLEY

2 TENNANT 3 BACUZZI

4 RUSSELL 5 HARRIS 6 TAYLOR

7 BUCHANAN 8 WILLIAMS 9 LAWTON 10 GOULDEN 11 CARKE

Referee:
Lt-Com. G. Clark, RN

Linesmen:
A.T. Ford
W. Vine

11 SOLOVIEV S. 10 BOBROV 9 BESKOV 8 KARTSEV 7 ARCHANGELSKI

6 SOLOVIEV L. 5 SEMICHASTNY 4 BLINKOV

3 STANKEVICH 2 RADIKORSKY

KHOMICH

Left – **MOSCOW DYNAMO** – Right

In the third minute a Blinkov pass found winger Archangelski, who cut inside, left two Chelsea defenders for dead, and smashed a left-foot shot into the side-netting. Two minutes after that the sandy-haired Bobrov, without apparent effort, struck the post with a rasping drive from just outside the penalty area. The Chelsea defenders looked at one another as if to say, 'What the hell is this?'

The Dynamos were not following any known script. In this first twenty minutes they seemed almost like supermen, changing positions on the run like a beautifully choreographed dance group, spinning into space and flicking the ball off to each other with a deftness that left their opponents looking leaden-footed. *Passovotchka* was the Russian name for it – the short passing game played at speed, all angles and anticipation, all sweet flowing movement.

And when their opponents had the ball the Russians were showing none of that reluctance to tackle or charge which had been so widely predicted. On the contrary, they were biting in, winning the ball, and then launching another exhilarating, graceful assault on the opposition goal. Where Chelsea stumbled they seemed to glide.

It was not all one-way traffic. After about ten minutes Bobby Russell and Len Goulden neatly linked up to create an opening for Reg Williams, who blasted over with only Khomich to beat, and a few minutes later the Russian keeper was forced to tip over a speculative thirty-yarder from Peter Buchanan. At this stage Lawton was playing deeper than usual, trying to escape the clutches of Semichastny, who was already looking a tower of strength at centre-half.

The other nominal centre-forward, Konstantin Beskov, was also lying deeper than a centre-forward was supposed to, but that was the way Dynamo played, with the two inside-forwards taking the main striking roles. One journalist would later say that 'it was almost impossible to decide whether Kartsev or Beskov was leading the attack', and it spoke volumes that he needed to know, as if putting a name to the man giving Harris such a nightmare would help to stop him.

Still the chances came and went. After a quarter of an hour Vassili Kartsev went for the heart, weaving his way into the area through several challenges and bringing Woodley to his knees with too straight a shot. A few minutes later it was Beskov's turn, as he hit the post from twenty-five yards with Woodley well beaten. It seemed only a matter of time before they scored.

And then, as so often seems to happen, the other team broke away and scored themselves. A Dynamo corner was cleared to Jimmy Bain, who sped down the left wing and threw over a hard and early cross. Lawton and Khomich reached the ball at roughly the same time, but the centre-forward, in his own words, 'managed to force it out of his hands and tap it sideways to Goulden', who gleefully lashed it high into the net. A goal would not have been given in the Soviet Union then, and it wouldn't be given in the Premiership now, but both sides had agreed to play by the British rules of the time. Completely against the run of play, Chelsea were 1–0 up.

They were still congratulating themselves when, straight from the kick-off, Bobrov was put through on goal with only Woodley to beat. He blasted it over the bar and stood for a second searching the heavens for a reason.

Worse was to come. In a situation of no apparent danger Stankevich and Khomich got their signals confused over a back pass, Reg Williams hopefully threw himself into the mix, and Stankevich's hurried clearance rebounded off the Chelsea player's body and into the net. Though they deserved to be at least two goals behind, Chelsea were two goals ahead.

One can only imagine what paranoid thoughts were running through the minds of the Dynamo players and staff. They knew they had played brilliantly, but at this rate they were going to lose 6–0. At that moment the weight of expectations back home must have felt almost crushing. Chelsea, by contrast, were suddenly playing with more confidence. Lawton still seemed firmly under Semichastny's thumb, but their own defence appeared to be getting the Dynamos' measure, with Bacuzzi and

Russell in particular making a series of timely interceptions and tackles.

Almost ten minutes went by with neither side making a chance, and half-time was looming on the horizon when Bobby Russell mistimed a sliding tackle on Konstantin Beskov in the penalty area and brought him down. He managed to come away with the ball, but Lieutenant-Commander Clark showed no hesitation in pointing to the spot.

Up stepped Leonid 'Snowy' Soloviev, probably wishing he was anywhere else on earth. Pressure was hardly the word. This was the man who according to the British press never missed penalties, but had in fact missed one in the last important match he had played – the Soviet cup final. Now, on an afternoon when his forwards had contrived to miss every chance that came their way, it had fallen on him to make amends. In front of him stood not only Woodley, but an intimidating wall of densely-packed fans on either side of the goal, leaning forward across the goal-line and actually pressing against the posts. As he ran up to take the kick the Russian must have felt their collective breath slowing him down.

The ball, cleanly but inaccurately struck, rebounded off a post and almost dislocated the neck of one of the spectators. A distraught Soloviev clutched his head in his hands.

Minutes later the deficit was nearly raised to three. Lawton, unexpectedly finding himself in a space only ten yards from goal, had a chance to put the game virtually beyond the Russians' reach, but Khomich made his first difficult save of the game. When half-time came two minutes later they were still only two behind, and in with a chance.

Yakushin's team talk has never been published, but it was probably a Russian variation on 'just carry on doing what you've been doing'. Shooting apart, his team had hardly put a foot wrong, and whether he knew it or not, the whole crowd was buzzing with the wonderful quality of the Dynamos' play and the amazing difference in styles. All that intricate close passing at high speed offered such a contrast to Chelsea's reliance on chasing the long ball. Most of the hundred thousand or so crammed into Stamford Bridge didn't really care who won: they'd come to see something special, and they hadn't been disappointed.

Among the Soviet section of the crowd the mood, not surprisingly, was rather less upbeat. *Moscow News* writer A. Yakovlev was with an engineer friend who doubled as a soccer coach. Asked at half-time what he thought of the game the friend didn't reply, but just reached for a cigarette. 'I understood how he felt,' Yakovlev wrote. 'Usually when two strong Soviet teams meet, a lead of two goals in the first half means eventual victory.' Soviet swimmer Leonid Meshkov, also watching, was just as worried. He was convinced that the excitement of their first game abroad had badly affected the Dynamo players, that their level of performance in the first half was well below what they were capable of.

The teams reappeared. Though substitutions had been agreed in case of injury none had been made. Play restarted with Chelsea defending the Shed end, and within two minutes Kartsev was presented with a chance which he drove over the bar. Then Bobrov drew a great save from Woodley. It seemed like a rerun of the first half, with the Russian forwards – and particularly Kartsev – stretching the Chelsea defence all over the place. The inside-right was soon clean through again, Woodley saving at point-blank range. In the press box the football journalists were all dragging out the old saw about foreigners not being able to shoot.

Lawton could shoot, as he showed soon after the hour mark, hitting the post from about twenty-five yards. The ball flew back across the goal behind the prone Khomich and was quickly cleared upfield.

As if inspired by the example, Dynamo finally scored five minutes later. 'Steady, comrades, steady,' Sinyavsky was telling the Soviet Union as Kartsev collected a short pass from Archangelski, jinked past both Harris and Taylor, and crashed home a drive from just outside the penalty area.

'He's through!' Sinyavsky yelled. 'He has scored! Yes, comrades, you can kiss him!'

But they didn't. Well-known kissers in diplomatic circles, the Russians could have been forgiven for smothering Kartsev in big wet ones, but like amateurs of old they just shook hands and ran back to the halfway line.

Raymond Glendenning, meanwhile, was handicapped by the lack of numbers on Dynamo shirts. 'Bobrov, a shot . . . it's a goal,' he announced with the well-bred voice of the times. 'Yes, he's scored . . . Kartsev, rather . . . Kartsev . . . a lovely goal.' And to show his listeners how much the crowd had enjoyed the Russian score he twisted his microphone round to catch the roar of approval still echoing around the Bridge.

There was no stopping the Dynamos now. In the seventy-fifth minute a quickly-taken free kick by Blinkov found Kartsev on the right, and he showed great footwork to draw in the Chelsea defence before slipping the ball inside to Archangelski. The winger's hard cross-shot took a slight deflection off Russell's leg, but was probably headed for the far corner in any event. The crowd first roared with appreciation of the Dynamo fightback, and then set about getting behind their own team, who now showed some fight of their own.

Lawton was at last getting some change out of Semichastny, and in quick succession two shots forced flying saves from Khomich. In the eighty-first minute his foot beat Khomich's hands to a lobbed ball in a crowded Dynamo goalmouth, but Semichastny got a head to his hooked shot, sending it high in the air. Lawton and at least two Dynamo defenders went for the dropping ball, the Englishman soaring above everyone else to head a glorious goal. It was the first and last time in the match that the Russians clearly came in second-best.

The last ten minutes were clearly theirs. Several times they simply walked the ball through the tiring Chelsea defence only to fail at the last. In these closing minutes their movement on the ball, according to several observers, seemed at least as fast, if not faster, than it had at the beginning. They were not only good, they were fit.

The final goal of the game came with five minutes remaining. Right-back Radikorsky won the ball from Goulden and sent Archangelski away down the right. His cross rebounded off someone to Bobrov, standing several yards offside, and he thumped it home to a huge roar of approval from the crowd. Most of the following day's papers thought that strictly speaking the goal should have been disallowed, but for once the *Daily Worker* and the *Daily Telegraph* found something to agree on – both claimed the ball had reached Bobrov via a Chelsea defender, who had thus played him on.

A minute later it was almost 4–3, as another Bobrov shot grazed Woodley's right-hand post, but when the final whistle blew, honours were still even. The crowd poured on to the pitch, and the Dynamos probably shared a few anxious moments as the fans hurtled towards them. But then they were surrounded by smiles and congratulations, several hoisted high and carried from the field like conquering kings. The Russians might only have drawn, but they'd won the hearts of 100,000 football fans.

'Listen, comrades in Moscow, Leningrad, Tbilisi, Berlin,' Vadim Sinyavsky shouted breathlessly into his microphone. 'We have passed our first exam with honour.'

7

'Not our type of game'

It is not hard to imagine the post-match excitement in the Dynamo dressing room. They had triumphed over nerves, a softer pitch and a harder ball than they were used to, a referee enforcing strange rules, their own profligacy in front of goal. The two teams might have scored the same number of goals, but there was no doubting who had won the moral victory. Here, in the home of football, they had done their country proud.

And the British crowd had loved them.

'The football was very good indeed . . . very good . . . Chelsea are fine . . . we want to play again . . . and again,' the players burbled to a *Mirror* journalist who had somehow managed to penetrate the screen around them. 'They are very tired; their emotions are jumbled,' Elliseyeva said sternly as she showed the intrepid hack the door. They might say anything.

The official response was left to the usual crew of Andreanov, Yakushin and Semichastny. The Chairman of the Ministry of Physical Culture expressed his satisfaction with both result and crowd, and he meant every word of it. This was how sports diplomacy was supposed to work. The Dynamos had given a great account of themselves, and the Soviet Union was going to bathe in their reflected glory. From this point of view a draw and a moral victory might prove the best of all possible worlds;

after all, it wouldn't do to humiliate the British at the game they still considered their own.

The Yakushin of the week before – Fleet Street's intense, silent Russian who watched the world through narrowed eyes – was nowhere to be seen. In his place was a man who seemed to be almost falling over himself to communicate. His players had not known at first whether the crowd was applauding their efforts, but after half-time they had no longer been in any doubt: 'We could see that the crowd were very friendly to our men and applauded them even more than the British. We are like artists on the stage. When the public approves of our game we like the public.'

There was the obligatory war reference – 'When we were two goals down we compared the game to Stalingrad when the Germans were outside the gates; we were not downhearted and certain that our time would come' – and a very diplomatic finale. Having watched his team expose any number of limitations in their opponents' style of play, he asked reporters to 'please tell your people we really admire the British way of playing'. Even the referee was praised for his fairness. It had been 'a lovely game', Yakushin said. 'Perhaps if our forwards had aimed a bit better we would have won,' he added modestly.

Semichastny agreed. 'I hope we didn't disgrace ourselves,' he told reporters with a perfectly straight face. 'We found a bit of difficulty in getting used to your English shoulder-charge, but perhaps our Russian method of nearly all of us blocking the way to goal harassed your men too.' This frank admission that both footballing nations had developed methods the other found hard to accept – the violent charging of the English, the penchant for obstruction and holding that characterised the Dynamo style of play – showed a diplomatic level of understanding on Semichastny's part which both sides, and particularly the British, would have trouble living up to over the next couple of weeks.

In the Chelsea dressing room the mood was a strange mixture of exhilaration, confusion and defensiveness. They knew they'd just experienced something special, but they were reluctant to look too closely at exactly what it was. 'The Russians were on the move all the time,' full-back Tennant said, as if that was a breach of the rules; 'we could hardly keep up with them.' Bobby Russell thought they played 'a different type of football . . . something we are not used to', but denied it was 'a better type of game'. Len Goulden agreed that the Russians 'knew their stuff', that 'their football was really amazing', but remained convinced that 'a good club side that had been well trained and was in good condition might beat them'. John Harris would be more thoughtful in his Sunday column, but in the immediate aftermath of the game he too found it hard to accept what had happened. The Dynamos had 'positioned themselves better', were much fitter, and 'they certainly showed us how to play', but then 'it was not our type of game'. Only manager Billy Birrell was prepared to dish out unqualified praise, or at least a patriotic version of it. The Russians, he said, had played the best football he had seen since leaving Scotland.

A still-panting referee was tracked to his hot bath by one intrepid reporter. The Russians had been very fit and the game very fast, he admitted between gasps for air. His linesmen were presumably either underwater or still struggling to get off the pitch. Either way, they were not questioned, which was a pity. One of them might have been able to clear up the arguments over the Dynamo equaliser, and both, with spectators literally leaning over their shoulders, must have had unusually interesting afternoons.

That evening Chelsea held a dinner for the officials and players of both clubs at the West End's Café Royal. Gifts were exchanged: enamel badges, white with a blue 'D' and a red star, for the Chelsea players; inscribed cigarette lighters for both teams. Chelsea were formally invited to Moscow for a return engagement; speeches were delivered by Andreanov and the British First Lord of the Admiralty, who teased the Russians about their marksmanship. It was, according to Lawton, 'a very happy little gathering . . . although neither could speak the other's language everybody seemed to be able to make himself understood'.

The Russian party drove back to the Imperial Hotel, where many of the players spent a mostly wakeful night. They knew they had played really well, but that hadn't blinded them to some of the opposition's qualities, and they had been particularly impressed by Lawton and Goulden. They had both given and attended a master-class, and their heads were full of what they as footballers might learn from their hosts in the coming weeks.

Moscow Radio's match report on the Tuesday evening was a very restrained affair. 'Our boys were visibly nervous in the first half,' the reporter admitted, 'and they failed to take advantage of a number of chances. In the second half they were able to prove the high quality of their play. It is to be hoped,' he concluded mildly, 'that, armed with this experience, the Dynamos will not stop at a draw in future games.'

By contrast, the British press reports on Wednesday left

few superlatives unused. 'The greatest club side ever to visit this island', trumpeted L. V. Manning in the *Sketch*. Here was 'skill without force, speed without flurry – football as it was meant to be played'. Dynamo were 'all set for a triumphant tour during which I doubt if they will be beaten'. Charles Buchan, who had predicted defeat at Stamford Bridge, could not remember a team giving such an exhibition of class football and failing to win. 'If Dynamo had won by a handsome margin they would have got no more than they deserved,' he wrote in the *News Chronicle*. In the *Evening News*, J. G. Orange thought Dynamo 'compared very favourably' with the best British teams.

There was praise for everything but their marksmanship. The Russians' high technical ability was clear: Buchan thought their footwork 'a real delight'; Alan Breck, in the *Glasgow Evening Times*, noted their excellent trapping. And it wasn't just a couple of the forwards: Harry Miller, in the *Glasgow Evening News*, thought the two full-backs a revelation. They kicked the ball 'cleanly with either foot, and partook in the teamwork with an occasional dribble and pass to a well-placed colleague'. Such a comment, of course, spoke volumes about the lack of those skills among British defenders.

The Russian passing matched their ball control. There was no 'Continental obsession with short passing', but neither was there over-reliance on the aimless British punt downfield. They used the short ball, the medium ball, the long ball – whatever suited the circumstances – and their passes seemed invariably to find an unmarked man. Manning was particularly impressed with the inside-forwards' accurate use of 'the long inside pass'.

Several individuals had caught the eye. Radikorsky, Semichastny and Bobrov were each singled out by several papers, and Khomich, Beskov and Archangelski all gained honourable mentions. But, as Buchan stressed, 'it was not individually that the Russians shone, but in teamwork'. Their movement off the ball, and the sense of positional play which informed it, were nothing short of sensational for 1945. Wagstaffe Simons of the *Sporting Life* considered 'the way they found and used the open spaces' positively uncanny. It was 'many, many years' since he had seen its equal. 'Immediately a player had parted with the ball he kept going. He did not wait to see what would happen to his pass.'

The Russian players' frequent abandonment of their allotted patch of turf completely bewildered ex-player Davie Meiklejohn of the *Daily Record*. 'They interchanged positions to the extent of the outside-left running over to the right wing and vice versa,' he said wonderingly. 'I have never seen football played like it. It was a Chinese puzzle to try to follow the players in their positions as it was given in the programme. They simply wandered here and there at will, but the most remarkable feature of it all, they never got in each other's way.' The English would still be flummoxed by such behaviour in 1953, when another famous team refused to let their positions in the programme dictate their movements on the field.

The flowing attacking moves were given the most attention, but the Russian defenders also came in for their share of praise. Despite their surrendering 'three paltry goals through momentary misunderstanding', Harry Miller thought the defence 'top grade'. Manning noted that the supposed Russian refusal to tackle had been exposed as the myth it was, adding generously that 'they took their knocks splendidly', and mostly eschewed 'the obstruction tactics we have had to endure from Continental teams'.

The Russians had played brilliantly and sportingly, but the British deserved much of the credit. Not only had they given the Russians the game and the sense of fair play; they had even supplied the tactical blueprint. Dynamo played 'strikingly like the Corinthians' according to Manning, who then half-contradicted himself by saying their style was pure Scottish. Wagstaffe Simons had been reminded of 1928's 'Wembley Wizards', but the *Glasgow Herald* delved even deeper into the past, editorialising on 14 November: 'The controlled pass along the ground, the swift thrust by half the team in concert, were not the invention of the Corinthians, as some bemused Englishman has claimed, but devices that the English borrowed from the northern end of the kingdom. And it is gratifying that the Soviet champions find them of service. We could do far worse,' the editorial voice concluded wistfully, 'than adopt them again ourselves.'

Even after the British had claimed half the historical credit for the Dynamos' brilliance, it was hard not to notice the light this shone on the current poverty of the domestic game. To compare these Russian players with those on display at the previous weekend's Hampden international between Scotland and Wales, thought Harry Miller, was to bring 'a blush to our football cheeks'. And Alan Breck knew exactly what was going wrong. The Russians were playing the same football he had played as a boy, but as soon as British schoolboys went into amateur or professional teams they were taught 'crude and negative methods which completely ruin the majority as footballers'.

Why, the implicit question went, had football developed that way in Britain but not in Russia? Such questions would be voiced more openly as the tour went on, but for the moment most people were simply eager for a second helping, too caught up in the wonder of it all to worry about the how and the why.

On the the day after the Chelsea game everyone seemed happy. The hosts had a few crush barriers to replace and four holes in the stand roof to reglaze, but their half of the £7,000 gate represented a very tidy sum in 1945. They had recouped a quarter of Tommy Lawton's transfer fee in one go; the current equivalent would be Manchester United netting £3m. from a single friendly.

The Dynamos were no doubt pleased with their fee, which after deductions provided a £2,500 contribution to the Stalingrad Fund, and the Soviet media, which devoted much radio time and many column inches to the game, were generally delighted with the team's playing performance. The tourists' greatly improved ratings off the pitch over the last few days were also doubtless appreciated in the Kremlin.

The British magazine *Cavalcade* was certain that Anglo-Soviet relations, 'bedevilled for decades by politics . . . only partly cemented by war', had been given a helping hand. For a brief space at least, 'the evil tradition of past misunderstanding' had been dissipated, and those who had witnessed the miracle at Stamford Bridge were 'not likely to forget their pleasure'.

The Football Association, for its part, seemed almost delirious at this juncture. Perhaps the early difficulties of the tour made the current success all the sweeter, but Stanley Rous's sudden announcement that he was personally in favour of England's rejoining FIFA – after a seventeen-year absence – was a welcome surprise for those perceptive few who had long lamented Britain's self-imposed and self-destructive semi-isolation from the world game. The *Daily Worker*, which alone printed this announcement, went even further, suggesting in an editorial that it was time for a European football governing body. The Dynamo visit certainly seemed to be casting British eyes outward.

In the meantime, Cardiff manager Cyril Spiers was looking forward to Saturday's second instalment with optimism. Though enormously impressed by the Russians at Stamford Bridge, he still believed that his Third Division South team could give them a stern test. His players, who were on average about four years younger than Chelsea's, could certainly compete in terms of pace. 'How we shall compare in skill,' he added honestly, 'I would not like to say.'

Who else the Russians would play was still up for negotiation. The Arsenal game was definitely fixed for the coming Wednesday, but beyond that nothing was certain. After the Chelsea game Rous was quick to say that he hoped Dynamo would stay for a long time, and that a match against an FA XI would, he hoped, follow games against Coventry on the 24th and Glasgow Rangers on the 27th or 28th. At that moment the Russians would probably have been granted political asylum and instant Football League membership if they had only bothered to ask. And to cap it all, the *Daily Mirror* had started referring to 'tall, immovably serious' Mikhail Yakushin as 'Mike'.

The Russians were obviously unprepared for such an outpouring of love. At this first moment of triumph someone – presumably someone in Moscow – seems to have suddenly got cold feet. Dynamo could not commit to any more games, Rous was told. The reason? Winter had come early in Russia, the ice hockey season began when winter did, and the Dynamo footballers were pledged to play for the Dynamo hockey team.

Some of the Dynamo players were indeed hockey players of some repute. Yakushin, though retired from football as a player, still played hockey, and Vsevolod Bobrov would go on to become an Olympic gold medallist on the ice. That said, it still strains credibility to imagine that the demands of a club hockey team would be allowed to take precedence over a tour of this importance. It seems far more likely that the story was thought up in Moscow on the spur of the moment as an apolitical excuse for bringing the team home, should the need arise. Victory over Cardiff and defeat by Arsenal, for example, and the team could bolt for home without having disgraced itself. Of course if both were beaten then the demands of the ice hockey season could be conveniently forgotten once more.

What mattered was to sound plausible, and fortunately for the tour's Soviet organisers, British ignorance made that a lot easier than it should have been. When Paul Irwin announced in the *Sunday Express* the previous weekend that the Dynamos were 'simply a set of very earnest amateurs – factory workers who train at night and go through the motions on their off-duty day', he was not flooded with letters or phone calls putting him right. The quality of the Dynamo play at Stamford Bridge might have started people wondering just how the Russians had got so good on such a regime – some even used it as evidence for their argument that British football should be reorganised on a part-time basis – but no one leapt up and said, 'These players are obviously full-time professionals in all but name.'

The Dynamos had categorically stated that they weren't. They told the FA they were neither amateurs nor professionals according to British rules. They were amateurs in the sense that they each had a trade and that they received no wages under contract for playing. But of course they could neither work nor earn while on tour – or during training for the tour – so the club made up the difference in so-called travelling expenses. And after the tour they might be rewarded for 'outstanding achievements', though none of the players could count on that. In other words, the Soviets claimed, their players were as unpaid as it was possible for them to be.

The British press didn't challenge this because they had nothing to challenge it with. Nor did they investigate the related topic of which players were actually eligible to play for Moscow Dynamo. Mike and his lads were obviously a sporting bunch who trained hard in whatever spare time their jobs allowed them. They were, in fact, rather like the mixed Anglo-Russian teams of Edwardian times, an impression underlined by *The Times* on 14 November when it announced, apropos of nothing, that back home Moscow Dynamo were associated with the 'Civil Service'. What a comforting image! It certainly sounded a lot more pleasant than the truth, which was that Dynamo's long-term development had been achieved under the aegis of Stalin's security police, the NKVD.

8

Sponsored by the gulag

Search the works of Lenin and you won't find many subjects that evaded his attention. Sport was no exception. 'Young people,' he said, not long after the Revolution had fully established itself, 'need the joy and force of life – healthy sports and recreation of all kinds.' Providing the means was, of course, a duty of the state. Football clubs and players, like everything else in the Soviet Union, would be subject to the rules laid down to promote and protect the new society. Stadiums would be built with public money when the plans dictated; clubs would be funded from the public purse; players would, like steelworkers or farmers, be workers in the public sector, albeit more privileged ones than most.

In return, football would help form the model Soviet citizen. Like the British public schools before them, the Bolsheviks saw team games as a means of moulding character, though their emphasis was more on the team than on the individual. Playing such games could promote individual creativity within the necessary collective framework, individual responsibility against a background of collective discipline. And of course Soviet football would be better than its bourgeois counterpart. Lenin didn't say so – it's hard to escape the suspicion that he wasn't a great football fan – but it's reasonable to assume that he shared the belief, common among the early Bolsheviks, that the spread of socialist principles and practice would improve the quality of just about everything, football included. More specifically, it was almost an article of faith among football-minded Bolsheviks that a new Soviet style of play, stressing collectivism rather than individualism, would one day prove too potent for the bourgeois teams of the unreconstructed West.

It might, of course, be a long time before this theory could be put to the test. For one thing, the revolutionary Soviet Union remained a virtual pariah state well into the 1930s; for another, the Soviets themselves never quite made up their mind whether they wanted to engage in sporting competition with the bourgeois West. The aforementioned Scandinavian tour of 1923 was followed by two internationals against Turkey in 1924–5 – the Soviet Union won 3–0 in Moscow, 2–1 in Ankara – but the emphasis thereafter, as Stalin asserted his control and drastically reduced intergovernmental contacts, was on supporting so-called worker sports under the aegis of the Red Sports International.

A typical visitor in this later period was the team representing the British Workers' Sports Federation which future *Daily Worker* journalist George Sinfield took, as player–manager, to the Soviet Union in 1927. The British were 'almost overcome by the warmth of the welcome', met everywhere by 'bands, banners and garlands of flowers', and paraded through Moscow 'like a team of prime ministers'. In the capital they were watched by a crowd of 35,000, supposedly the biggest the Soviet Union had ever seen, but it can hardly have been impressed by the standard of the British team. A couple of heavy defeats were interpreted by Sinfield as 'a rude shock to British soccer prestige', but in truth the day was long gone when a cobbled-together team of politically correct amateurs and semi-pros could provide any real opposition to the top Soviet teams.

Domestically, the Russians had taken up where they had left off in 1914. As early as 1918, with the civil war consuming large parts of the country, the traditional Moscow v. St Petersburg game was revived, the Muscovites winning 9–1 against a war-depleted opposition. Over the next few years most of the pre-revolutionary clubs were taken over by varying combinations of local workers, soviets and Party committees. One Moscow regional committee, for example, took over two local teams, merged and renamed them, and then received sponsorship from the young Communist organisation, the Komsomol. In the following twelve years this team regularly exchanged its organisational sponsors – going through a cigarette manufacturer, the food workers' union and a retailing cooperative, among others – before finally emerging as the footballing arm of the multi-sports society Spartak. Through all these various incarnations the team was dominated by the four Starostin brothers, who came to occupy an almost legendary niche in Soviet football history, for reasons that would go way beyond football.

The Charnocks' Morozovtsi had made a simpler journey. Immediately after the Revolution an internal security agency was set up to defend Red gains and thwart any possibility of a White comeback. It had many names over the next seventy years – Cheka, GPU, OGPU, NKVD, MVD, MGB, KGB – but the idealism which inspired some in its first days was an early casualty. Felix Dzerzhinsky, its Polish chief, thought sport essential for developing 'strength, dexterity, courage and endurance' among the agency's several thousand members, and in June 1923 he set up the Dynamo Sports Society to provide the necessary facilities and organisation. At first the society was restricted to GPU operatives, but this was soon widened to include all personnel under the GPU's general umbrella, including family members. The OKS, the old Morozovtsi, which had already been taken over by the Electrical Trades Union, now found itself the Moscow footballing section of the fast-growing, nationwide Dynamo Sports Society.

There was, however, still no national football league in which teams like the newly christened Moscow Dynamo could compete. National tournaments would be organised at sporadic intervals during the next decade, but they would feature only representative city teams. The clubs competed in local leagues, a fact that did little to encourage the quality of play. The conduct of players had noticeably dipped since the Revolution, with fights and over-violent play becoming far too common for the authorities' liking. Football, far from spreading socialist values, often appeared to be undermining them, but no one seemed too sure how to address the problem. Higher refereeing standards would obviously help, and in the Soviet Union of the time much emphasis was given to raising the cultural awareness of the players through museum and theatre trips, but as the 1920s gave way to the 1930s it began to look as if a major reorganisation of Soviet sport was needed to encourage overall standards of both performance and conduct.

Football was still growing in popularity, and crowds packed into the small grounds that had been inherited from the pre-revolutionary clubs, despite the almost complete lack of facilities. According to Robert Edelman in his book *Serious Fun*, even the largest of these grounds only had 'five thousand places on rickety wooden bleachers. Most fields were only partially covered with grass. Scoreboards and public address systems were non-existent, while toilets and food concessions were minimal. Dressing rooms, when they existed at all, were primitive.'

The first Five-Year Plan featured an extensive stadium-building programme, and not surprisingly Dynamo, with the clout of the security service behind it, was the first club to benefit. In 1928 a 35,000 all-seater horseshoe-shaped arena was completed in Moscow's Petrovskiy Park; much to the players' delight it featured hot showers. Stadiums in Leningrad, Tbilisi, Baku, Yerevan, Odessa, Kharkov, Stalingrad and Kiev followed over the next few years, and in 1935 the Dynamo Stadium in Moscow was fully enclosed with the addition of another 15,000 seats.

While this basic infrastructure was under construction, much thought was being given to how Soviet sport as a whole should be organised. The solution, when it emerged in 1935, bore similarities to what was happening elsewhere in the society – sport, like agriculture, was essentially collectivised. The myriad single-sport teams connected to particular workplaces were slowly gathered together in city-based multi-sport societies. The Dynamo and Red Army societies were the precursors, but they were not union-based like the newly-created Lokomotiv (for railway workers), Torpedo (car workers), Stroitel (construction workers) or Spartak (cooperative workers). Thirty-four of these new societies were formed, each with its own colours, badge, banner and rules. They would staff and equip themselves, and build their own amenities, all out of union dues. And together with the two existing societies they would supply the football teams required for an all-Union league.

The necessity for such a league was rapidly becoming obvious to everyone involved in Soviet football. Hitler's accession to power in 1933 led to an abandonment of the

Comintern's disastrous policy of confrontation with more democratically-minded socialists and an espousal of its opposite – a united popular front of the left. In the context of football, this meant the playing down of purist worker sports and a greater willingness to play so-called bourgeois teams. The results achieved were by no means bad, and in the late summer of 1935 a Ukrainian representative side even managed to hit six goals past the French First Division team Red Star in Paris. This glorious dawn – 'Bourgeois Europe must take notice!' one Soviet sports paper declaimed – dimmed somewhat a few months later when a joint Spartak-Dynamo team played Racing Club de Paris in the same city. The Muscovites, who included Mikhail Yakushin in their side, lost 2–1, and those who took part in the subsequent post-mortem were loud in their support of an all-Union league. Soviet players were as good as any, it was claimed, but a national league was necessary for promoting more sustained competition for the better sides, and for bringing through new players. They could then close the gulf that still existed between the best foreign and Soviet teams. With 6 million players and the world's most perfect social system, Soviet teams should be leading the world, not lagging behind.

Stalin's enthusiasm was tested by means of a match in Red Square. It was originally intended that Spartak and Dynamo should contest this showcase game on a vast green carpet, but the latter pulled out, allegedly for fear that a mishit pass might strike Stalin or roll blasphemously into the maw of the Lenin Mausoleum. So Spartak played Spartak reserves in a well-rehearsed game featuring a varied selection of goals, the two captains keeping a careful eye on an official who was standing close to Stalin. This man was supposed to wave a white handkerchief when the 'Friend of All Sportsmen' began to look bored, but the planned thirty minutes had lengthened to forty-four when Stalin himself finally called a halt to the proceedings. Soviet football had received the only seal of approval that mattered.

The all-Union league and an all-Union cup competition were both inaugurated later that year, the former with four divisions of seven to eight teams, the latter open to just about anyone. There would be much chopping and changing over the next few years, but this basic division of labour would remain, just as it has in Britain, with the league used to hone quality and the cup to broaden the numbers involved. Right from the start both competitions proved popular, and by 1938 First Division crowds would be averaging just under 20,000, with many more attending the big matches.

The quality of football steadily improved, but in just about every other respect problems persisted. Many of the ground facilities were still decidedly primitive, and the fans behaved accordingly. After queuing for hours at a single entrance, then suffering cramped seating during play and more endless queues for food at half-time, it didn't seem particularly unreasonable to first litter and then invade the pitch, especially when there was no public address system or programme to forbid it. After one particularly violent episode in Leningrad it became standard procedure to ring the pitch with soldiers.

Inside the ring the players were not behaving much better. Soviet sports magazines were still demanding that Soviet players, in addition to being the world's technical best, 'should be models of discipline, culture and high moral values', but kicking prone and injured opponents seemed to be on the increase. Forty-three separate incidents of player 'hooliganism' were reported to the League's disciplinary committee in the first two months of the

1936 season, and each team's 'political guide' was kept busy denouncing the errors of his comrades' ways, tongue firmly in cheek.

Sport and sportspersons were supposed to be setting an example of how to behave in a more civilised society, but the opposite seemed to be happening. The state could draw consolation from the fact that football was discouraging political opposition by effectively creating a world of its own – in Nikolai's Starostin's words 'football was the only, sometimes the last, possible hope for maintaining in one's soul some small piece of humane feeling and humanity' – but that had not been the intention.

Nor had anyone set out to encourage the creation of a privileged sporting élite, but the development of an all-Union league, which further blurred the line between amateur and professional status, made that inevitable. Before 1936 it was an open secret that players were remunerated in a variety of ways: some were expensively rehoused, some were paid for jobs they didn't do, some were just given a pile of roubles under the table. All this was discussed in the Soviet press, reprovingly but also understandingly. It was no secret that football took up a lot of time, with three days' practice a week and a match day, not to mention a month's pre-season training in the Caucasus while the northern snows were melting.

The league, with its bigger crowds and long-distance travelling, simply made it harder to keep up the pretence. Yevgeny Eliseyev, who played for Dynamo in the 1930s, recalled that he was paid to play football but actually registered as an instructor of physical culture; he was a professional in all but job description. The authorities could have simply accepted the reality of the situation and declared all the players professional in the Western sense, but the creation of such an obvious élite would have gone against the ethos of the times, so the pretence had to be sustained. And not only that: when it came to attracting players, the various societies were forced to compete with each other in creating ever more lucrative falsehoods.

The system that encouraged such abuses of truth was also prone to abuses of power. The early years of the league coincided with Stalin's Great Terror, and men who thought nothing of sending thousands to their executions and millions more to the gulags were not likely to be over-fussy about exercising their personal power in the Soviet football arena. They could of course have taken drastic action in pursuit of their supposed aims – executed players who spectacularly failed to set the correct socialist example on the pitch, for example – but they preferred interference on behalf of their favourite teams. They were fans first and socialists a long way second, if it all.

The first famous instance of such meddling from above came with the Basque tour of late summer 1936. The select team of Basques, which was touring the Soviet Union as a thank-you gesture for Soviet help in the Spanish Civil War, played six matches against top Soviet teams, winning five and drawing one. It was then prevailed upon to play an extra two games, a second against Dynamo and a first against Spartak.

These two teams were already dominating the Soviet league – they would win three each of the first six championships – but there was more to the rivalry between them than just football and a shared city. Dynamo stood for the Soviet regime in general and the NKVD in particular; Spartak, sponsored by the politically more neutral Komsomol, had always attracted those with anti-Establishment sentiments. Supporting Spartak was one of the few safe ways to give the regime a two-fingered salute.

So when another Dynamo defeat was followed by a Spartak win – and a win, moreover, that owed everything to the award of a disputed penalty by the Spartak-supplied referee – Dynamo's powerful supporters were suitably enraged. Wheels were set in motion, and the referee ended up being banned for life.

Robert Edelman blames Lavrenti Beria for this decision, but in 1936 the ex-player and keen Tbilisi Dynamo fan was still based in Georgia. After his transfer to Moscow as deputy chief of the NKVD – he succeeded chief Yezhov a few months later – Beria seems to have adopted the capital's Dynamo team, and on match days he was usually to be seen with his cronies in the special government box at Dynamo Stadium. Spartak remained the main enemy, of course, whichever Dynamo side they were playing, and in 1939 the Starostins' team beat Tbilisi Dynamo with a single disputed goal in a cup semi-final. Spartak went on to beat Stalinets Leningrad in the final, but then had to replay the semi-final when Beria and his NKVD chums brought their powers of persuasion to bear on the football authorities. Spartak won again, but the Starostins would eventually pay for their temerity.

Their friend and protector, Komsomol boss Kosarev, had by this time fallen victim to the purges, and later in 1939 Nikolai Starostin himself was saved only by the fact that his daughter was best friends with the daughter of Stalin's acolyte Molotov. Three years later, with the war into its second year, Beria at last had his revenge: all four Starostin brothers were arrested on a charge of plotting to kill Stalin during the famous match in Red Square. Even he couldn't make this ludicrous indictment stick, but after prolonged interrogation the accused confessed to making several critical remarks about Soviet sport. Each would serve many years in the gulags, though Nikolai at least would spend most of them as a football coach, often with provincial Dynamo teams.

The Soviet league closed down for four years during the war, the cup for only three, with a truncated competition taking place in the late summer of 1944. Matches were played throughout the conflict, though, and often deliberately arranged by the authorities as morale-boosters. The Leningrad Dynamo team toured the Soviet Union in 1942, and in their grimly besieged home city games attracted crowds of 8,000 despite widespread starvation and the constant threat from shelling. Soon after Stalingrad fell, a match was held in the city's rubble-strewn stadium between a select team of locals and Tbilisi Dynamo. And most famously of all, a side mostly composed of Dynamo Kiev players took on and beat a German *Luftwaffe* team, knowing that the price of victory was execution. Recent research has cast some doubt on this story, with claims that those executions that followed were not actually contingent on the result, but it was widely believed at the time.

In 1945, when the Dynamos came to Britain, these events were all in the very recent past, and the history of Soviet football, like the history of the state from which it sprang, was masked by the aura of heroism in a common struggle which the team projected. Behind the mask lay another history altogether. As in many other parts of Europe, there had been prodigious technical development on the pitch, with increasingly skilled players and coaches ready to enter the post-war world in a spirit of adventure and experiment. But in their own natural habitat those same players were no more sporting than their British counterparts and no less wholeheartedly devoted to football as a career and provider of livelihoods.

The Dynamos were not linked to the 'Civil Service', or anything vaguely like the British conception thereof. Their connection was to an organisation that had recently overseen, both before and during the war, the wiping out of millions. The coaches and players were not members of the NKVD, but they knew who paid the bills and they knew whom they had to please. Yakushin, for example, had played with Nikolai Starostin in representative matches abroad, and he presumably knew all too well why his erstwhile team-mate wasn't to be found at Spartak's ground any more. His and his team's penchant for silence was no accident. Back in Moscow, Comrade Beria was likely to be following the tour very closely indeed.

9

Dunkin' footballs

On the morning after the Chelsea game several of the Dynamo players went to see the sick Mariavkin in Westminster Hospital, thereby alerting the ever-vigilant British press to the fact that he was there. They reportedly told him that what had worried them most in the Chelsea game were the narrowness of the pitch and the height of the crossbar; the latter, according to the dubious intelligence supplied by the *Daily Mail*, was higher in Russia than in England. At White City that afternoon Yakushin had the players practise their shooting and the British shoulder-charge, and that evening, as part of their continuing education, they studied newsreel footage of English matches.

Not all the players had their minds completely immersed in what they were watching. According to Vadim Sinyavsky, in the first of several reports he filed for *Soviet Weekly*, Leonid Soloviev was agonising about his missed penalty, and his no-relation namesake Sergei was waiting for news of his wife, who was expecting their baby before the end of the month. Yakushin had 'a far-away look' because the ice hockey season was about to start without him, and 'engineer-planner' Mikhail Semichastny was worried about some Moscow building project.

The tourists might be thinking of home but they liked London. Sinyavsky found a 'remarkable orderliness in the streets', with people keeping to the pavements and cars to the road. It was hard remembering to look right when he was used to looking left, but knowing hardly any English was not proving a problem. 'Sportsmen have their own language,' he wrote mysteriously, using the liftman at the Imperial Hotel as a case in point. This non-Russian-speaker could pass on all the day's news in only a few seconds.

The only hint of criticism came in an aside about the White City Stadium. The tourists had been 'astonished' to learn that such a stadium, with its 'wonderful field, beautiful grass, convenient grandstands', hosted no matches. In Moscow there were not enough grounds for clubs who wanted to use them. 'Ah well, each city has its own ways and habits,' Sinyavsky noted philosophically, but the implication was clear – this was a wasteful use of resources. It would not be allowed in a sensibly planned society.

'We are waiting with impatience for our next game,' he concluded, adding that 'perhaps our sick players will be well by then, and this will make our team more homogeneous'. There was clearly no chance that Mariavkin would recover in time to make the journey to Cardiff, so by 'sick players' he can only have meant Dementiev and Trofimov. And it's hard to see how the team could have been made more 'homogeneous' except by increasing the number of regular Moscow Dynamo players in the line-up. All of which offered further circumstantial evidence for the supposition that Bobrov and Archangelski – the stand-ins for the injured Dementiev and Trofimov – were the only guest players in the party.

In Cardiff preparations for the visit were, with a few exceptions, well advanced. By a remarkable stroke of luck the King and Queen were visiting the city on the Wednesday as part of their Victory tour, so there was no need for the town council to go overboard on a fresh set of decorations for the Russians. Flowers were flowers, bunting was bunting – all that was required was the substitution of hammer-and-sickles for the Union Jacks.

The moment the Royals were safely *en route* for Swansea, huge Soviet flags were draped over the entrance to Central Station and raised above City Hall, with smaller versions hanging from any and every convenient pole in the Welsh capital. A young Welsh miner's portrait of Stalin had been chosen to provide the focal point of a floral display at Cardiff City's Ninian Park ground, and the question of what mementoes to offer their guests in return for the expected bouquets was finally decided in favour of miniature miner's lamps. The first suggestion, a bunch of leeks, had for some reason been voted down.

At this stage City were expecting at least 65,000 for the match. Both seats and the standing enclosure were already sold out, and in the light of events at Stamford Bridge it was deemed essential to take extra precautions. The usual admission price was raised to 2/6 – men in uniform a shilling less – in an attempt to keep the numbers at manageable levels, and an unprecedented 300 policemen were ordered for the day. The latter were to be coordinated by state-of-the-art communications: according to L. V. Manning 'as complete a loudspeaker packing system as I have ever seen on any sports ground'. To supplement this technological marvel, men were busy tarring the stand supports with cart grease as a deterrent to would-be climbers.

All they needed now was a crowd, and the signs were that the Valleys were going to do the Russians proud. The mining village of Mardy, whose left-wing tendencies had earned it the soubriquet 'Little Moscow', was expected to be represented in force, and so were many others. It would be 'the Russians' first contact with the industrial masses', the *South Wales Echo* enthused. 'Nowhere in Britain will they receive a more stirring welcome. It will be an international occasion.'

On Thursday morning the Dynamo party, minus Mariavkin and the sick Trofimov, was driven across London to the GWR's Paddington terminus. On the platform the players were recognised by a group of soldiers, and the party's reserved first-class coach – the Embassy had obviously forgotten to stress that socialists travelled in third – was soon besieged by young boys, porters and servicemen. While the Dynamos leant from the windows and happily signed autographs, the journalists in attendance tried to work out what was in the boxes that were being loaded aboard. Russian food was a popular guess, though one case clearly 'bore the name of an American canning company'.

The train left on time at 11.55, and for much of the journey the Dynamo players stared out of the window, enjoying their first look at the English countryside. Like most visitors from far away, they were amazed at how green it was and how little the sun shone. Some of the players had a quick English lesson – 'I am liking coffee,' Khomich was heard to say – and the senior players discussed what tactics they would be employing against Arsenal in six days' time. That, after all, was the big one.

Three hours after leaving Paddington the train drew into Cardiff Central, and the members of the Soviet party were duly overwhelmed by the splendour of the decorations that greeted them. They were personally welcomed by Cardiff City Chairman H. H. Merrett, who also happened to be one of South Wales's most prominent businessmen. He promised the Russians a civic reception the following morning and a choice of tours afterwards, and then escorted them a couple of hundred yards down the road to the Central Hotel, where a huge banner welcoming the Soviet guests had been plastered across the four-storey Victorian façade. While the Dynamo officials explained to the hotel manager that they'd brought all their own food the players were shown to their rooms. The lucky ones had a view down St Mary Street towards the city centre; the less fortunate had to make do with the railway tracks they'd just come in on.

Most of the hotel seems to have been taken over by the Russian party. After dining on their own food many of the tourists sat around the lounge piano and sang old Russian songs, before someone in authority reminded everyone that Moscow Radio's nine-o'clock news was imminent. The announcement of their own arrival in Cardiff was duly cheered, and several members of the party were then persuaded to visit the hotel ballroom, where a bevy of local girls just happened to be waiting for dancing partners. Several waltzes ensued. 'Dynamos are jolly good dancers' was the eventual verdict, but most if not all of the players were playing dominoes in their private lounge. Perhaps dancing was considered unwise with a match only two days away, but it seems more likely that they were still not trusted to converse with the British on a one-to-one basis.

The following morning brought bad news for the Soviet Union. The atomic-bomb talks in Washington between the US, Britain and Canada had reached a conclusion, and it wasn't the one Moscow wanted. 'No Nation Must Have Monopoly', screamed the *Daily Express* headline, but that was exactly what was being proposed. A Special Commission of the UN would be set up in January to ban the destructive use of atomic energy and promote its peaceful application. When 'effective and enforceable safeguards' against the former had been worked out – they never would be, of course – the US and Britain would let other nations in on the industrial secrets of the bomb's creation. 'Atom Bomb Stays Secret' was the more truthful headline in the *Daily Sketch*, while a *Times* editorial felt compelled to point out that 'the long-term diplomatic drawbacks of secrecy in encouraging unwanted suspicion and mistrust may well outweigh any temporary advantages'.

Perhaps some members of the Dynamo party read the headlines, or asked Elliseyeva what was in the papers that morning. Perhaps some even guessed the importance of what was happening, and over breakfast that morning had intimations of the Cold War in waiting.

Perhaps not. The party split up into small groups: one visiting the docks, one driving out to the Powell Duffryn Colliery at Abercynon, one taking in the National Museum of Wales and a reception given by the Lord Mayor at City Hall. The Mayor swapped speeches with tour manager Andreanov, the Russian explaining that the tourists had felt honour-bound to visit Wales because they knew how much the Welsh had admired the Soviet war effort. The Mayor was then dragged outside and asked to point out the red flag flying for the Soviet photographers.

The Abercynon group were not taken underground, merely given a tour of the surface. When asked what he thought, one player explained through Elliseyeva that since he didn't know anything about mining he couldn't express an opinion. Tea was offered and refused on the grounds that they only ate and drank at set times, but despite this less than effusive attitude the departing

Russians were heartily cheered on their way by a crowd of miners queuing for their pay-packets at the pit office.

During the day there were occasional signs of a continuing thaw. 'It has taken Wales to break the ice,' one member of the party told a British journalist, while another confessed that he and his compatriots had found the principality more welcoming than the 'vast loneliness' of London. Out in the open, in stage-managed excursions surrounded by reporters, each Russian reaction was still rigorously controlled, the natural urge for spontaneity still carefully repressed, but the strain of maintaining polite silences and neutral expressions was apparently beginning to tell.

That evening the tourists let down their guard for the first time. For reasons best known to themselves they allowed the Russian-speaking reporter Olga Franklin to share time with the Dynamos at the hotel. Perhaps they were swayed by beauty, perhaps they just felt safer with a woman. Or perhaps they decided it was time to let a hundred Dynamos bloom. Whatever their reasons for accepting her fly-on-the-wall presence, she made good use of it. Her simple account in the *Daily Sketch* of what she saw and heard was probably more illuminating than the Soviets would have wished.

That evening the Dynamos' favourite form of entertainment was gawping at magazines. Unable to read the text, they lingered over pictures and advertisements, and voraciously consumed any pictorial articles, even those – like one on Thomas Dewey's US presidential election campaign – that didn't at first sight seem particularly promising. Franklin watched them 'pore for hours over photographs of luxury kitchens and Hollywood belles. Several copies of a fashion periodical are worn ragged after being handed from one footballer to another.

Soloviev, who felt some explanation was needed when I saw him disappear clutching the fashion paper, said that he worked in ladies' fashions in Moscow.'

A likely story. Meanwhile, war hero Vladimir Subdunin, in his second and last tour cameo, sang beautifully to Sinyavsky's piano accompaniment. Bobrov, the other Soloviev and two others played dominoes; over in a corner 'a quiet, tall man' read a book about Ivan the Terrible. Semichastny stared at a photograph of embracing Hollywood sweethearts, whereupon two of the younger players yanked the magazine out of his hands and dissolved into giggles. The team captain smiled benevolently at their youthful prank.

The Russians explained to Olga that Soviet papers did not contain pin-ups. Nor, for that matter, luxury kitchens. She felt 'so elated that when the Dynamos really start talking they do not stop, and to find that "the mysterious Russians" are just charming ordinary boys'. Only when she asked about wives and girlfriends did they clam up – such matters were not for public airing.

Predictable stuff, all in all, but was this the way the Soviet authorities wanted their footballers characterised, as a bunch of lads hungering for semi-naked women and Western consumer goods, and desperate for news – almost any news – of the outside world? By allowing Olga Franklin access they'd got across the message that the Dynamos were just ordinary boys, and perhaps that was exactly their intention. Who, after all, would want a war against boys like these? Who could fail to trust their fathers with the secrets of the atom bomb?

But in delivering this message they'd lost track of another. If there was nothing special about the Dynamos, then perhaps there was nothing special about the Soviet Union. And if state socialism wasn't the future, then it was just another version of the present; a version, moreover, in which glamour pin-ups and luxury kitchens were obviously in short supply.

The Cardiff City team the Dynamos were due to meet on the following day was probably slightly better than its lowly Third Division status suggested. During the war, manager Cyril Spiers had concentrated on scouring the immediate area for good young players, and over the past couple of years several of these had grown up together in the team. In 1943–4 Fred Stansfield, Arthur 'Buller' Lever, Danny Lester, Colin Gibson and Billy Rees had joined Alf Sherwood, Roy Clarke and Beriah Moore as first-team regulars, and in 1944–5 the same eight, with the addition of Terry Wood, had formed the backbone of a young and settled side. Their winning of the wartime League West that season was hardly a sign of greatness – Swansea and Bristol City were the only other regular Football League teams to compete – but it was certainly evidence of competence. In the current season they were in the South section of the Third Division South, and of the thirteen games so far played they had won eight, drawn one and lost four, scoring forty-nine goals – the highest number in any division – and conceding twenty-one.

There were some fine players in the side, as their future records would make clear. Sherwood, Rees and Clarke became regular Welsh internationals; both Lever and Stansfield won solo caps. Gibson played once for England B, and like Clarke was eventually transferred to a big English club. Ken Hollyman, who had played as a teenager before the war took him abroad, would eventually supply much of City's midfield energy through two successful promotion campaigns.

But it was the marvellous team spirit that turned the side

into more than the sum of its parts. They even trained on Sunday mornings after playing on Saturdays, according to Buller Lever.

> If we played away, on a Saturday, or something like that, then we'd perhaps go to the local hop or whatever it was. If we stayed overnight, no matter where we stayed or where we went to, everybody went. They all went together. I remember playing Torquay the year we won promotion. It was a gorgeous day and we were just coming past the prom on the front there and someone mentioned a swim. Spiers was in charge: 'Stop the bus,' he said, 'stop the bus.' All the boys put their shorts on in the bus and they all went in the water for a swim. And that was after the game. That was the spirit, you see.

The players certainly weren't motivated by the splendour of the financial rewards. Fred Stansfield showed me the contract he signed for the 1946–7 season; it promised him £5 a week through the winter – £6 if he was in the first team – and £2 a week in the summer. In exchange, he agreed 'to play in an efficient manner to the best of his ability for the club'. Wages were eventually topped up by the Providence Scheme, whereby the club annually put aside a lump sum – Buller Lever thought it must have been about £150 in 1945 – for when the player retired. For those players earning close to the maximum it wasn't, by the standards of the time, a bad living, but neither was it a particularly good one.

Most players weren't on the maximum, of course, and those in the lower divisions often supplemented their football pay with a second source of earnings. During the war several of the Cardiff players – Sherwood, Rees and Lever among them – had worked down the pits as

Bevin boys, and several others had been taken into the forces. Some were still beyond Spiers's reach; one was becoming available just in time. Old-timers Billy James and Billy Baker, who had volunteered for the Territorials in 1941, had only just been reported safe in Jakarta after several harrowing years of Japanese imprisonment. Baker would eventually resume his career as a first-team regular, but James would never be the same again. Ken Hollyman, recently returned from duty in Nova Scotia, was waiting for his demob in Hednesford when a telegram arrived with the news that he'd been selected to play against the Dynamos. That Friday he hitchhiked down to Cardiff in his newly-issued demob suit.

Hollyman knew about the Dynamo tour, but it had never occurred to him that Cardiff would entertain the Russians. He certainly had no doubts as to which side would be better prepared: the Cardiff lads wouldn't be as fit and they wouldn't have had the chance to train together. Even those who attended the training sessions lacked faith in the process. 'All we had to do was run round the field,' Fred Stansfield recalled. 'We couldn't have the ball on the pitch then. It wasn't the fact that balls were in short supply – they didn't want us kicking the pitch up. And the trainers didn't know much in those days. There was no real coaching or training.'

Prepared or not, City had one trick up their sleeve. On the eve of the match, as the Dynamos drooled over Hollywood belles, the Cardiff backroom staff were busy at work. In those days players used to leave the toes of their football boots immersed for days in a solution of water and household soda; they came out 'like concrete', Ken Hollyman remembered, leaving him ready for any tackle. 'Get stuck in, kick the ball, the ball's going with you.' And that evening at Ninian Park, as he happily dunked his boots, watching father-in-law Jim Merrick had an idea. 'He says, "We'll do that with the balls."

'So we took four balls . . . I can see my father-in-law now . . . he took the four balls and he immersed them in this ordinary household soda. We got a quarter of a pound of soda in each bucket, we immersed the balls and left them overnight.'

Close your eyes and you can almost see the two of them, leaving a darkened Ninian Park with impish grins on their faces. And you can also imagine, if only for a moment, the scene in Moscow had Comrade Beria discovered that the success of his beloved Dynamos – not to mention the future of the post-war world – had been put at risk by a pound of soda and a row of buckets. No gulag would have been too distant for Ken Hollyman and his father-in-law.

10

After the goal rush

If the football press corps had received any intelligence of balls hardening overnight it hadn't affected their predictions for the game to come. The *Daily Mail*, after admitting that on paper the Cardiff youngsters had no chance, covered its bets by adding that 'Welsh unknowns have upset longer odds before today', but such hopes were rare. The *Sketch*, in expecting the Dynamos to run up a cricket score, was much more typical.

The *Daily Worker* scribe used the occasion to have a go at his fellow football reporters. He noted that these 'critics are now, after their patronising remarks at the beginning of the tour, pleading that before the tour ends the FA must get together a side guaranteed to give the Russians a tanning. Well, perhaps not in so many words, but that's the gist of their stuff.'

At least no one was still claiming that they were so slow you could hear them think. That morning a Dynamo party had been driven out of Cardiff, and north up the autumnal Taff valley to the Treforest Trading Estate. Here they wandered round one of the earliest industrial parks, a British version of the future as seen from 1945. Why this particular piece of sightseeing was offered to the Russians is hard to imagine, particularly with the dramatic splendours of Caerphilly Castle only a few miles away. One would have thought that a medieval castle would prove more interesting to men from Moscow than a few light industries, but perhaps the local authorities were keen to show the Soviets that they held no monopoly on visions of the future. In 1945 people looked forward with rather more optimism than they do now, and in those days tourism still catered to artefacts of both the future and the past.

In Cardiff the red flags were hanging limply from their lampposts, but nothing much seemed to be denting the enthusiasm of the fans thronging the city centre. Many had arrived the evening before, but few had found paid accommodation. Some were put up in a school by the local authorities; others had roamed the town centre all night, keeping the residents awake with their football talk and attempts to keep warm. At least the night had been dry – now the trains arriving at Cardiff Central from as far afield as Liverpool and Manchester were disgorging fans into a cold and persistent rain. By the end of the morning a steady stream of rain-soaked people were making their way down Tudor Street in the direction of Ninian Park.

Even late arrivals had no problem securing a place. A combination of the rain, the higher admission charge and fears of Stamford Bridge-style trouble kept the attendance far below the expected 65,000. Many later said they hadn't come because they hadn't thought there was any chance of getting in. Still, 40,000 was the largest crowd Cardiff City had seen in years, and those who had turned up were in for a treat.

Despite there being plenty of space, despite the obvious lathering of gunk on the stand supports, several fans tried, with a notable lack of success, to climb them, and presumably spent the rest of the afternoon wondering how they were going to explain the state of their clothes to mothers and wives.

Under the main stand the balls were taken from their

buckets, and one at least was given to the referee, Mr A. E. Davies of Pontyclun. What he thought of its rock-like consistency has not been recorded.

The Dynamos arrived at the main entrance on Sloper Road, where they offered Stalin's portrait 'especially admiring looks' before making their way to the dressing room. Thirteen players were soon out on the wet pitch for the now-familiar warm-up, a number that encouraged several Cardiff supporters to think the Russians were in for an unlucky afternoon. According to the threepenny match programme, Dementiev for Bobrov was the only change from the team that had played Chelsea, but there was no sign of the diminutive inside-left, and Bobrov's retention of his place was duly announced.

Cardiff fans already knew that international full-back Alf Sherwood and top-scorer Billy Rees were both sidelined with injuries. The inexperienced Marsh Raybould took the former's place, Billy Gibson moved to centre-forward and Beriah Moore filled the vacated right-wing position. Like Chelsea before them they would be wearing red versions of their usual blue kit.

First, though, there was some singing to do. Moscow Radio, which was taking the match live, had put in a special request for 'Aberystwyth', 'Cwm Rhondda' and 'Abide With Me', and the uniformed band led the crowd through these three before finishing with 'Land Of Our Fathers'. As the fervent tones of the 40,000-strong choir disappeared down the throat of Sinyavsky's microphone, the flags of Britain, Wales and the Soviet Union fluttered together in the light breeze. It all gave the occasion 'an international appearance', thought the *News of the World*, for once living up to its name. In the seat next to Sinyavsky, his pretty new assistant Miss Strelkova was looking the part of a Russian Hollywood belle.

Right – **CARDIFF CITY** – Left

McLOUGHLIN

2 LEVER 3 RAYBOULD

4 HOLLYMAN 5 STANSFIELD 6 LESTER

7 MOORE 8 CARLESS 9 GIBSON 10 WOOD 11 CLARKE

Referee:
Mr A. E. Davies

Linesmen:
Mr W. C. Bucknall
Mr C. O. Hancock

11 SOLOVIEV S. 10 BOBROV 9 BESKOV 8 KARTSEV 7 ARCHANGELSKI

6 SOLOVIEV L. 5 SEMICHASTNY 4 BLINKOV

3 STANKEVICH 2 RADIKORSKY

KHOMICH

Left – **MOSCOW DYNAMO** – Right

The teams came out and lined up opposite each other. This time there was only one bouquet, and Cardiff captain Fred Stansfield managed to look pleased with it – the flowers would end up on his sister's mantelpiece. The Dynamos were each presented with faintly glowing miniature miner's lamps, and stood there clasping them, their eyes flickering restlessly around the murky ground and the dark Welsh hills beyond. The ceremonials over, Mr Davies, who was wearing a light-coloured jacket over his shirt and shorts, called the captains for the toss. He may even have apologised for the ball.

* * *

City started the game as if they were determined to justify their reputation for speed, rushing hither and thither, biting into the tackle, and actually putting together a couple of good attacking moves. In the first Beriah Moore and Eric Carless combined well on the right, in the second Terry Wood was pulled down just outside the penalty area, and Marsh Raybould's high free kick was gathered by Khomich. The Cardiff supporters could have been forgiven for wondering whether all this fuss about the Russians was just newspaper talk. Maybe Chelsea had been worse than anyone thought on the previous Tuesday. And even then the Dynamos hadn't beaten them.

The illusion lasted six minutes. A tricky run by left-winger Sergei Soloviev was halted only at the last moment, and in their next attack Evgeny Archangelski was brought down by Raybould. Right-back Radikorsky took the free kick quickly, crossing for the blond Bobrov to glance a header home. The crowd was still recovering from this shock – the usual moaners were still complaining about the free kick – when Bobrov drew Stansfield out of position and threaded a perfect ground pass through the resulting space to Beskov who shot low past the hapless McLoughlin from about twelve yards. These were the chances they had missed against Chelsea – Cardiff, it seemed, were not going to be so lucky.

But neither, it appeared, were the Welshmen going to lie down and die, and for the next fifteen minutes it looked as if they might yet get back in the game. The half-backs and inside-forwards were tigerishly contesting every ball, and for several minutes Semichastny looked more uncomfortable against the lightweight Gibson than he had against Britain's best. A corner was forced, pushed out by Khomich, headed back, saved again. Clarke, Carless and Moore all had on-target shots saved by the Russian keeper, who then had to pluck the ball away from the diving Gibson's head. At the other end Dynamo drew two easy saves from McLoughlin before Soloviev skinned full-back Lever, raced diagonally in on goal, and forced the Cardiff keeper to fist away his rasping shot at full stretch.

In terms of possession, in terms even of goal attempts, the game seemed fairly even, but the more knowledgeable fans could see that City's non-stop effort was barely coping with the Dynamos' superior skill and movement off the ball. In the twenty-fifth minute another swift interchange of ground passes through the centre ended up, via a Cardiff defender's leg, in the path of the racing Archangelski, and his cross-shot was billowing the net before McLoughlin hit the ground. 3–0 to the Dynamo. The weight of the ball didn't seem to be causing them undue concern.

The game now entered a quieter period, with the Russians seemingly content to sit on their laurels. One Clarke shot forced a characteristic leaping save from Khomich, but generally speaking the Cardiff attacks failed to make much headway against the Dynamo defence. The Russians frequently had eight men behind the ball, and on those rare occasions when the Cardiff forwards managed to bypass the forward screen of inside-forwards and wing-halves, they found themselves up against a back three with near-telepathic understanding.

When half-time arrived the early pace of the City youngsters was all but a memory. The Dynamos left the field at a canter, the Cardiff team trudging tiredly in their wake. It wasn't a good omen for the second half.

Dusk seemed to have come early, and the myriad cigarettes glowed against the gloomy backdrop as the band came out for its half-time gig. The lucky members of the crowd warmed themselves with a cup of tea while

Sundry Dynamos – most of them reserves – in training at White City. *From left to right:* Nazarov, Dementiev, Ilyin, Oreshkin, Bechtinev, Petrov, Archangelski, Khomich, and Mevedev.

Dynamo fans flying the flag at Stamford Bridge.

Mikhail Yakushin leads the Dynamos out at Stamford Bridge.

The Chelsea flower show: a study in embarrassment.

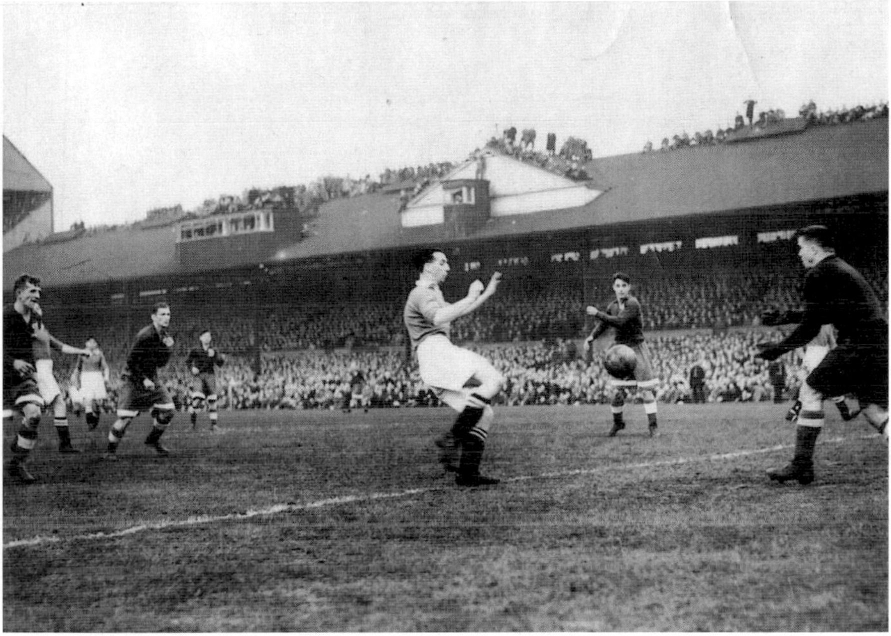

Lawton moves in on Khomich in the lead-up to Chelsea's first goal.

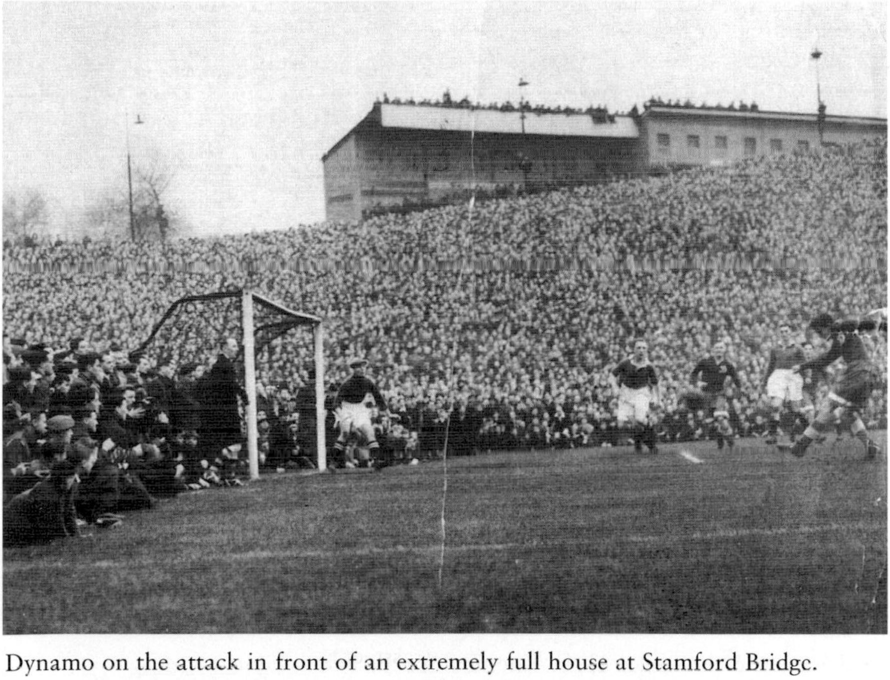

Dynamo on the attack in front of an extremely full house at Stamford Bridge.

The Dynamos are presented with miniature miners' lamps. These, as one reporter noted, 'would have been a fine idea if the Russians had worn them; Cardiff would have at least seen which way the Russians were going'.

Fred Stansfield challenges Alexei Khomich for the ball at Ninian Park.

Players and other party members relaxing around the piano in the lounge of Cardiff's Central Hotel.

Khomich gathers the ball at White Hart Lane as Arsenal's George Drury looms menacingly out of the fog.

Victory dance: the Dynamos take to the floor of the Lyceum on the evening of their triumph over Arsenal.

Five in a line: the Dynamo attack swarms forward during the first half at Ibrox.

A grounded Jimmy Smith watches his deflection enter the net for Rangers' first goal.

Radio sports commentator Raymond Glendenning introduces the Dynamos from the stage of the Scala Theatre during the tourists' farewell bash.

The final shot: a Soviet cine-cameraman aims a lens over the head of FA secretary Rous and captures Northolt Airport for the NKVD's (Stalin's security police) files.

everyone took guesses as to how many the Russians would score. A statistician might have pointed out that Cardiff had taken nine shots to the Dynamos' ten, and were therefore rather unlucky to be behind. But then statisticians never learn.

The second half began like the first, with a period of Cardiff pressure. This time they dominated the first ten minutes, one Gibson shot scraping the outside of a post, but the last reserves of Welsh energy were being used up. In the fifty-fifth minute the Dynamo forwards mounted one of those fast sweeping attacks at which they excelled, the ball travelling across field to the racing Soloviev, whose instant return pass caught the Cardiff defence wrong-footed and allowed an impudent Beskov to back-heel the ball home.

The crowd cheered – 'if they were at all partisan', the *News of the World* commented, then 'they were guilty of this fault in favour of the visitors'. Bobrov had already become a favourite, and whenever he took off on one of his elegant runs, someone in the crowd would shout, 'Come on, Sandy!'

Four minutes later Khomich made a flying save from Hollyman. The Russian goalkeeper, who had so caught the imagination of the Stamford Bridge crowd, was enhancing his reputation at Ninian Park. There was no doubt that he was, in school playground parlance, a bit of a show-off, exaggerating his leaps rather more than some of the shots seemed to require. But he also saved the ones that would have left lesser goalkeepers clutching air, and he made very few mistakes, either in handling or in judgement. Considering that he was used to Russian rules, which offered far more protection to goalkeepers than the British rules of the same period, he was coping remarkably well with his new vulnerability to physical challenge.

Most of all, he was obviously a character. British fans loved the way he took goal kicks as if it was the last minute and his team were one down, so unlike the British habit of languorously collecting the ball, carefully spotting it, counting the paces backward and then finally, as a sort of afterthought, kicking it downfield. They also loved his habit of responding to applause by flapping his hands at the spectators, as if he was modestly trying to shut them up.

The cheers for his save from Hollyman were still dying down when Dynamo suddenly seemed to rev themselves into another gear, or even another dimension. Perhaps it was just that City were slowing down, their stamina finally sapped by the exertions needed to keep their opponents in sight, but at Chelsea too it had seemed to many of the onlookers as if the Russians actually played faster as the game progressed.

In two minutes, the sixtieth and the sixty-first, they scored two more goals. First Bobrov was on the end of one spectacular wide-sweeping movement, then Archangelski put the finishing touch to another. In the next morning's *Sunday Pictorial* Peter Wilson called this sixth goal the 'greatest piece of football wizardry I've seen in more than six years'.

The Dynamo forwards were now close to humiliating the Cardiff defence, not so much by the score as by the way they were playing. The swift inter-passing was leaving defenders spinning almost randomly; the Russian forwards seemed to be arriving in groups right under McLoughlin's nose. It was possible to imagine them passing round a cigarette while they decided who still needed a goal for his hat-trick.

Beskov got his in the sixty-fourth minute, shooting home from close range after a Kartsev body-swerve had sent half the crowd the wrong way. Bobrov's hat-trick came a minute later: a simple tap-in after McLoughlin dropped a corner. This was unfortunate – despite the score, the keeper had been one of Cardiff's best players.

At 8–0 the Dynamos finally relaxed, and instantly paid the price. During a Cardiff attack the ball squirted out to the right of the goal, and Beriah Moore hooked it across and over Khomich into the far corner. The crowd applauded happily, and several of the Russians could be seen cracking a smile.

Three minutes later one of the Dynamo defenders handled in the area and a penalty was given. Terry Wood, who'd already had one shot from similar range acrobatically saved by Khomich, hit the ball firmly to the goalkeeper's left, but the 'Tiger' got enough finger on the ball to divert it against the post. Scrambling up, he still managed to reach the loose ball a split second before the onrushing Cardiff players, suffering a bruised wrist for his pains.

Two minutes later he made another great save from Moore, and that was the end of Cardiff's comeback. Twice more, in the eighty-second and eighty-eighth minutes, the Dynamo forwards strolled through the revolving door of the Cardiff defence, Beskov picking up his fourth, Archangelski a hat-trick to equal Bobrov's. When the final whistle blew, the 10–1 scoreline represented the biggest-ever defeat inflicted by foreigners on a Football League team.

Arthur Lever recalled that they 'just came off and shook hands and everybody was laughing, as much as to say it's just a game and that was it. It was such an enjoyable game. It's silly to say that, I know, when we got beat 10–1, but we did enjoy it.' It had been played in the best of spirits.

'There was nothing on the pitch at all . . . there was no animosity in those days really. The supporters took it all in good part; most of them who watched the game, they thoroughly enjoyed it, because we had as much of the game as they did. It's like somebody said,' he added with a grin, 'they broke away ten times and scored.'

The Dynamos had enjoyed it too. Back at the hotel their high spirits overflowed into a singsong round the piano, before they set off for the reception dinner organised by City. The *News of the World* reported the presence of the Soviet Ambassador, Gusev, but few other details survive, and the personal reminiscences of the Cardiff players provide a wonderful example of how, more than half a century on, the memory plays tricks. Ken Hollyman was certain that there had been no dinner, and further denied that there had been any off-pitch communication between the Cardiff players and their Dynamo counterparts. 'We never spoke to them,' he said. 'They couldn't speak English and we couldn't speak Russian.'

Fred Stansfield and Arthur Lever both remembered the dinner, and both were pretty sure it had been at the Angel Hotel on Castle Street, which that afternoon had prominently advertised itself on the front page of the match programme – 'Visitors in connection with the football matches are specially catered for at reasonable rates.' But when it came to communicating with the Russians, the two remembered things differently. Fred Stansfield agreed with Ken Hollyman that the teams' ignorance of each other's language was virtually complete, but remembered having a lovely evening anyway: 'somehow or other we managed to chat'. But not about politics: 'What we talked about was nothing like that. From what we could get to know of them, they were happy enough.'

Arthur Lever, by contrast, recalled that a lot of the

Russians could speak English, and had an anecdote to prove that at least one of them did. After the match he had asked one Dynamo why they had that thick white line around the bottom of their blue shorts, and had been told that when players were running head down with the ball, a flash of white out of the corner of an eye made it easier to pick out a team-mate. At the dinner itself, he found the Russians friendly, though they kept their distance – 'I don't think they mixed really.' Interpreter Elliseyeva, he noticed, seemed much more at home with the 'hierarchy' than with the players – 'that was the problem there'.

The three Cardiff players' recollections of the game were generally consistent with one another. They all agreed that Dynamo had been brilliant – 'a cracking side', 'a glorious side, a marvellous side', 'supreme football players' – and that the various reports in the press of their slowness and reluctance to head or tackle had been exaggerated. The Russians had asked for the ball to be replaced twice during the game, but the extra heaviness had not, as Hollyman ruefully admitted, noticeably slowed them down. On the contrary, their 'technique and support play had us chasing shadows'.

Arthur Lever was convinced the Dynamos' passing movements were worked out in advance; like chess players they had a series of 'set moves' to suit different situations. Fred Stansfield agreed: 'They played to a plan, they didn't kick the ball far, they played possession football.'

All three agreed that the Russians played fair. Stansfield thought them 'very clean', and denied that they used their arms a lot. Lever said they 'didn't have to play dirty because they played such good football . . . there was no nonsense at all going on, no kicking or anything like that – not like you see today, grabbing the shirts and all that nonsense'.

When it came to the two sides' comparative fitness, opinions differed rather more. Hollyman thought the City players were 'nowhere near as fit as them', but the other two denied there was such a gap. According to Stansfield, fitness just wasn't the issue: what had really made the difference were City's tactics of standing off and letting the Russians play. Prior to the game, he said, manager Cyril Spiers had told him that 'because of relationships with foreigners, "If you knock somebody down, pick them back up" . . . In other words, he was telling us not to get stuck in.' This, Stansfield thought, was 'like somebody said, "Don't bother, just play a game." Whereas if it had been a league match he'd have said get stuck in and don't let them settle.'

Instead of getting stuck in, they had just stood off their opponents. 'You can't,' Stansfield concluded, as would any decent centre-back, 'play football that way.'

Spiers's instructions apparently didn't reach Hollyman. He had never seen much point in instructions anyway; it wasn't that difficult working out what needed doing. 'You know it yourself . . . you're playing against good players . . . the first thing I would do if I was marking you and you were Tom Finney, I'd say, "I'm on top of you, boy . . . you're not going to get the ball." ' When I asked Hollyman if he thought City had soft-pedalled against Dynamo, his answer was 'No bloody fear – I wouldn't soft-pedal in any game.'

Of course, only Spiers and Stansfield know what passed between them before the game, but the substance of the latter's claim is in itself illustrative of the gulf in footballing style that lay between the two teams. The City defenders went out to mark men. 'We played the game we normally do – marking,' Stansfield said. 'I took the centre-forward.' Hollyman took the opposing inside-left, who happened to be Bobrov, though the Cardiff right-half 'didn't bother to take his bloody autograph'. Raybould took Archangelski, Lever took Sergei Soloviev, Danny Lester took Kartsev. And they all stuck to their charges, even though the Dynamo forwards showed no inclination to patrol the part of the pitch traditionally reserved for them. They moved all over the place, taking their defenders with them, destroying Cardiff's defensive coherence with positional play alone. Add superior ball skills, and a massacre became almost inevitable.

Lever later said that Cardiff had been given a football lesson, but what had been learned? There were only two positive responses to the sort of football the Dynamos were playing: match it on its own terms or make up the skill difference with work-rate and sheer determination. Cardiff couldn't do the former, and if, as Stansfield claims, they were prevented from doing the latter, then indeed they had no chance of keeping the score even vaguely respectable.

All three Cardiff men, in their different ways, accepted that the Dynamos were a great side, and yet all three also held on to the feeling that if things had somehow been a little different – if they'd been fitter, if they hadn't been asked to soft-pedal, if they'd played them two years later – then somehow they might have matched them. And these three Welshmen were far from alone in thinking that way: variations on the same theme would be commonplace throughout the tour from players, press and public. British football was still the best, they claimed, even when all the evidence staring them in the face screamed the opposite. The Germans had looked stronger in the war, but they'd been beaten. And not by fancy work either.

Three days after their encounter with the mighty Russians, Lever and Stansfield took a special trip east on the train and queued in the north London fog like ordinary fans for the chance to see them from a rather less fraught perspective. No doubt they were hoping that Arsenal would restore both British honour and the stars to their proper courses by beating the Dynamos, but I would also guess that, as professional footballers, they knew that they had seen something really special in the murk at Ninian Park, something of the game's future, and that a part of them was eager to see it again.

In Moscow the mood was exultant, and no time was lost in making the obvious political point. 'Why don't we trade?' the resident Brits were asked. 'We'll give you some footballers in return for the atom-bomb secret.' Rarely had a joke concealed more resentment, but half a century later it's hard to believe that Britain would have suffered from such a trade.

The only other printed Soviet responses to the win came from Yakushin. 'I am pleased,' he told the *Daily Worker*, 'but our players made some mistakes. I hope they will play better in future and make no mistakes. You know we Russians never stop at one stage; we always wish to go one better.' The *Mirror* didn't so much quote as fictionalise the Dynamo coach. Not happy with his players' 10–1 victory, 'coach Mike Yakushin gave them a couple of dressing-room lacings during the afternoon. Although they played noughts and crosses with the bewildered Welshmen, Mike was far from satisfied. For one thing, Vassili Kartsev was repeatedly offside. "You don't see Tommy Lawton do that," Mike pointed out, "so turn it in." Or words to that effect.'

The rest of the British press was not feeling quite so light-hearted. It had been thoroughbreds against hacks, the *Sunday Express* said somewhat unkindly; the miner's lamps 'would have been a fine idea had the Russians worn them. Cardiff would at least have seen which way they were going.' In Monday's *Daily Mail* Geoffrey Simpson thought the Dynamos played 'a brand of football which in class, style and effectiveness is way ahead of our own. As for its entertainment value – well, some of those who have been cheering their heads off at our league matches must be wondering what they are shouting about.' Cardiff manager Spiers's observation that Dynamo were 'a machine and not an ordinary football team' was widely quoted.

Why were they so good? Well, for a start, they were fitter. Roy Peskett in the *Mail* thought them 'strong as Cossacks, and as hardy as the steppes', which seemed suspiciously like racial stereotyping, a sort of Eastern European version of Brazilians having natural rhythm. He pointed out that in the 'two games played to date, not one player has received attention from the trainer', adding mysteriously that he believed few of them wore shin-guards. Hardy indeed.

But the main reason for their success was observation of the fundamentals. There was 'nothing revolutionary in the Dynamos' technique', according to the *Western Mail*. Quite the reverse, in fact: 'It was fashioned on the old accepted principles of ball control, positional play and intelligent anticipation.' Their reporter had seen the past at Ninian Park, and it worked.

The past, of course, was mostly British. All the Dynamos were doing, Geoffrey Simpson thought, was 'playing the football we used to play. They are showing us the fundamentals, which in our mad helter-skelter style of big kicking and fast running appear to have been forgotten.' And how had they received the word in the first place? Well, they were 'the spitting image of the Austrians, who were trained by Jimmy Hogan'. In which case, the *Sunday Graphic* decided, 'in some East European fashion the art and craft of Association Football transmitted itself eastward from Austria through the Balkan countries to Russia'. On a camel train, perhaps.

But even if it was possible to believe that the Dynamos had, in some strange and mysterious way, learned everything they knew from itinerant British football gurus, it was obvious to all but the most blinkered that the Russians were now the teachers. 'They showed up our methods as crude and in need of renovation,' the Chelsea programme bluntly admitted on the day Dynamo played Cardiff. English football was not in the same class as twenty years ago, Geoffrey Simpson argued. 'Science has been sacrificed to the mad craze for speed. The first-time kick has superseded the controlled pass. The ball is put into the air instead of on the ground.'

He went into specifics. The Dynamo wing-halves supported their forwards; their British counterparts didn't. The Dynamos brought the ball under control, then drew and beat an opponent before passing; the British hit first-time passes to men who were marked. The Dynamos concentrated on delivering short passes to men in space which were easy to take; the British hit long balls to men who were marked, and often with their backs to goal.

In the *Sunday Dispatch* Stanley Walton took a wider but equally perceptive view. 'The shoddy state of British football has been thoroughly exposed by the men from Moscow,' he began.

> For long enough we have deluded ourselves that our quality and style were exquisite and that those who raved about the Preston Invincibles and the Queen's Park of long ago were dotards to be laughed at. It did not take the

> Cardiff débâcle yesterday to convince me that English football was on the slippery slope. I have seen better football in Egypt during the war, and even the primitive blacks of East Africa can teach us something in adroit manipulation of the ball. All the Russians are the product of coaching on sound basic principles, and the sooner the FA appoint approved coaches in all our schools and minor clubs the better it will be for the future of the game. We are far too complacent and pleased with ourselves. And that applies also to the players, who do not devote enough study to the science of the game . . . Tearing about all over the field on a Saturday with not an idea in the noddle does not constitute football as we used to know it . . .

The Dynamos' play might evoke the British past, but there was also a growing recognition that they had something of their own to offer. The *Weekly Mail and Cardiff Times*, while noting that the Russians believed in the old-style 'five forwards moving as a line', also realised that there was more to it than that. 'They were so successful because each player thought a few moves ahead, and showed such intelligent anticipation in running into unmarked positions.'

How did they do that? Well, several answers emerged. The *Western Mail* reported that the players were encouraged to play chess, in the hope that it improved their ability to think both quickly and several moves ahead. The *Daily Mirror* put the Russians' fast and free-flowing style down to ice hockey, which they apparently played as an eleven-a-side game on flooded and iced-over soccer pitches. The *News Chronicle* revealed that 'the beautifully coordinated moves that brought the Moscow Dynamos a 10–1 victory were all carefully worked out beforehand –

on a blackboard which had travelled with the team from Moscow'. A reporter asked to see the magical artefact, but was told by Elliseyeva that the players were tired after their long train trip back to London. 'Well, can I see it later?' the persistent scribe asked. 'It is very difficult,' Alexandra told him.

The *Sunday Graphic* pointed out that the Russians' strange practice of tiring themselves out with a pre-match warm-up actually made sense. The statistical department of the Army Physical Training College at Aldershot had worked out that 35 per cent of football injuries occurred in the first seven minutes of a game, before the muscles had really warmed up.

There were still, of course, those who refused to believe. L. V. Manning, for one, was far from convinced. It was hard, he thought, to assess the Russians on the strength of two games against teams that were far from top grade. And more than that, English football as a whole was at such a low ebb that the Russians might well look better than they really were. Their success was entirely due to exceptional teamwork and positional sense; their players were not individually superior. Even Cardiff had 'revealed the Russians' vulnerability to the quick tackle', their full-backs and wing-halves 'would crack under expert pressure'. Stanley Matthews, Manning was sure, would make left-back Stankevich 'look very ordinary'.

Alex James, the heart of the successful Arsenal team of the thirties, thought much the same. The Dynamos' success, he asserted confidently in the *News of the World*,

> lies in teamwork which is to a pattern. There is no individualist in their side, such as a Matthews or a Carter. They play to a plan, repeating it over and over again, and they show little variation. It would be quite

> easy to find a counter-method to beat them. This lack of an individualist is a great weakness. They have no one player who can 'stand on the ball', hold it, and use it. The Russian plan is to keep the ball moving. Give me the pick of, say, thirty or so of the cream of British footballers and, if you let them play together for a time, I have no hesitation in saying that the Dynamos would not live with them.

The Dynamos were really pleased to meet Alex James in the Ninian Park dressing room – he was still probably the most famous British footballer in the Soviet Union – but if they read this article they can't have been too impressed. James claimed he could devise a counter-method to the Russian style, but there's no sign of one here, not unless a single player 'standing on the ball' counts as such. Examined closely, it's no more than a statement of blind faith in the virtues of British individualism. Why, he seemed to be saying, would anyone bother about tactics when they had a Matthews in their side?

11

England expects

Chelsea had never won the league or Cup, and Cardiff City's sole triumph had been at Wembley in 1927, courtesy of as soft a goal as ever graced a Cup Final. Their victims that day, by contrast, had been the dominant side of the interwar era, winning the Cup twice, the league on five occasions. Arsenal's manager and players had been the prime movers of the tactical revolution which followed in the wake of the 1925 change in the offside law, and the finest exponents of the style of play that evolved from that revolution, the style that still dominated British football in 1945. Abroad, the name Arsenal was almost synonymous with English football. It was no surprise that Dynamo had specifically requested a game against them, or that Semichastny, when asked to pick out which English footballer he would most like to play against, had selected the Gunners' Ted Drake.

Semichastny would not get his wish – Drake had been forced to retire during the war – but on Wednesday 21 November the Dynamos would get their game against the legendary Arsenal. After their moral victory over Chelsea and the ten-goal thrashing of Cardiff the Russians could have been forgiven for suspecting that British football was stuck in a tactical rut, but only by beating Arsenal could they be certain that they had bested the master, and not just a couple of unworthy disciples.

The origins of association football go back almost as far as recorded history. The Chinese are said to have had kick-abouts, the Roman legions to have played friendlies against local Britons, and there's ample evidence of riots thinly disguised as games regularly convulsing medieval villages. What can be said with some certainty is that slowly and surely the game shrank, in just about every particular. The pitch contracted from several miles in length to less than 200 yards, the number of players was reduced from hundreds to twenty-two, the level of allowable violence and the parts of the body with which one could touch the ball were both curtailed. By 1863, and the first codification of the rules, the game was taking on the basic shape it has today.

The one huge difference was the definition of offside as simply being ahead of the ball. Of course this prohibited any forward pass, but at the time that didn't seem particularly strange. Both the rugby and association codes had evolved from the rolling village maul, and in 1863 individual movement with the ball – dribbling with the foot, in soccer's case – was still considered the normal way to advance. The birth of deliberate passing – of actually giving up the ball voluntarily to a team-mate – was the first great tactical innovation.

The rules were adapted to accommodate this new reality in 1866: from then on, a player was only offside if fewer than three members of the opposing team were nearer to the opposition goal-line than he was. This revolution – the real beginning of football as we know it – took time to manifest itself, with players often preferring the old dribbling habits to the newfangled pass.

But the potential implicit in the new rules was bound to become apparent at some point, and when it did – in the Queen's Park team of the 1870s – there was no going back. After ten years of Scottish dominance – England won only two of the first ten internationals between the two countries – the passing game spread throughout England, and reached an early apotheosis in the play of two particular teams – the Royal Engineers and the Corinthians.

The passing revolution had also shifted the balance between attack and defence. In the early 1860s, when the ineligibility of the forward pass enormously favoured defences, most teams played with at least six forwards, but even with the three-man offside rule the development of the passing game had, by the end of the 1870s, shifted the balance back in favour of the attack. Teams were now lining up in the formation that would feature in British match programmes for most of the next century, with two full-backs, three half-backs and five forwards. The famous Preston North End 'Invincibles' won the first league–cup double playing this way in 1889, and for the next thirty-five years all British teams played to roughly the same style and pattern. The centre half-back was a key player in this system, with both defensive and attacking duties.

This was the football that Britain gave to the world in the decades before the First World War, but by the early 1920s there were increasing doubts its potential for growth. The game was getting monotonous to watch, the number of goals scored declining year by year. Technical skill on the ball seemed in ever-shorter supply, and no one appeared interested in tactical innovation. English teams were even beginning to lose to foreign teams, though that fact was mostly ignored by press and public alike.

The offside law was identified as the main culprit by the football authorities. It certainly was *a* problem – it was far too easy to frustrate opponents by repeatedly playing them offside – but there were others of equal importance. The league structure, and particularly the fear of relegation, made teams reluctant to take risks with tactics, or with players better known for mercurial artistry than for stamina and full-blooded commitment. In turn, this reluctance exacerbated the traditional British distrust of 'fancy work' in any form, and deepened the ingrown prejudice against a consistent application of thought to the game and how it could be played. You ran the players round and round the training pitch until they were fit, and then you sent them out to get stuck in. That was the way it was done. The whole notion of coaching was considered suspect, an unnecessary interference in the natural order of things, and not surprisingly most of the best British coaches ended up working in Europe.

There was no reorganisation of the domestic game, no commitment to developing ball skills or imaginative training routines, but there was a change in the offside law: from 12 June 1925 only two players were required between the attacker and the opponents' goal line. As defences struggled to cope with the new rule the number of goals conceded rose quite substantially, but the apparent increase in entertainment value was short-lived. The new season was only a couple of months old when Arsenal manager Herbert Chapman and team captain Charles Buchan decided on the formation change that would once again revolutionalise British football: to stem the flood of goals they moved the centre-half back between the full-backs as a permanent defender. From being the most versatile player on the pitch, he became the most one-dimensional: the 'stopper', who needed no ball skills to speak of, only a head made of granite, power in the foot to kick high and long, and the body strength to knock centre-forwards off their feet.

With the centre-half now gone from midfield, and the wing-halves also forced on to the back foot by the new offside law, the necessary balance had to be maintained by withdrawing one or both of the inside-forwards. The game, which had become increasingly compressed in midfield as teams became so adept at playing opponents offside, now spread out again. More goals were being scored, but there was no parallel rise in the quality of play. Rather the reverse, in fact, because with players spread out across the pitch the long-ball counter-attacking game came into its own. Stamina and strength became more important, individual technique and positional play less so.

Arsenal had the players to make this formation work for both attack and defence – Alex James, in particular, seemed born to the crucial pass-spraying role in midfield – but most other teams had to settle for its purely negative potential, and as the interwar years drew towards a close the football diet on offer at British grounds was becoming depressingly one-dimensional. Hulking centre-halves and centre-forwards fought for long balls and crosses, inside-forwards and wing-halves covered every inch of the pitch, dribbling wingers ran at full-backs. British teams, according to the famous Austrian coach Hugo Meisl, 'base their play on force and speed, seeking to arrive at the opposing goal by the quickest possible route, moving the ball with long, high passes, always making use of their physical endowment'. The close-passing game of the late nineteenth and early twentieth centuries had all but died out in Britain; the game had become more frenzy than football, with every league match resembling a knock-down, drag-out cup tie. As long as everyone played the same way no one was going to get too much of a shock, but the British were no longer the only people playing football.

Meisl and his equally innovative Italian counterpart Vittorio Pozzo had begun their work before the First World War, and by the early 1930s Continental teams were providing the clearest of warnings that British football was in trouble. In 1931 Scotland lost heavily in both Italy and Austria, while England suffered a 5–2 thumping by the French in Paris. At the end of 1932 Austria came to England and lost 4–3, playing, in L. V. Manning's words, 'first-class Corinthian with a kick in it, and at twice the pace'. These precursors of the Dynamos gave English football a scare, but after a while the usual complacency reasserted itself. Everyone who'd seen the Austrians had been impressed by them, but no league club bothered to try out the modified 2–3–5 formation which had given England so much trouble, or introduced any new training routines designed to improve the average player's ease on the ball.

It was easier to play safety-first. After all, neither England nor Scotland had lost at home to a non-British side in the whole interwar period, and as long as a decent veil could be drawn over results on the far-off Continent, it was possible to assume that there was really nothing to worry about. Foreigners might have a few tricks to teach us, be a bit nifty on the ball, but they couldn't shoot to save their lives, they couldn't head the ball and they certainly didn't like it 'up 'em'.

If only foreigners could be relied upon to live up to their stereotypes. In their first two matches the Dynamos had all but destroyed the illusion of British supremacy, but many still clung to the possibility that there was less to the Russians than met the eye. Put them up against the best that British football could offer and the result would surely be different.

And this was more than just a hope, it was a need. The tour was now two weeks old, and in that time the Dynamos had won the admiration and respect of the British footballing public. But over the next few days, in the interval between the matches at Ninian Park and White Hart Lane, something changed in the public mood, or, to be more accurate, in that mood as it was supposedly reflected in the British press. In late November of 1945 there was so much less to Britain than met the eye, and sustaining the illusion of football supremacy was part and parcel of a wider, mostly unconscious clinging to the centuries of imperial grandeur. The Dynamos had been admired – now it was time for them to be beaten.

Whether the Arsenal team could achieve this was an open question. The club seemed to have more first-team players still abroad with the services than most, and its recent form hardly suggested the glories of pre-war years. Four successive defeats had dropped the club to eighteenth in the League South standings on the day before Dynamo's arrival, and there was no sign of a Tommy Lawton galloping to Arsenal's rescue.

The fixture had been arranged only a few days into the tour, and that gave manager George Allison around a fortnight to collect as strong a team as he could from Arsenal's widely scattered playing staff. Added impetus was provided by a visit to Lancaster Gate, where he was interviewed by Mikhail Yakushin and the referee who was to officiate in the match, Nikolai Latyshev. According to Allison, in his book *Allison Calling*, he was asked where he lived, how he spent his time, where the players lived and how they spent theirs. An English-speaking

Russian – Allison didn't say it was a woman – interpreted each question and answer and the referee scribbled it all down in his notebook. 'And so it went on, question after question, all of an intimate character, touching on my personal life, the personal life of the players and even of the ground staff. Some of the questions were almost impertinent. The Russians wanted to know what kind of food we ate, how much we paid for our services, how we spent our holidays, what we did in off hours, how we trained. What bearing it had on the Dynamos' visit I will never know. It was more like a secret police quiz than a football parley.'

Allison would eventually have plenty of reasons for feeling hostile towards the Russian tourists – and the coming of the Cold War would of course make such hostility routine – but it's hard to discern from this 1948 account of the 1945 meeting just why he felt so offended. The Soviets, in their thorough, plodding and often insensitive way, were just doing research. They knew next to nothing of how English clubs worked so they were asking any and every question they could think of. At least they believed there was something to learn from foreigners. Allison, given a wonderful opportunity to improve his own knowledge of the game beyond Britain, seems to have asked no questions at all. Rather, he 'tried to stick it out manfully for the sake of international sport'.

But then he got hungry. 'Anyone's stomach is liable to rebel after nearly three hours at a round-table conference,' he recalled. He was, he admitted, 'just a little irritable', and told the interpreter it was time they got around to arranging the match. 'There is no need to tell you my feelings when back came the translated answer: "We have nothing to do with the match arrangements. You must contact the Soviet Embassy for that." It was not only my stomach that felt rebellious after I escaped from the round table and its NKVD quiz.'

It seems safe to assume that he left Lancaster Gate more determined than ever to put out an Arsenal team capable of beating the Dynamos. Certain key players were clearly out of reach – Bryn Jones in Italy, Denis Compton and George Curtis in India, George Male in Palestine – but he immediately applied to the service chiefs for the release of those in Northern Ireland, Belgium and Germany: George Marks, Eddie Hapgood, Leslie Compton, Reg Lewis and Bernard Joy.

On 10 November the *Daily Express* reported that Lewis, Hapgood and Leslie Compton would be released, but this news proved premature. Four days later it was revealed that Southampton's Roper had been asked to guest on the right wing, but three days after that, on the eve of the Dynamos' match against Cardiff, Roper was absent from the team that Allison announced he was trying to bring together. This comprised Griffiths, Scott, Hapgood, Leslie Compton, Joy, Leslie Jones, O'Flanagan, Drury, Lewis, Bastin and Cumner. It contained only one non-Arsenal player, the Cardiff goalkeeper Wyn Griffiths, and he had been a regular guest since the start of the season.

By Sunday, however, the picture had changed again. Leslie Jones was definitely injured, and the Army had refused to release either Reg Lewis or Leslie Compton, both of whom were touring Italy and Austria with a services XI. 'If that is what the authorities think of the reputation of British football in a situation of this kind, we can hardly be blamed for fielding guests,' the *Daily Express* remarked sanctimoniously on Monday morning.

The call went out that day. In his autobiography *Feet First*, Stanley Matthews claims that he was hoping the

Dynamos would come to Stoke, 'or that a match would be arranged against an England XI, so that I might get the opportunity to try my luck against them'. When he heard that Allison was having trouble raising a strong team, he and team-mate Neil Franklin asked their manager to ring Allison and offer their services. 'The Arsenal manager was delighted, but pointed out he had had word that Bernard Joy would be able to get home from Germany, which meant Neil was not required. I was more fortunate as Arsenal were without a right-winger.'

In fact, they had two – both O'Flanagan and Southampton's Roper were available – but neither could be described as Britain's greatest footballer, and Stanley Matthews could. At some point on the Monday someone had impressed upon Arsenal that a win was expected, and that players should be chosen with that in mind, regardless of club affiliation. Stanley Matthews's inclusion was particularly requested by these 'higher authorities', Bob Crisp claimed in the *Express*, adding that 'here I ought to make it clear that the FA insist they are not the "higher authority" concerned'.

So who made the phone call? Someone in the Government? Someone at the Palace? There's no way of knowing. Arsenal officials, questioned the following day as to the identity of their mysterious superiors, refused to supply a name but made no attempt to deny the essence of the story.

Allison, meanwhile, got on with the job of strengthening his team. Five of his chosen XI – Griffiths, Joy, Drury, Bastin and Cumner – were now definite, which left six places to be filled. If Laurie Scott failed a fitness test and Eddie Hapgood didn't make it back from the Continent, then Tottenham's Ralph Ward and Fulham's Joe Bacuzzi would deputise. Reg Halton from Bury was brought in to take Leslie Jones's spot at left-half, with Cliff Bastin moving back into Leslie Compton's berth at right-half. Matthews had already been chosen for the right wing, and it was decided to make up the forward line with Fulham's bustling Ronnie Rooke – 'the ablest all-round leader in the country, excluding Lawton', said Frank Cole in the *Daily Telegraph* – and Blackpool's young England star Stanley Mortensen. If both Scott and Hapgood played, there would be six Arsenal men in the team; if neither did, only four.

There were objections, and not just from the Dynamos. Bob Crisp wrote that 'by labelling this team Arsenal, neither George Allison nor the FA are going to save any reputation at all. In fact, if the Russians get beaten by this team labelled Arsenal a lot more harm will be done than if a genuine Arsenal side was beaten 10–0. And what sort of satisfaction are Arsenal going to get out of such a victory?' The *Mirror* thought that Dynamo were 'being asked to tackle a needle game with an Arsenal team that is Arsenal in name alone . . . Arsenal will be a near-England eleven.'

Allison, meanwhile, was one minute claiming that he'd been forced into choosing such a side by the unhelpfulness of the service chiefs, the next minute insisting that his selection represented a tribute to the Russians. The latter, not surprisingly, were unimpressed by the verbal gymnastics. They made a long and reasoned protest at the FA offices, but stopped short of threatening to withdraw from the match. They weren't even indignant, Rous said, just disappointed that they were not playing the real Arsenal. They thought Allison should have consulted them before making the changes, and were worried that defeat at the hands of a team containing so many guest players might be misunderstood in Russia.

A statement was released to the press under Semichastny's

name. We were given a list of Arsenal players, he said, and the team we have been presented with contains names that are not on the list. We have therefore concluded that we will be playing a representative England team.

'I hoped that the Russians would welcome the opportunity of testing their skill against a more experienced team of English players,' Allison responded on the same day, 'rather than have the privilege or pleasure of toying with immature material.'

They did not, and it later transpired that the 'immature material' – those Arsenal youngsters omitted to make room for the stars – were just as angry as the Russians. 'We have been loyal to the Arsenal all season,' one said after the game. 'Many of us have come long distances at great inconvenience to play for the Arsenal on Saturdays and we think it unfair that we should have been left out of what, after all, was an unusual match. We wanted badly to play against the Dynamos.'

Allison denied it all. He hadn't received a single protest from those left out. Quite the contrary: the youngsters had been relieved that he had spared them such an ordeal.

The 'higher authorities' who insisted on Matthews's inclusion in the team may remain a mystery, but there were several known precedents for such interference – the Soviet Government was not alone in viewing sporting events in a political light, or in manipulating those events for political ends.

In the 1920s the Soviet-inspired British Workers' Sports Federation had branches all over the country for organising sport and spreading the word. Under its aegis George Sinfield's London Workers XI toured the Soviet Union in 1927, and three years later a return invitation was issued to a team from the Don Basin coalfields. The Home

Secretary declined to grant the necessary visas on the grounds that he had no wish to encourage a 'political approach' to sport. Secretary of the Football Association Sir Frederick Wall was more than sympathetic – he made it clear that the Russians would have been banned from FA-controlled grounds in any case. 'Football in dear old England,' as Sir Frederick stated several years later, 'is merely a sporting entertainment . . . England regards international matches as a game, but Continental countries look upon these matches as a test of strength, spirit and skill. Victory increases national prestige, and defeat is a sign of decadence. To them, success is vital.'

As if to prove the point, an FA-arranged match between England and Germany at White Hart Lane in 1935 was allowed to proceed despite a storm of protest from left-wing political groups, London union branches and Jewish groups. The TUC petitioned the Home Secretary, who retreated behind the farcical assertion that the match had no political significance.

Three years later, with the British Government desperately clinging to its policy of appeasement, England played Germany again. This time Berlin was the setting, and the players were pressured by both Government and FA into giving the Nazi salute during the performance of the German national anthem. 'We were appalled,' Stanley Matthews wrote later. 'I have never known such an atmosphere in an England dressing room . . .'

But they saluted nevertheless. None was willing to defy the higher authorities, whether footballing or political. In this instance, as in many others, it was probably hard to tell the difference.

Through the days of rumbling controversy that surrounded the composition of the Arsenal team, the

Dynamo players went about their usual business as athletes, ambassadors of sport, and would-be friends of the British people. The siren call of the Soviet ice hockey season seemed to have faded after the Cardiff result, and on the Monday morning the tourists were doubtless amused by a *Daily Mail* cartoon which showed a grim-looking Joe Stalin dressed in Dynamo kit. As usual he had a pipe in his mouth, but on this occasion he also had a bouquet of flowers tucked under his arm. One booted foot was resting on a ball, which happened to be the globe, and he was standing in front of a trophy cabinet. There were cups for Germany (home), Poland (away) and the Balkans; a vacant space had been made ready for the US Atom Arsenal.

On a more jovial note several papers carried a picture of Field Marshals Zhukov and Montgomery sharing a laugh over lunch in Berlin. And on the other side of the Atlantic US scientists were urging their Government to open new talks with Britain and the Soviets about the dangers posed by atomic weapons. One moment the wartime alliance still seemed like a living reality, the next it appeared no more than an empty shell.

The Dynamos had Arsenal to worry about. They were invited to train on the Highbury pitch, but preferred a two-hour session at White Hart Lane, where the match was to be played. Khomich's wrist, injured at Cardiff, was reportedly still giving him trouble but he appeared after a while and seemed fit. Tottenham full-back and captain Ralph Ward, who was now unofficially on stand-by for the Arsenal, watched the Russians' shooting practice and expressed admiration for the way they struck the ball. The Tottenham Secretary, Yorkshireman Arthur Tanner, was just plain impressed. 'By goom! Hot stuff!' was his considered opinion.

Elsewhere on the sidelines, Yakushin and Elliseyeva were fielding questions about the Dynamo diet. After six years of war and culinary boredom the British people were obsessed by food, and right from the beginning of the tour there had been enormous interest in what the Russians were eating. They had supposedly brought in a busload of their own food, but soon after their arrival Elliseyeva was claiming that 'while they are here in England they will eat good plain English food and nothing else'. Breakfast on that morning had included some very British-sounding porridge and sausages, while lunch consisted of beef, cabbage and potatoes. Three days later an official admitted, 'his eyes agleam', that rump steak was the players' favourite, and that they also enjoyed the local white bread and beer. They seemed to eat a lot – three evening meals in quick succession in Cardiff – but it was also claimed that their meals at the Embassy were procured with ordinary British ration cards.

Getting at the truth wasn't easy, and by this time a purely prurient interest in the Russians' eating habits had been replaced by a more self-serving curiosity. Was there a connection between the Dynamos' obvious fitness and their diet? If so, what was their secret?

Caviare, according to the headline in Monday's *Evening Standard*. Perhaps, according to the column of text below. 'Lavish quantities of red and black caviare appear at every meal,' Evelyn Irons reported. 'Even at breakfast. There is always a bowl of gherkins, too. Fresh vegetables, except potatoes, are not usually eaten except in soup, and their favourite sweet is stewed apple mixed with raisins.'

How all this fitted in with team doctor Naygonosov's 'muscle-making diet' was far from clear. Carbohydrates and proteins were the most important elements, Yakushin explained through Elliseyeva, the 'brisk little woman interpreter'. Vodka was not permitted during the season, and although smoking was, only one player – Radikorsky – occasionally indulged.

As for meals, well, that morning the players had eaten meat, potatoes, bread, cheese, butter, tea and sugar. For lunch, which was usually taken around two in the afternoon, they would have meat soup, meat and potatoes, and a sweet dessert. Supper, at around nine, would be a rerun of lunch without the soup. It wasn't the sort of diet that Arsène Wenger would endorse, but the ingredients were all British. 'We brought nothing from home in the way of food,' Yakushin insisted.

That evening they went to see the musical *Sweet Yester day* at the Adelphi Theatre. On arrival they mistakenly brushed aside welcoming theatre director Lee Ephraim, and headed straight for their seats in the stalls. The unfortunate misunderstanding was soon corrected, and at the interval some team members were taken backstage to meet Anne Ziegler and Webster Booth, the stars of the show. The *Daily Mail* carried a picture of a star-struck Alexei Khomich.

There was no interval rush to the bar by the others, and those who were drinking had only lemonade. Left-back Stankevich expressed his surprise that smoking was allowed in the auditorium – it wasn't in Moscow – and decided it must be hard on the singers. After the show the Russians said they had enjoyed it, but that they would like to see a straight play before returning home.

Tuesday was a day off for the Dynamos; some went sightseeing in a foggy London, others just hung around at their hotel. At some point during the day they probably discussed the report compiled by their observers at Arsenal's weekend game against Plymouth, even though its value was obviously limited. For one thing, the Gunners' line-up had included only four men scheduled to face Dynamo; for another, their opponents had been reduced to ten men after only twelve minutes.

At a Lancaster Gate meeting on the previous day it had been confirmed that the Russians would play Glasgow Rangers at Ibrox on Wednesday 28 November, so an early return to Moscow was now no longer possible. The game against Coventry, on the other hand, was definitely off. It had been provisionally scheduled for the coming Saturday, but the Dynamos had decided that with several players already suffering from minor injuries they could ill afford another game before taking on the mighty Rangers. A later game against an FA XI was said to be still under discussion, and Charlton Athletic had just issued a formal invitation to the 100,000-capacity Valley. In November 1945 the south-east Londoners were probably England's finest team, and certainly boasted the most efficient defence.

There didn't seem to be any shortage of people who wanted to see the Dynamos in action. Long queues for seats had curled around White Hart Lane on Monday, and a 65,000-plus crowd was expected on the day. Perhaps fearful that people would be put off by the press predictions of a full house, the Tottenham assistant manager insisted that there would be plenty of room. Prices would not be raised, the basic ground admission remaining at 1/6. The gates would open at noon.

The only likely problem was the weather. The fog had come and gone throughout the day on Tuesday, and the forecast for Wednesday was for low temperatures, local outbreaks of rain and a light southerly wind. It would be dull, with perhaps some fog.

12

The fog of war

A wet and foggy dawn greeted the many spectators who had spent the night huddled up against the walls of the Tottenham ground. Most of the morning papers headlined the opening of the war-crimes trials in Nuremberg, and the *Express* carried a picture of an unrepentant-looking Hermann Goering in the dock. It was another ending for the old world, another reminder that the new one still needed to be organised. Now that the common enemy had been brought to book, what else could Britain and the Soviets share? Other than football, of course.

Several spectators had arrived around midnight, having journeyed many miles in a bid to see the Dynamos. One queue was headed by three women, two from Cheltenham and a third from Staffordshire; another was anchored by seventy-six-year-old Arsenal supporter David Wilson. A few fans behind him stood St Petersburg-born Alexander Raghinsky, who had lived in London for over a quarter of a century, but was still proudly sporting a blue and white rosette, complete with a pencilled-in 'Dynamo' in Cyrillic script. All of them were wet and getting wetter, but at least they were close to the front. Outside Manor House tube station the police were soon having trouble controlling the huge queues of people waiting for trolleybuses.

By mid-morning there was no obvious improvement in

visibility, but people continued arriving at the ground in their thousands, and the general feeling – based, no doubt, on a mixture of optimism and experience – was that the fog would eventually lift. Soon after 10.30, worried by the vast numbers now eddying around the ground, the police ordered the White Hart Lane officials to open the gates. The crowd poured in, and as if on cue the fog did begin to lift. Happy groups of boys, who had obviously been excused school for the day, clung to the walls around the pitch, ate their sandwiches and counted the minutes to kick-off.

It soon became apparent, however, that the fog was not so much lifting as thinning. Visibility had improved, but when referee Nikolai Latyshev arrived sometime around noon the conditions were still close to unplayable. By the end of the day Latyshev would be much less popular than he was at the beginning, but there seems little doubt that at this particular moment he took the only possible decision. With 40,000 people already in the ground, and the local experts assuring him, through the inevitable interpreter, that conditions were likely to improve, he had no choice but to announce that the game would go ahead.

Neither team's composition was given out until the last minute. Eddie Hapgood had not made it back from the Continent, so Joe Bacuzzi would get a second guest appearance against the Dynamos, partnering the recovered England international Laurie Scott at full-back. Otherwise the team was as advertised, and a formidable one it was too. The defence in particular, thought Armour Milne in the *Mirror*, 'would inspire an unhealthy inferiority complex in any British team'. And then there were the guest forwards. 'I expect to see the Russians beaten,' Frank Coles wrote in that morning's *Telegraph*, and proceeded to explain how and why. Arsenal would win 'by opening up the play . . . by swinging the ball about'. If they used the long ball to launch swift counter-attacks, then Matthews, Mortensen and Rooke would be racing through the Russian lines like the Gunners of old.

In Tuesday's paper Coles had categorised the game as a contest between the Dynamos' teamspirit and the 'pronounced individualist merit' of the Britishers. Socialism versus capitalism, and this on the day that the Government announced the nationalisation of electricity, gas and the railways.

The Dynamos' team selection contained one surprise: Evgeny Archangelski had been dropped to accommodate a fit-again Vassili Trofimov. The latter had a high reputation, but considering how well Archangelski had played in the first two games – he had scored four goals, after all – his omission added weight to the suggestion that Yakushin was intent on picking regular Dynamo players if and when he could.

Otherwise the Russians were unchanged. Khomich's wrist had mended but Dementiev's pulled muscle had not, and Bobrov had once again made the team after failing to make the programme.

The Dynamos emerged into the murk for their twenty-minute warm-up at around 1.45 Several of the forwards peppered Khomich and his goal with fierce shots while the other track-suited players ran the length of the pitch several times, inter-passing at speed as they did so. At this stage visibility was just about acceptable – it was possible to see players on the far side of the pitch, and occasionally even the red flags fluttering above the grandstands could be glimpsed – but any further deterioration and the game would be hard to play and even harder to officiate.

In the officials' dressing room Latyshev was giving last-minute instructions to his two English linesmen, Jack Weller and W. E. Ross Gower. The Soviet system had been explained to Weller at a friendly Embassy get-together the night before, and now Ross Gower was initiated into its mysteries. He would take one touchline, Latyshev told the two Englishmen through the interpreter, and they would share the other. He didn't want any help when it came to decisions in the penalty area. The linesmen didn't argue: as one told a reporter, 'We have been asked to give him all cooperation, and we will do our best. For all the work he is taking on he will have to be extremely fit.'

Right – **ARSENAL** – Left

GRIFFITHS

2 SCOTT 3 BACUZZI

4 BASTIN 5 JOY 6 HALTON

7 MATTHEWS 8 DRURY 9 ROOKE 10 MORTENSEN 11 CUMNER

Referee:
Mr N. Latyshev

Linesmen:
Mr. J. Weller
Mr. W. E. Ross Gower

11 SOLOVIEV S. 10 BOBROV 9 BESKOV 8 KARTSEV 7 TROFIMOV

6 SOLOVIEV L. 5 SEMICHASTNY 4 BLINKOV

3 STANKEVICH 2 RADIKORSKY

KHOMICH

Left – **MOSCOW DYNAMO** – Right

George Allison, who had listened in on the officials' conference, was less open-minded. 'It was too late to start an argument,' he decided, 'much as I felt like it.' His players were just sitting in their dressing room feeling miserable. 'There seemed absolutely no prospect of the match being held,' Cliff Bastin wrote, 'and we morosely awaited the inevitable news of cancellation.' It never came, and the first intimation the Arsenal players had of their opponents' warm-up routine came as the two teams walked out together. Centre-half Bernard Joy, finding himself alongside goalkeeper Khomich, noticed with some surprise that the Dynamo goalkeeper was already 'smothered in mud from head to foot'.

Writing several years later, Cliff Bastin described how the Russians 'marched out of the tunnel and into the middle of the field with military precision', and how there was 'something unnatural about these young men, who were always so restrained and unspontaneous in their manner'. He also claimed, with scarcely-concealed sarcasm, that he was 'looking forward to receiving a huge bouquet of flowers from the dour, rugged Semichastny'.

Perhaps the hostility came later, or perhaps he had already been influenced by Allison's attitude. Certainly, as captain and manager, these two must have exercised a strong influence on the way the team as a whole approached this encounter. 'I feared at the time that they regarded the match with Arsenal as being of political rather than sporting importance,' Bastin wrote, but if this was true of the Russian authorities and players – which seems more than likely – it was also true of their British counterparts. It was not a real representative eleven that took the field at White Hart Lane that afternoon, but the 'Arsenal' players were in no doubt that they were playing for their country. This would not be a game to lose gracefully.

'A complete fog. I can't see anything. Where's the ball? What's happening?' These words, taken from Vadim Sinyavsky's radio commentary on the game at White Hart Lane, might have been spoken, at some point in the afternoon, by any member of the 54,000 crowd. The density of fog varied through the ninety minutes of the game, but visibility rarely exceeded fifty yards and often fell as low as thirty. Even a man rooted to the centre spot would have had trouble seeing everything, and most spectators saw considerably less than half the action.

Given such conditions, the exactitude with which so many controversial incidents were later described seems miraculous. One is left with the impression that this fog had magical properties, not only blinding people when they wished to be blinded, but enabling them to see what, and only what, they wished to see. If there hadn't been a fog at White Hart Lane that afternoon someone would have had to conjure one up.

Dynamo's opening goal, scored in the very first minute, offered a clear example. Bernard Joy described it in some detail in his book *Forward Arsenal*:

> They scored before we had even touched the ball. The centre-forward tapped the ball to the inside-right who pushed it back to the left-half. Straight through came the pass to Bobrov, the tall, David Jack-type of inside-forward. Immediately the centre-forward went to the left wing, not half-heartedly in the hope of receiving a pass, but at full speed as though the ball was already there. I was well after him before I realised the mistake. The middle was open and I doubled back to close it

> again. Too late. Bobrov pushed the ball into the gap, just wide of my outstretched foot, inside-right Kartsev took the ball in his stride and slipped it past the oncoming Griffiths.

Sounds convincing, doesn't it? Cliff Bastin, in his book *Cliff Bastin Remembers*, distinctly remembered a free kick being awarded, although no one knew what for: 'Joe Bacuzzi was right on the spot, and he was completely mystified by the referee's decision.' One of the Russians took the disputed kick quickly, slotting the ball through to Beskov, who scored.

Joy thought Kartsev was the scorer, Bastin thought Beskov. Bastin's account included a free kick, Joy's followed the ball in one seamless movement from kick-off to net. Which was true?

Neither, seems the most likely answer. The *Daily Mail*, *Star*, *South Wales Argus*, *Daily Telegraph* and *Evening Standard* – to name but five – all agreed that Sergei Soloviev supplied the killing pass and Bobrov the final strike, and three of them also noted that Soloviev received the ball from Semichastny. Not one paper mentioned a free kick, disputed or otherwise, yet ten years later, in his book *Soccer Nemesis*, the usually perceptive Brain Glanville was repeating Cliff Bastin's account of this goal – and indeed the whole game – as if it was the gospel truth. Sometimes, it seems, the fog was in the eyes of the beholder.

In these opening minutes the conditions were as good as they were going to get all afternoon, with the two grandstands facing each other like ghostly eminences. On one touchline Mr Latyshev's dark kit could still be distinguished from that of the players – later in the first half he would receive several passes – while on the other the two linesmen's state-of-the-art luminous flags glowed faintly in the grey. The players could just about see from one end of the pitch to the other, though judging the trajectory of long balls and crosses was already difficult.

The fog thickened almost immediately, hiding the two stands from each other's sight, and for the next ten minutes or so visibility extended only about three-quarters of the way across the pitch.

The Dynamos forced a corner, which was tipped over the bar by Griffiths. On the western side of the pitch – the press and radio side – Stanley Matthews beat three men with a jinking dribble and pushed the ball inside to Drury, who moved it on and out of sight. Matthews put in several crosses, which, to judge from the distant applause, were well handled by Khomich.

Then Arsenal – or 'the English team' as Vadim Sinyavsky was calling it in his radio commentary – equalised. Some good work from Cumner was just about visible on the far side of the pitch, the ball came across, and Rooke slammed it home from close range. As if in celebration, the fog lifted slightly, and once again the flags above the stands fluttered faintly in and out of sight.

The game swung from end to end, from clarity to a whirl of dim shapes, with both defences holding firm. In the twentieth minute Leonid Soloviev went down under an Arsenal challenge close to the East Stand touchline, and it was immediately obvious that he couldn't continue. 'Before Soloviev was helped off, Oreshkin had taken up his place,' the *Daily Mail* said, providing fuel for the later accusations that the Russians had taken advantage of their substitutions to play parts of the match with twelve men. 'A player went off the field and another passed him on the way to the pitch,' was the way the *Glasgow Evening Times* saw it.

The game resumed, and a Kartsev shot from long range flashed past the post. A couple of minutes later a free kick for a foul on the Dynamo inside-right was taken quickly, and Bobrov was suddenly away on his own. As Scott closed in he slipped the ball sideways to Sergei Soloviev, who seemed certain to score. But the winger's last touch was not quite good enough, allowing Wyn Griffiths to claim the ball bravely at his feet.

The goalkeeper had already taken one knock on the head in his vain attempt to prevent Bobrov from scoring, and he received a second here. It took three minutes to convince the trainer that he could continue, and if there had been a replacement at hand Griffiths would surely have come off. An appeal was immediately issued over the sound system for QPR keeper Harry Brown, who was known to be in the ground, to report to the dressing room, and those spectators surrounding Charlton keeper Sam Bartram in the West Stand enclosure persuaded him to offer his services just in case. Griffiths, meanwhile, was playing out the rest of the half, considerably the worse for wear. When half-time arrived he had no idea what the score was.

A quarter of the match had passed. Stanley Mortensen was tripped as he tried to weave his way through the centre of the Russian defence, but Matthews's free kick was scrambled away. At the other end Sergei Soloviev beautifully nutmegged Laurie Scott only to be neatly dispossessed by Bernard Joy. The Arsenal defence was matching the Dynamos' positional play, and the Russian attacks were not looking nearly as incisive as they had in the previous two games. At the other end Mortensen was proving a handful for Blinkov, and then there was Matthews. Arsenal trainer Tom Whittaker described

> one great moment . . . when the mist momentarily lifted

> down the touchline in front of us, and we saw that Stanley Matthews had four of the Russians frantically changing feet and gear, back-pedalling, restarting and reversing, and then, like the supreme master showing the pupils how it was done, he leisurely dribbled the ball through the whole four of them before being swallowed up by the fog.

At other times the Dynamos refused to be left. Stankevich was using his arms rather too much for the crowd's liking, and was being frequently pulled up for it by the Russian referee.

Looking back, it's impossible to pick out the moment – if indeed there was one – at which this game turned nasty, or to say which, if either, of the two sides was more responsible. The injury to Soloviev may have incensed the Russians, the injury to Griffiths the British. The *Bulletin & Scots Pictorial* reporter thought that 'in the early stages the football was clever and clean, but when the Russians indulged in crude charging and even held on to the Arsenal men, the Englishmen retaliated'. The 'even' in this statement is significant: British players and press instinctively felt that holding on was more reprehensible than mere crude charging.

Matthews, in particular, was being subjected to methods that the Arsenal players considered thoroughly unsporting – shirt-pulling, elbowing, pushing, blatant obstruction. But the Russians had their complaints too. 'The referee has stopped the game,' Sinyavsky told his listeners back home. 'He very rightly gives a free kick to the Russians for an attack on the goalkeeper, such a rough one and completely unnecessary. I should say the game is now very sharp.'

It was no secret that the countries interpreted the rules

differently, but up until this point a collision course had been avoided by Soviet deference and British refereeing. The British players had been allowed to play it their way, and the Soviets, particularly in the Cardiff game, had been doing well enough not to care. Now a Soviet referee was trying to run a game according to unfamiliar British rules in dense fog, a game, moreover, between two fairly well-matched sides, both of whom desperately wanted to win. There seems no doubt that Latyshev made a number of dubious decisions and that the Arsenal players reacted badly. 'The wrong decisions by the referee irritated our fellows so much that the game got rather out of hand,' Bernard Joy admitted.

Nothing much seems to have happened off the ball, even with the conditions providing such perfect cover. Visibility was still around the forty-yard mark, and spectators followed those parts of the game they couldn't see by listening to the roars and boos of those who could. On either side of the goals large posses of cameramen waited with their magnesium flash bulbs for a forward about to shoot, a goalkeeper about to make a save. For a few seconds the action would be transfixed by blazing light, and then the gloom would descend again, seemingly twice as dark and impenetrable. In the stands, wrote L. V. Manning, 'a thousand men lit a thousand cigarettes and it looked like a thousand bonfires'.

On the pitch Arsenal seemed to be gaining the upper hand. Bastin thought that 'in view of the fact that our team had never played together before, and was recruited from no less than six different clubs, it was displaying astonishing teamwork'. The Dynamos, by contrast, 'were playing so badly towards the end of the first half that we might well have been three or four goals in the lead'.

They went one up about six minutes before the interval.

Bastin himself started the move with a lovely through ball to Rooke, who flicked it into the oncoming Mortensen's path. The Blackpool man drove it powerfully past Khomich with his right foot.

The Dynamos were still reeling from this blow when Matthews undid their left flank for the umpteenth time. After dancing past Stankevich with the ball apparently glued to his toes, he put an inch-perfect cross on to Mortensen's head, and the young Blackpool player scored again.

Perhaps Arsenal relaxed, but the third goal in four minutes came from the Russians. Beskov, sent gliding through in the inside-left channel, coolly shot across Griffiths to cut the arrears. Two minutes later Mr Latyshev blew for half-time.

In 1945 the British football regulations called for a five-minute break, but George Allison suggested an immediate turn around. They should make the most of the light, he argued, though it's not exactly clear who he was arguing with. If it was the referee he must have found an interpreter at short notice.

If he did receive such a suggestion, Latyshev ignored it. Five minutes went by, and then another five. The Arsenal players sat in their dressing room and wondered what was going on. 'It dragged out to a quarter of an hour before we got restarted,' Bernard Joy complained.

In the Dynamo quarters there was much more excitement, or so the subsequent tales would have us believe. When the Russians reached their dressing room they found eleven cups of steaming tea waiting for them. According to Bastin, they 'took one look at the tea, picked up their cups, and splashed the liquid right across the floor. Then they drank vodka!' His source for this story was the 'Russian-speaking Englishman' who had been thoughtfully placed in the Dynamo dressing room to make sure things were running smoothly.

The same man no doubt passed on the details of the infamous conversation between Yakushin and Latyshev. According to Allison, it was a Russian-speaking friend who had overheard the Dynamo manager tell the referee that if Arsenal held the lead he was to abandon the game, but if the Dynamos came from behind it would have to be played to the finish. 'At this my resentment and irritation grew,' Allison wrote with admirable restraint.

Both Brian Glanville and Bernard Joy endorsed these stories in their own books, and later authors – Jack Rollin, for example, in his *Soccer at War* – have accepted them, at least in part, as historical truth. But there is nothing in the way of independent evidence to support them, and common sense suggests that they were nothing more than smear stories. Why would finely-tuned athletes – as everyone agrees the Dynamos were – start drinking vodka in the middle of a crucial match? And why would anybody with an ounce of intelligence allow such a conversation as the one alleged to be overheard?

If the stories were true, it seems rather strange that they didn't emerge for several years. No journalist got so much as a whiff of them on the day, but once the Cold War had fully set in, any old anti-Soviet junk could be passed off as the truth.

Through the extended half-time interval the fog showed signs of lifting, but the players were no sooner out on the pitch than conditions worsened again. Harry Brown had answered the call, and now took his place in the Arsenal goal. Sam Bartram was probably a relieved man: he had once stuck to his post in a fog-bound goalmouth until a team-mate came to find him – the game had ended fifteen minutes earlier.

Brown didn't have the best of starts. Three minutes into the second half Soloviev – blatantly offside, according to the Arsenal players – crossed for Kartsev to put a weak header through the goalkeeper's hands. A linesman had apparently raised his luminous flag, but the referee, who had swapped his dark blazer for a white shirt to make himself more noticeable, ignored him. 'The whole of our defence stood still, confidently waiting to hear Latyshev's whistle,' Bastin wrote, but if all the referee's decisions in the first half were as bad as the Arsenal players claimed, then one wonders where such confidence came from.

The sides were level once more, the Arsenal players a little angrier than before. A few minutes later Mortensen went hurtling through the Dynamo defence only to be upended by an outstretched Russian foot. Latyshev waved away the Arsenal appeals for a penalty, further stoking the resentment.

Not long after that, Khomich gathered the ball in his goalmouth and was aggressively charged by Rooke. Khomich went to ground and one of the Dynamo defenders put himself, none too gently, between Rooke and the goalkeeper. George Drury waded into the fray, eager to let out some frustration in a good cause, and was seen to throw at least one blow. Latyshev took Drury aside, and according to most of those in a position to see, ordered him from the field. The Arsenal man pretended not to understand, and quickly lost himself in the fog.

Play continued, the conditions slowly worsening. With almost half an hour remaining and the scores level, Allison, according to both the *Express* and the *Mail*, tried to get the game abandoned. The Dynamo staff said no, but when Ambassador Gusev sent a message from the box suggesting the same thing, Yakushin agreed to a consultation with Allison and the referee. The threesome met down on the pitch, where the visibility seemed markedly better than it had from the stand. At this point either Allison agreed that the game should go on, or he was overruled. In his book the Arsenal manager refused to admit that any such conversation had taken place. He had appealed to the First Secretary of the Soviet Embassy, he wrote, and had been refused. He had made this appeal, moreover, when the score was 4–3. A most sporting gesture.

The controversies kept on coming. Soon after the abortive touchline conference Trofimov was substituted by Archangelski. He 'walked off no more the worse for wear than the majority of the Dynamo team', said the *Glasgow Herald*, but Bastin doubted whether he had gone off at all. 'For twenty minutes of the second half the Russians were playing with twelve men,' he claimed. His evidence: 'The fog prevented me from seeing very much,' he wrote, 'but I had a feeling that the Russians had one man more than us, at throw-ins on the other side of the field.' Bernard Joy thought Archangelski had entered the game while 'Trofimov was still on the pitch, limping picturesquely', but didn't think the two men had overlapped for more than 'a brief spell'.

The *Daily Mail* provided a simple, credible version: 'Archangelski ran on to the field, sought out the referee, and while apparently asking for permission, glimpsed the ball, and set off after it. Meanwhile, Trofimov, the man he was replacing, walked slowly from the field.' Not exactly legal, but hardly cheating on the grand scale. So much for the myth of the Russian twelve men.

Visibility was now closer to thirty yards than forty. Again Soloviev received the ball in an apparently offside position, again play was allowed to continue, and Bobrov memorably shot home on the run from just outside the penalty area. 4–3 to the Dynamos.

The number of 'tousy incidents', as the *Bulletin & Scots Pictorial* colourfully dubbed them, multiplied. One in particular stuck in Arsenal memories. With about twenty minutes to go Ronnie Rooke – who had already, in the words of the *Mirror*, been the 'cause of several stoppages for rough play' – picked up a loose ball some forty yards from the Dynamo goal and carried it at speed towards the penalty area. According to Joy's version of events, the Fulham man was just about to shoot when

> Semichastny jumped on his back and was shaken off by so vigorous a blow that he carried a black eye for several days. Rooke steadied himself and beat Khomich with one of his pile-drivers from twenty-five yards. As we ran to congratulate him we saw the referee was pointing to the spot where Rooke had been fouled. This was unfair, we thought. He should have allowed play to go on under the advantage rule. Imagine our consternation, when he gave a free kick against Rooke.

A well-known English ex-referee, who happened to be standing behind that goal, later told the *Daily Record* that no infringement had taken place. Since he must have been at least thirty yards from the incident, in conditions of not-much-more-than-thirty-yard visibility, his judgement was somewhat open to question. And in any case, even the Arsenal players admitted that two infringements had taken place – Semichastny had thrown himself at Rooke, and had been elbowed in the face by the Englishman in retaliation. But in fact the referee had already blown for a third infringement: handball against Rooke. The inside-forward denied it: 'Handle it – I never had a chance to use my hands, they were both tied behind my back!' Which raises the question: how did he get his elbow in Semichastny's eye?

Dynamo dominated the last twenty minutes. The Arsenal defenders were clearly tiring, and on several occasions a Russian through ball almost brought a fifth goal. Many of the crowd had long since left by this time; some had spent a good portion of the second half sitting in nearby cafés, warming themselves with cups of tea and listening to Raymond Glendenning lament the fact that he couldn't see anything either. Now the foggy streets filled in earnest, children gripping fathers with one hand, hammer-and-sickle flags with the other. On the Tottenham High Road the police fought a losing battle to keep the queues honest as the trolleybuses sailed serenely out of the mist.

In the ground behind them Nikolai Latyshev blew his whistle for the last time, and the players tramped off in the general direction of the dressing rooms. Moscow Dynamo had beaten the famous Arsenal by four goals to three.

It had been a close result, but the mood in the two dressing rooms must have been very different. Both sets of players would have carried some anger off the pitch, but in the Dynamos' case the sense of hard-won triumph must have swept all before it. They had beaten a virtual England eleven! As for Arsenal – some of their players were still seething at the injustice of it all years later.

The club had arranged a dinner at the Lyceum for later in the evening, but there doesn't seem to have been any socialising between the two camps. 'Social intercourse by the Russians seemed to be forbidden,' Bernard Joy wrote, adding somewhat gratuitously that the supposedly injured Trofimov was the only Russian who took to the dance floor. Perhaps the Arsenal contingent left early, because the following morning's newspapers were full of the 500 girls who scrambled to dance with the shy Russians, and pictures of happy Dynamo players shaking a leg on the Lyceum floor. One non-playing member of the party, obviously somewhat the worse for wear, told a reporter that he was thinking of staying in England. 'There is something about this place I do not understand,' he said philosophically. 'Perhaps it is your girls.'

Yakushin had more than the result to smile about. Chelsea manager Billy Birrell, who had been scouring White Hart Lane for the Dynamo trainer and the five footballs borrowed two weeks earlier, had been successfully evaded, and the balls were safely back aboard the maroon coach.

13

Black eyes, ballet and a Clapham housewife

The newspaper inquest began next morning. Should the game have even been played?

No, was the general consensus. 'The most farcical match that has ever been played', the *Mail* called it; 'It bore not the faintest flicker of resemblance to a game of football,' the *Sketch* stated. Yakushin had no argument with them: according to the *Glasgow Herald*, he agreed after the match that it should never have been started. His players told L. V. Manning that they'd had no desire to begin or continue a game in which neither side could play football. They had believed they were obliging the crowd.

As, no doubt, had the referee, but in his case the criticism was almost universal. His decision to place himself on one touchline and the two linesmen on the other was generally ridiculed, not because it ill suited the conditions – which was true – but because it was a stupid system in itself, which was much more debatable. Davie Meiklejohn accused him of obvious bias: 'The Russians got all the breaks . . . body-checks, elbow work, all went by unpunished, but not so with the Arsenal. Some of his decisions bordered on the ridiculous.' Manning, who thought that Latyshev had 'only an elementary idea of the tackle rules and made the most astonishing decisions', seemed even more incensed by the referee's 'pip-squeak whistle, which sounded' – the ultimate insult – 'like a French train starting'.

Bastin, of course, thought that Latyshev had been the Russian's twelfth man, 'that as long as the Dynamos got the ball into the net, even if they carried it there, the referee was going to award them a goal'.

At this distance, without even a foggy film record, it's impossible to tell whether Latyshev was deliberately biased throughout, unconsciously biased by unfamiliarity with traditional British rule interpretations, or simply used as a convenient scapegoat. It is possible, though, to point out bias in the British reporting of the game. Take the George Drury incident as described by Roy Peskett in the *Mail*: 'Drury, thinking the Dynamo keeper Khomich had dropped the ball, went in after it, only to be hauled off by a Russian defender. The Arsenal inside-right brushed his opponent away, and was immediately pounced on by the referee.' A telling use of verbs: the nasty Russians hauled and pounced, the nice Brit just brushed. Peskett forgot to mention that what the nice Brit actually did was punch the Russian in the face.

The referee was accused of bias, the Dynamos condemned for their use of foul tactics, but the violent antics of the British team were simply ignored. 'There was a little more feeling in this game than in the others the Russians have played,' the *News Chronicle* reported diplomatically, 'but it was obvious that the trouble was due to over-anxiety on both sides rather than bad blood.'

The British press preferred to dwell on the virtues of Matthews, rather than on the vices of Rooke and Drury. He had been the best player on display, and the fairest, 'practically the only player on the field at the end of the game who was not guilty of infringements'. Glasgow Rangers manager Struth, at White Hart Lane to scout the Dynamos, thought Matthews the man of the match, and Stanley in his turn promised to visit Ibrox during the coming week with a few helpful tips on how to beat the Russians.

Only the *Mirror* dissented from the chorus of adulation, accusing Matthews of over-elaboration, of making 'so many rings around the Dynamo backs that he made himself dizzy and, as a result, failed to make as many openings as he ought to have made'.

The British side might have had the best player, but had the right team won? For all the complaints about the referee, ex-Arsenal star Charles Buchan was in no doubt. 'The Russians were worthy of their victory,' he wrote. Their defence had been troubled by Matthews, Mortensen and Rooke, but their attack had been 'superb'.

Moscow was predictably cock-a-hoop. 'We have become the second motherland of football,' Moscow Radio crowed, 'drawing with Chelsea, winning brilliantly over Cardiff, and now winning over the all-England team of professional clubs. The English are amazed. They are flabbergasted. They marvel at the play of the Soviet masters. Their papers are full of enthusiastic articles and descriptions.'

Izvestia even had Dmitry Shostakovich's seal of approval. The composer had always thought British football the best in the world, but Soviet footballers had now demonstrated 'a game of much higher class'. And just to add to England's humiliation, the English-language *Moscow News* carried an interview with the Moscow Torpedo goalkeeper, Anatoly Akimov. He thought the Dynamos were doing reasonably well, but that there were probably five other teams in the Soviet Union that were just as good. The Dynamo attack had been praised by the British, but the Central House forward line was definitely better.

The same paper took great care to ram the political point home:

> The performance of the Moscow Dynamo team and its victory over such a strong eleven as Arsenal came as a surprise to the British public. Indeed, for many, the Dynamos were as much a 'discovery' as were the Soviet chess players who recently beat the Americans. We feel that it is an excellent opportunity to offer a little advice to all such 'discoverers'. To avoid surprises of this kind, wouldn't it perhaps be just as well to get to know us better? Knowledge of us might perhaps help foreign observers to understand other things about us besides sports.

Some members of the British public might have been listening and learning, but most of the country's football journalists were more interested in finding a team that could teach the wretched Russians a lesson. The tour had been a huge success, the *News Chronicle* thought, and now the Dynamos 'deserved the compliment' of a game against an FA XI. The *Sketch* had no doubt that 'an FA XI of England class' could beat the Russians, and Charles Buchan made it easier for Rous and co. by selecting a team for them: Swift (Manchester City), Walton (Manchester United), Scott (Arsenal), Dearson (Birmingham City), Davies (Nottingham Forest), Burgess (Tottenham Hotspur), Matthews (Stoke City), Carter (Sunderland), Lawton (Chelsea), Mortensen (Blackpool) and Smith (Aston Villa).

If the Russians couldn't be persuaded to play an FA XI, then one of the stronger clubs should be pushed into the breach. Writing in the *News of the World*, George Harrison was convinced that any decent attacking side with a solid defence could defeat the Russians. They were only unbeaten so far because the FA had given them such poor opponents. 'Charlton would have given much better value. So would Villa, Wolves, Blackpool, Chesterfield, and half a dozen more . . .'

There were more thoughtful pieces. Frank Coles made the interesting point that Arsenal's long-ball game was bound to have suffered more from low visibility than the Dynamos' close-passing style, 'for the simple reason that no one could follow the flight of the ball accurately'.

Stanley Matthews reckoned the Arsenal team had been unlucky not to draw. The Dynamos, in his opinion, were a good side but not world-beaters:

> You cannot fault their forwards. They move into position better than any Continental team I have ever played against. Their wingers are skilful and strong-running and they have shrewd inside men who are able to make the ball do the work. Yet they cannot be rated a great XI until their defence is stiffened. It is too stereotyped and easily beaten by forwards who hold the ball.

Jimmy Hogan, who had coached in Europe for many years, focused more on the British reflection in the Russian mirror. While the Dynamos were playing the old British game at a faster pace, the British were stuck with 'an up-in-the-air, get-the-ball-if-you-can-style style', punting the ball down the middle to marked centre-forwards, failing to use wingers or width, just hoping for mistakes rather than trying to be creative.

Bernard Joy, writing on the day after the match, also thought Arsenal had deserved a draw, but he had no real complaints. The key to the Russian success, as he saw it, was their positional play. The man on the ball was given so many options by the movement of others. He did not need to beat an opponent, he could let the ball do the work. British players, who had lost this art, were forced either to dribble or to pass to a marked opponent. 'We emphasise individual play rather than the blending of individuals into a good team.'

The Russians were not hidebound by stereotypes. It wasn't always the centre-forward who was left upfield; it wasn't always the outside-right patrolling that touchline. They took turns, they interchanged positions as a matter of course. And since their style of play involved attacking and defending in numbers, the Russians needed to be very fit. But rather than simply running round the training pitch twice as often as their British counterparts, they took the whole subject at least twice as seriously. 'They had interwoven coaching with training,' Joy thought; they took everything into account – health, diet, relaxation, leisure, psychology.

All of which was very perceptive, perhaps too much so for the times. Joy himself admitted that such Russian methods were 'revolutionary, and to our minds perhaps, un-English', and concluded with the comforting thought that Britain still produced not only the best natural players but also the most sporting: 'we accept defeat more generously than most other nations'.

The British weren't so good at ballet dancing. C. B. Fry in the *Sunday Graphic* thought the key to the Dynamos' success was their position in Soviet society, which, he explained, was very similar to that enjoyed by Soviet ballet. Both were 'standing institutions, popular to a degree, and regarded as a national asset, a national value, worth preserving intact even in war'. The players' standard of athleticism was obviously high, and there was no way of producing such 'excellence of poise and movement' unless, at the back of the players' minds, there was a fine ideal of athleticism. 'The rosy shadow of the ballet and what it means to the Russian mind' lay across the football pitches of the Soviet Union.

In the *Sunday Dispatch*, Lester B. Wilson was more interested in the rosy shadow cast by the new Labour Government:

> When Arsenal met Dynamo
> With all the tickets sold
> The English climate showed itself
> As sadly uncontrolled,
> For chill, reactionary fog
> Was clearly never planned
> In England's newly socialist
> And green and pleasant land.
>
> And those who bought admission
> But were thwarted from the skies
> Can see in this the woeful thoughts
> Of private enterprise;
> These factors point a moral when
> considered all together,
> So forward, Mr Morrison – and
> nationalise the weather!

The Dynamo officials were round at Lancaster Gate again on the Thursday for a conference on the tour's future. Once more Rous tried to sell them the idea of a game against a representative XI – something the Russians had explicitly rejected in their famous fourteen points seventeen days earlier. He suggested Wednesday 5 December, most probably in Birmingham.

Perhaps the victory adrenalin was still rushing through their veins, but the Soviet officials didn't refuse the invitation out of hand. They were still keen on the idea of a game at Wembley. They would refer the matter to Moscow, and let the FA know sometime in the following week.

Rous had no choice but to accept the decision, or the lack thereof. Arthur Elvin, the managing director of Wembley Stadium, was more forthright: 'They state that they will make up their minds next week. It will be too late, as we wouldn't have time to print the tickets.'

In the House of Commons, meanwhile, Devonport MP and future Labour leader Michael Foot was asking whether a minister could find time to pressure the services into releasing a couple of full-backs capable of standing up to the Dynamos. There was no answer from the Government.

The Dynamo players were having the day off, resting from their exertions in the fog and on the dance floor. No one in the Dynamo party had said anything to the press on the previous evening about the confrontational tone of the afternoon's game; the Russians, initially at least, seemed willing to accept victory as compensation for any criticism that might have come their way.

Perusal of the morning's British press must have changed their minds. Finding themselves under concerted attack for unsporting play, they decided to use their own media to respond in kind. 'The English played very roughly,' Yakushin told Moscow Radio, 'and I saw many methods used that are considered unsporting by us.' He also had a wonderful piece of visual evidence – Mikhail Semichastny's black eye. The Dynamo captain cabled the Soviet Committee of Sports in Moscow, claiming that he had been struck twice in the face by one of the opposing side, and that goalkeeper Khomich had been struck once.

As intended, the British press picked up both stories. The punches hadn't been deemed newsworthy in themselves, but complaints about them certainly were. What did Arsenal and the FA have to say? Not a lot. 'Suggestions that Russian players were struck have astonished football officials in Britain,' one paper spluttered. Arsenal officials pronounced themselves 'amazed' by such accusations.

With both sides refusing to back down, it looked as if a row might develop which could engulf the tour, and someone in Moscow must have realised as much. Sports diplomacy would not be served by accusing the British of unsporting behaviour; there were some things a nation could not be expected to accept. Turning the other cheek, however, would win them even more friends. They had won the war at White Hart Lane, and now they could win the peace as well.

The following day the Dynamo publicity machine went into reverse. Semichastny had a black eye, but he had received it in training at White City on Thursday, and certainly not in the Arsenal game. Elliseyeva, cornered by a reporter, said that she knew nothing, but that she would fetch Semichastny. She came back alone. The Dynamo captain had told her it was nothing at all, certainly not worth talking about. And he hadn't got it in the game on Wednesday.

The argument rumbled on, but only the British were arguing. 'It was important for the Russian players to be told that they must not resent their goalkeeper being charged when he is holding the ball,' the *Sketch* lectured. 'Such resentment had caused more potentially explosive incidents than the Semichastny black eye.' Ronnie Rooke, meanwhile, was still playing the innocent. 'Throughout the game,' he claimed,

> Semichastny always stood away from me, and, therefore, his tackles when the ball was in the air were always late and made when the ball was gone. Perhaps that is the way they play in Russia, but in this country any centre-half who continually meets the centre-forward late is penalised by the referee under the rule of ungentlemanly conduct.

Rooke would have been well-advised to take a lesson from Stanley Matthews, who realised that nations differed not only in how they interpreted the laws of the game, but also in how they emotionally graded the various transgressions. He recalled that he had twice had his shirt pulled out of his shorts at White Hart Lane, but that the Russian concerned had obviously been unrepentant. Such behaviour was not considered particularly unsporting in Russia, Matthews had been told later. After all, you couldn't get a broken leg or bruised knee from somebody pulling your shirt.

Meanwhile, another source of controversy was bubbling up. Throughout the tour nagging doubts had persisted among British commentators as to the bona fides of the Dynamo players – was this truly a club team or a cunningly disguised Soviet representative XI? The Soviet protests over the composition of the Arsenal team – and the annoying fact that they had beaten it – had unwittingly refocused attention on the composition of their own. Rumours that several members of the Dynamo team were guest players – rumours fuelled, no doubt, by the vast increase in person-to-person Anglo-Soviet contacts which the organisation of the tour necessitated – were now gaining ground.

The Soviets attempted to scotch them. British

journalists were assured once again that the Dynamos were not professionals in the British sense, that they were all serving in the armed forces or fully employed, and that they definitely all belonged to the same club.

Not all the Soviet officials were on the same page, however. The line taken by the *Moscow News* was based on the understandable assumption that sooner or later some eager British journalist would notice that Bobrov had been playing for Central House throughout the previous season. Its football correspondent took the bull by the horns. 'Some British sportswriters,' he began,

> try to justify the defeat of the English team on the grounds that Dynamo itself is a reinforced Arsenal. This contention, however, does not bear up under scrutiny, as a comparison of the Dynamo line-up in this season's USSR championship play with the team appearing in England shows. The only moot point may be the position of Vsevolod Bobrov, who this season took part in title play for the first time in his soccer career and, since he was in the Army, played for Central House.

The writer didn't explain how a non-Russian-speaker could find evidence of Dynamo's line-up in the league that season, but he was probably speaking the truth as regards the team that initially took the field against Arsenal. Since neither Archangelski nor Dementiev had been in that side, Bobrov's status was the only bone of contention.

Soviet transfer rules, the writer stated rather cheekily, would not have allowed Tommy Lawton to move from Everton to Chelsea just in time to face the Dynamo. Soviet players could only switch clubs between seasons, and that, he implied without actually stating it, was what Bobrov had recently done. Before the war he had been a member of the Dynamo Sports Society, and there was 'nothing strange, therefore, in the fact that he should now be playing on the team of his society'.

The following season, there would, of course, be nothing strange about his playing for Central House once more, but by then nobody in Britain would be looking. And once the Cold War got into its stride, neither side would let facts get in the way of a good story. In 1955 Allison's assistant, Tom Whittaker, could happily claim that 'the Moscow Dynamo team was a club in name only. The players had been specially assembled from four towns, were the pick of the players from the whole of Russia, and had been drilled into a brilliant machine sent to this country on a political mission with orders that they must not fail.'

In Britain the Dynamo players were mostly kept safe behind the walls of their hotel and the language barrier. 'They are not allowed to roam London,' the *Star* reported plaintively. 'They spend hours looking at illustrated papers, go to bed early, rise early.' On those rare occasions when one or two were allowed out in Elliseyeva's company, they were careful to keep to the script. In an interview for the BBC, Mikhail Semichastny and Konstantin Beskov blandly answered a series of prearranged-sounding questions, and even managed to make a couple of inoffensive political points in the process.

They still had a high opinion of British football, but were now also of the opinion that the British had something to learn from them, both on and off the field. Neither man went into details on the footballing side, but Semichastny was prepared to criticise British stadiums. The pitches were fine, but he'd been surprised to see so many people standing. In the Soviet Union, of course, around 90 per cent of the spectators were seated. It was hard to imagine scenes at home similar to those that had taken place at Stamford Bridge, with spectators crowding round the goalposts. It was all rather primitive, he implied, without actually saying so.

Beskov's list of Britain's notable features – London parks and architecture, bomb damage, left-hand traffic, beautiful Welsh singing, theatres and fog – merely served to emphasise how cloistered the touring party had been, but the passing reference to 'old-fashioned gas lamps side by side with modern electric street lighting' carried the same intimations of backwardness. In the Soviet Union, one was forced to assume, modern lighting was the norm.

If this was criticism, it was all offered in the most friendly spirit. Semichastny had found British football crowds very knowledgeable; Beskov stressed the hospitality of the British people. And there was always the war to come back to. Some of the Dynamo players had taken up arms, others had worked in war production industries. We were fighting the good fight against our common enemy, they told the British public. Just like you were.

On Thursday evening the maroon coach carried most of the players south across the river, to the Manor Place Baths on the Walworth Road, where they watched a display of amateur boxing. The following morning they were again on the Surrey side, visiting the works of Mr Claud Butler in Clapham. The Dynamo Sports Society had ordered a hundred racing cycles from Butler, and the ex-champion cyclist threw in another eleven free of charge for the Dynamo team.

The *Daily Worker* even managed to make some

political capital out of this event. After stating, quite erroneously, that the Dynamo party had ordered a hundred bikes on the spot, the writer explained that the decision both reflected well on 'our British makes' and illustrated the Russians' 'all-round knowledge of sports'. It was already well known that the Dynamo footballers were also ice hockey players, skiers and cross-country runners; if they were 'cycling experts to boot' it only went to show how good the facilities were back in the USSR.

He didn't mention Mrs Tapsell, the Clapham housewife who had made the Russians' day. She had left home that morning with shopping in mind, but on her way to join the queues in Clapham High Street had bumped into five Moscow Dynamos. Having recognised them, she did what few other Clapham housewives would have done – she began jabbering excitedly to them in Russian. 'The Dynamos gathered round her,' the *Mirror* reported,

> talking excitedly and temporarily forgetting the racing cycles they were to inspect at the works of champion Claud Butler. Mrs Tapsell explained in Russian to them and in English to her slightly amazed audience that she had worked in a Moscow clothing factory for two years. Afterwards she was so excited she couldn't remember half of what the Dynamos said.

All human life, as they say, was there. The standard of reporting echoed that accorded the tour as a whole: no one bothered to ask Mrs Tapsell how, why or when she had worked those two years in a state that was virtually cut off from the rest of the world. More importantly, the vision of these five Dynamos, so excited by this Russian-speaking Englishwoman whom fate had thrown their way, this unique chance to talk on an open street with an ordinary human being, said everything there was to say about this tour as a failure of real communication. And the vision of Mrs Tapsell, so excited to meet them, said everything there was to say about how much ordinary people would have wished it otherwise. It was everyone's loss.

14

Porridge, herring and tartan ties

On the morning the Dynamos met Mrs Tapsell, the streets of central Glasgow contained the longest queues in living memory. It had been decided at the beginning of the week that the match at Ibrox would be all-ticket, and at 9 a.m. on Friday morning a sizeable proportion of the 90,000 available went on sale at Russell Moreland's on Argyle Street, the Sportsman's Emporium on St Vincent Street and Lumley's on Sauchiehall Street.

Large queues had actually begun forming by mistake on Wednesday evening, a fact that presumably encouraged people to arrive even earlier on Thursday. As soon as the working day ended the lines started to stretch out, and by the time the pubs closed there were several hundred people in each of the three queues. All classes and both genders were represented; they brought stools and folding chairs to sit on, rugs to wrap themselves in, and presumably the odd nip of something liquid to help keep out the cold. They talked and sang and slept, and when dawn finally turned black into grey the police estimate had the three queues stretching more than two miles in total.

The Russell Moreland queue, which by 5 a.m. hadn't reached much beyond the Central Station railway bridge – the 'Hielanman's Umbrella' in local parlance – had by six snaked round the corner into Oswald Street, by eight passed down Midland Street to Jamaica Street, and before the doors had opened extended right up Jamaica and Union Streets, the tail of the queue passing within sight of its head. The Sportsman's Emporium queue, which began less than a quarter of a mile to the north-west, stretched along St Vincent Street, then twisted through several lanes before turning back on itself down Bothwell Street. Thomas Reid was the happy man at the front; he wanted two tickets, one for himself and one for a brother who was due back from India on Saturday.

The Lumley's queue, a further quarter-mile to the north, was the longest of the three. It had reached Renfield Street as early as 10 p.m., and continued to grow through the night, turning back along Renfrew in the early hours and then gradually retreating up that street, across Hope, Cambridge and Rose, before ending a few yards short of the Art College. May Eastcroft headed this queue, and she wanted tickets for her father and his friend. A little way behind her, Allan Stewart was reflecting on the Scottish Cup victory in the twenties which had ended a long dry spell for his team. That had been the best day he had known in forty years as a supporter, but on this coming Wednesday he was hoping for something even better.

He was presumably satisfied when nine o'clock finally arrived and he could buy his ticket, but many of his fellow queuers were not quite so happy. The late opening of one shop provoked angry remonstrations from those outside, while word was already spreading back through the other two queues that tickets were limited to two per applicant. At the rear end of each shuffling stream, men fresh off the night shift grumbled away at their misfortune.

The mounted police watched and waited. At ten o'clock a rumour swept along the Russell Moreland queue: there were tickets on sale at the Scottish FA offices and only a dozen people waiting. A mob of several hundred people swept down Jamaica Street, over the Jamaica Bridge, and along the riverside Carlton Place to the offices in question, only to find that the rumour was false. The Scottish FA, in receipt of an allocation slightly beyond its needs, had sold a few excess tickets to casual callers, but there were none left now. An even more desperate group of people swarmed back across the Clyde, and a series of fights broke out as they tried to reclaim their places in the original queue.

At eleven o'clock Russell Moreland's ran out of tickets, and those now at the front of the line discovered that they had been queuing for six hours in vain. The other two outlets also soon sold out, leaving many thousands ticketless. Some would spend another night in a queue, this time at Ibrox Stadium – Rangers, who had announced that they would not charge higher prices for the Dynamo game, had decided to offer a 1/6 ground-admission ticket to anyone who paid 9d to watch the Saturday reserve match. This sleight of hand was not appreciated by the *Sunday Record*, which found it 'suspiciously like one of those things shopkeepers were prosecuted for during the war'.

By the time the tickets went on sale the Dynamo advance guard had reached Glasgow. Yakushin, Semichastny, Beskov and an Embassy-supplied interpreter named Evgarov took the night train from Euston on Friday, and before breakfast on Saturday morning they were being checked into the Beresford Hotel by welcoming SFA officials. They had brought a Soviet flag with them, and soon it was fluttering against the grey sky alongside the blue and white cross of St Andrew.

Their main reason for coming north ahead of the main party was to get a look at Wednesday's opposition, and after lunch the Soviet foursome were driven down to Motherwell's Fir Park ground. Perhaps it was the Scottish air, perhaps the absence of a coterie of officials, but the Scottish journalists found the Dynamos as amiable and talkative as the language barrier allowed. Over Scots cake and tea at half-time the Russians expressed their surprise at the speed of the game; they had obviously been expecting something closer to the old Scottish style, not this Caledonian variant of the English game which they already knew all too well.

Rangers won the match, but their performance can hardly have struck fear into the watching Dynamos. They went one down without touching the ball, recovered to take the lead late in the first half, and then grimly hung on through the second. Still, there was no doubting the club's recent pedigree. Rangers had been champions in 1935, 1937 and 1939, and had won every wartime Scottish league they had entered between 1940 and 1945. Supporters might be grumbling that they were no longer the team they had once been, that many of the side's better players were now getting a little past it, and it was true that only four of the side's seven current internationals – Dawson, Smith, Johnstone, Gillick, Shaw, Young and Waddell – would be regulars in the 1946–7 season. But if the side that faced the Dynamos was undergoing a period of transition, then it could hardly have been smoother: Rangers were leading the Scottish League South, and they would again be league champions in three of the four post-war seasons.

Trainer Arthur Dixon's main worry was the fitness of his players, most of whom were part-time professionals. Employers had been understanding, and most of the team had got extra hours off for training, but getting them all together at the same time was not easy to arrange.

The watching Dynamos at Fir Park would have noted Young's strength at centre-half, the sound covering of the defence, Watkins's energy in midfield, and Waddell's skill on the wing, but they would have seen nothing to worry them unduly. They weren't going to be outpassed by this side, and they had seen nothing on the tour to suggest that any British side could outrun them.

Observing the Soviet footballers, scribe Harry Miller put into words something that had somehow eluded all his fellow reporters. There were two things, he said, that made the Dynamos stand out in a British crowd. One was Konstantin Beskov's old-fashioned, velvet-collared topcoat, the other was that they were so obviously in top physical condition. 'You could not compare the ordinary run of our footballers with such obvious athletes,' Miller wrote. The difference was unmistakable, 'even in civilian clothes'.

That evening an article in the *Glasgow Evening News* entitled 'Dynamos as diplomats' must have pleased those in the Soviet Embassy who were monitoring the touring party's reception. 'It was a first-rate diplomatic idea of Russia's to send her famous football team, the Dynamos, to Britain,' writer William Power thought. 'Whether we understand her psychology, she evidently understands ours.' This was like a Native American chief thanking the Europeans for realising just how much his people liked beads, but Power was just getting started. As far as the architects of Soviet sports diplomacy were concerned, the news just kept getting better.

'An English crowd may well have been surprised at the spectacle of hefty footballers bearing floral tributes,' Power admitted. But there was a lesson to learn here: 'The Russian people have reminded us that impressive virile achievement of a manifold sort may and should be accompanied by communal respect for intellect and art. Therein lies their true greatness.' Not only was the rosy shadow of ballet lying over their football pitches, but the rosy light of football was bathing their theatres.

Sport could just be sport, but it could also serve 'a great world purpose by promoting a human understanding between peoples'. Football might not have the greatest track record in this regard, but perhaps its day had come.

> A people who love football and can produce a team like the Dynamos cannot be so very different from ourselves. Such is our reflection. It is a big step towards the kind of understanding on which the fate of mankind depends. It may be that the biggest victory in history – the victory over mutual understanding and suspicion – will have been won on the football fields of Britain.

Here the Soviets had it all. Not only did the Dynamos reflect a superior society – one in which art, intellect and sport flourished in classless harmony – but their very excellence on the football field meant that they were just like the British. There was something to emulate but there was nothing to fear.

The Soviet Union's PR men were now working overtime. On Sunday the *Glasgow Sunday Post* carried details of the 'science of football proficiency test' which all Soviet players had to pass. Each entrant had to prove he could run a hundred metres in under thirteen seconds, and fifty in six and a quarter, kick and head the ball correctly under severe test conditions, exhibit sufficient muscle strength in ankles and legs, and demonstrate the stamina to last two hours of all-out play. Each player was also expected to live by a regular routine, eschew alcohol, and consult a psychologist if he was inexplicably off his game.

Such a scientific approach naturally required the backing of a progressive-minded state, and the success of the Dynamos, Moscow Radio insisted on Monday, proved that the Soviet Union was just such a paragon. The Government was spending millions of roubles on facilities and equipment, and at the Central Research Institute of Physical Culture in Moscow – 'the fountainhead of athletic science in the Soviet Union' – dedicated staff were researching methods of training and ways of achieving peak performances. 'Physiologists of world renown' were studying the most minute movements, and passing on their findings to trainers and coaches throughout Soviet sport.

The appliance of science was all it took; that and the necessary progressive outlook. And if Soviet scientists could create such footballers, then the challenges of the future – like the building of an atom bomb, perhaps – would surely prove easy to meet.

In London the rest of the Dynamo party had also been watching football. Some went back to White Hart Lane to watch Spurs play Chelsea, others visited Upton Park for West Ham versus Derby, but the largest group descended on Craven Cottage to watch Fulham take on league leaders Charlton Athletic. Two rows of seats had been reserved for the Russians, but so many turned up that the club officials had to move a row of paying Brits.

Sinyavsky was on top form that afternoon, describing the Fulham ground as 'packed to the utmost limit with spectators squeezed into four stands like sardines – preserved not in oil but in fog. But once again, what a wonderful field! And how neatly they mow the lawns.'

When the teams came out he was 'surprised' to spot 'two old acquaintances from "Arsenal".' Here they were again, playing in the same positions, Rooke (centre-forward) and Bacuzzi (full-back). 'I recognised them by the aggressive, sharp style of their play, especially Rooke.' Sinyavsky didn't stoop to mention that Arsenal had managed to find a full side from their own staff for the day's match against Plymouth, but then the *Daily Mirror* had already done that, and every bit as sarcastically as the Soviet commentator could have wished for.

Sinyavsky was impressed by the enthusiasm of the British spectators, although his belief that they 'submitted implicitly, just like the players, to the referee's decisions' probably said more about Soviet crowds and players than he intended. Soviet spectators, he said, tended to favour mass two-fingered whistling, which often lifted the pigeons off neighbouring rooftops. Or they yelled 'Castor oil! Put your glasses on! Get off the field!' at the referee. Sinyavsky himself seemed to prefer the British habit of booing, which he found, when performed *en masse*, to be both 'solemn and effective'. He didn't bother to explain how such behaviour could be considered implicit submission.

As for the game – Charlton displayed championship form, romping home more easily than the 4–2 scoreline suggested. Sinyavsky refused to be impressed: if Charlton faced the Dynamos without any guest players he was certain that the Russians would win.

The Dynamos continued their sightseeing on Sunday. Some of the London party went to the zoo, where two of the players were photographed holding pythons, while the advance guard in Scotland trained for an hour at Ibrox and talked with Rangers' players Jock Shaw, George

Young and Jimmy Smith. They then visited Third Lanark's Cathkin ground and the famous Hampden Park, whose sheer size bowled them over. Beskov was sporting a brand-new Cameron tartan tie when they arrived at the Alhambra Theatre to see *Hot Ice*, and before the show the band played 'Two Lovely Black Eyes' for Semichastny, who laughed when the joke was explained to him. After the show they suppered on milk, bread and sardines before dancing with local girls at the hotel.

By this time the London party was aboard the night sleeper from Euston, and at 6.45 the following morning, some half an hour late, the train wheezed to a halt alongside Glasgow Central's Platform 2. The Lord Provost Hector McNeil, Chief Magistrate Robert C. Smith and the delightfully-named Mr W. S. Unkles were among the dignitaries waiting to greet the Russians, and each member of the thirty-nine-strong party was dutifully introduced by Mr Karavsev from the London Embassy. Keen-eyed journalists noticed that there were two women in the party – Elliseyeva had been joined by Miss Strelkova, who would once again be assisting Sinyavsky with the radio commentary – and that goalkeeper Khomich was carrying a string of six footballs, five of which presumably belonged to Chelsea. Billy Birrell did not, however, suddenly spring out from behind the luggage trolleys to snatch them away.

At some point in the ceremonials a bystanding Argyll and Sutherland Highlander named Warburton stepped forward and presented one of the Dynamo players with a sprig of white and purple heather. 'Good luck,' he said simply, and went on his way. These days, of course, he would have been wrestled to the ground by security guards before he got close enough to smell the players' aftershave.

The party boarded the two special buses waiting to take them to the Beresford Hotel, and gazed rather bleary-eyed at the short kaleidoscope of Glaswegian streets which comprised their journey. Disembarking in the hotel forecourt they were offered shouted greetings by three tramcar crews, who had made unofficial stops in the street outside for just that purpose.

Breakfast followed, and it hardly sounded like health food. They ate butter 'in lumps from their forks', a surprised reporter noted; 'they rubbed it into their porridge, making it take the place of milk'. Since they were in Scotland the Dynamos demanded fresh fried herring, and after that they piled jam and marmalade on to the Scots bread. They spooned sugar on to everything but the herring, and then several members of the party lit up Russian cigarettes, filling the specially reserved dining room with smoke.

They retired to the lounge, where one player practised his English numbers while others tried to make sense of the morning papers, one of which even had a headline in romanised Russian – apparently 80 per cent of punters predicting Wednesday's match winner at fixed odds of 6–5 were backing Dynamo. Another had a short snippet about the people who'd been turning up at the Beresford Hotel throughout the weekend, vainly hoping to buttonhole a Russian with enquiries about the whereabouts of relatives in the Soviet Union and Soviet-occupied territories.

One of the players sat down at the piano and played a mixed bag of songs, some Russian, some Western swing. Others sang along as Elliseyeva told the invited reporters that they'd had a comfortable enough train journey, but were sorry it had been at night as there had been no chance to see the Scottish countryside. A few ventured out on to the Glasgow streets for some late-morning window-shopping, and once again the journalists following them were surprised to find the Russians anything but reserved. Approached by passers-by on Sauchiehall and Renfield Streets the Dynamo players smiled happily, willingly signed autographs and politely raised their snap-brim hats.

Around noon they were driven out to Ibrox Stadium for a training session. As eight or so Rangers players looked on from the directors' box, Yakushin put eighteen of the Dynamos through their paces, watch in hand. First they limbered up, then they ran twenty times round the pitch, and finally they practised with the ball, the forwards with the goalkeeper, the rest inter-passing. There was no cheerful banter, but neither was there any sense of harsh regimentation. The watching Rangers' manager remarked that they obviously didn't regard it as work – you only had to look at their happy faces.

Both Elliseyeva and Strelkova were also in attendance, the former rather more chatty than usual. She didn't really know much about football, she admitted, but the name Dynamo had a connection with engineering – it symbolised the spirit of movement. She did know that Glasgow was colder than London, and that she could have done with an extra coat. Strelkova, meanwhile, was practising her tackling on one of the Dynamo reserves, and bursting into gales of laughter when she managed to take the ball off him.

In the afternoon several of the players were taken to see a rugby match between Glasgow High School Former Pupils and a Royal Australian Air Force XV at the Old Anniesland ground. They arrived after the kick-off and left before half-time, obviously underwhelmed by the spectacle.

Back at the hotel, sprigs of white heather had been

arriving all day from well-wishers, causing one member of the party to remark that 'the Scots were as strange as the English'. It had been a full day, and it wasn't over yet: there was still the evening's official reception to get through. This was held in the banqueting hall of the City Chambers, and featured the usual ragbag of political big-wigs – including two former Lord Provosts – local worthies from government and football, and sundry assorted celebrities. Once again the language barrier presented an insuperable obstacle to any real contact, but as usual the Dynamos proved convivial guests. They enthusiastically joined in with 'Auld Lang Syne', pumping arms so vigorously that one columnist expected a Cossack dance to follow. Another wryly noted that the last football banquet in Glasgow had been for the Germans, the tables dotted with little swastika flags. There had been menace in the air that night, but there was none on this occasion. This was not a future enemy they were entertaining, went the unspoken thought.

At this point on Monday evening the Scottish FA might have disagreed with him. Behind the façade of the tourists' busy first day in Glasgow a row had broken out which threatened the cancellation of Wednesday's match.

On the day after the Arsenal game, Rangers' manager Bill Struth had recognised how unhappy the Russians had been with the London club's policy of fielding guest stars, and had pledged that Rangers would, 'if at all possible', stick with their own players for the Ibrox game. As stipulated by the Dynamos' original agreement with the English FA, the Glasgow club had duly forwarded a list of eighteen players from which their side would be chosen.

However, when officials of the two clubs met that morning to finalise the arrangements, the Scots sprang a surprise. James Caskie, a young and talented outside-right, was in the process of being transferred from Everton, and they wanted to include him in their team for Wednesday's game.

He's not on the list, the Russians said. But he'll be a Rangers player by Wednesday, the Scots insisted. And through an increasingly acrimonious morning, both sides refused to budge. He was playing, the Rangers officials said. Then there'd be no game, the Dynamo officials responded. Chairman James Bowie and his fellow directors were reportedly 'greatly taken aback by this attitude', and the Dynamos were presumably no less incensed. They had made their protests clear enough when Arsenal had, as they saw it, tried to cheat them, and they were in no mood to be taken advantage of again.

After lunch, in a bid to convince the Russians, Scottish FA Secretary George Graham was brought into the discussions. He patiently explained to the Dynamo officials that Caskie's papers were now in the post, and that when they reached the SFA office the outside-right would be a Glasgow Rangers player. The Russians were presumably impressed by the SFA's touching faith in the GPO, but not by the argument. Caskie was not on the list, and that was all there was to it. If they said yes to this, then what was to stop Tommy Lawton and Stanley Matthews turning up in the Rangers dressing room on Wednesday afternoon?

The talks were broken off for the dinner reception and resumed once it was over, but if any of the Soviet officials had been mellowed by liquid good cheer it didn't show. According to one of the Scots present they were now questioning even centre-half George Young's inclusion, on the specious grounds that he hadn't played for several weeks.

Bowie and Graham must have had intimations of how

Western diplomats felt after a day with Molotov. It was galling, but at least there was only one player's inclusion at stake, not a people's future. Facing a calamitous PR disaster, not to mention a huge loss of revenue, the Rangers officials finally bowed to the inevitable and agreed not to select Caskie.

The following morning the papers were full of the Russian refusal to let him play; 'The impression is that the Russians are more concerned about the result than the mere game of football,' the *Glasgow Evening News* complained somewhat disingenuously. Of course the Russians cared more about winning, but then so did Rangers. The Scottish club had not spent a day arguing for Caskie's inclusion because they thought the winger would weaken their chances.

Ironically, the one lasting legacy of the affair was to make the result even more important. If the Scottish side had wanted to beat the Dynamos before, they were now even more determined to do so. A game with edge to spare had been given a little more.

Early on Tuesday afternoon a large Soviet party – which only included half a dozen of the players – was taken aboard the Clyde Navigation Service tug *Clyde* for a cruise down the river of that name. As in Wales, there was no attempt to seduce the visitors with natural beauty or historic interest, only a determined effort to demonstrate industrial virility and the British contribution to the war effort. The Russians were taken past working shipyard after working shipyard, and invited to feast their eyes on the 45,000-ton battleship *Vanguard*. It was pointed out that most of the wartime Arctic convoys had set sail from these very docks.

There were other messages for the Russians, chalked or

painted on the hulls of unfinished ships, or simply shouted out. Ordinary Glaswegians, it seemed, were more amused than angered by the Dynamo refusal to play Caskie. 'Who's afraid of Caskie?' one shipworker yelled out with a big grin on his face. 'We want Caskie!' others yelled with mock indignation. Forecasts of Wednesday's result were much in evidence, ranging from 10–1 in Rangers' favour to victory by the odd goal, but there were also cries of 'Good old Joe Stalin!' and a fair sprinkling of red flags among the blue. The Russians smiled back, obviously pleased that the jokes were all in good humour.

Back on dry land, they were shown, in quick succession, Glasgow University, Jordanhill Training College, the Mitchell Library and the Kelvingrove Art Galleries. The Jordanhill visit had been specifically requested by Dmitry Ionov, the Soviet Director of Athletics, and here they stopped long enough to witness a physical training session and an exhibition by the Scottish swimming star Nancy Riach. After this they returned to the hotel for dinner, and then set out once more, this time for Glasgow's La Scala Cinema, where they watched a Donald Duck cartoon, a newsreel and *It's A Pleasure*, a romantic weepie in which Sonja Henie struggled to rescue her skating partner from the demon drink. The Dynamos had been in the West for just over three weeks, but on days like this it must have seemed like months.

A call for further instructions had been made to Moscow from the hotel on Monday, but as yet there was no reply. Perhaps the Rangers match on the following day would be the last, perhaps not. If the Dynamos won, then the temptation would surely be to call it a day, rather than risk sullying their record against the crack team the English FA would probably put together. If they lost, then it might be worth staying in hope of registering another victory. Yakushin had doubtless advised his political masters that the tour was taking its physical toll on players already tired by a full season in the Soviet Union, and there were also the psychological stresses to consider. These players were not so much touring a foreign country as touring an alien planet, and some of them would be very homesick by this time. How such stresses would make themselves felt on the pitch was an interesting question, and in later years Yakushin and his colleagues might have felt that they were on the footballing equivalent of a Mir space station, carefully watching for the effects of exile in foreign space to reveal themselves.

15

A very Scottish penalty

Wednesday dawned mild and sunny with a slight breeze – ideal weather for football. Thousands had poured into the city the previous day, filling everything from the best hotels to the worst park benches overnight, and thousands more arrived that morning. The city's only topic of conversation, on the buses and trams, in shops and eating places, was the match and how it would go. Not surprisingly, such interest was fuelling inflation: 1/6 ground-admission tickets were now going for 10/-; 21/- stand tickets for as much as £10.

The newspapers were not so keen to forecast this one. L. V. Manning reckoned that Rangers would score three, but that it might not be enough. A lot depended on the referee, Englishman Tommy Thompson, whom Manning didn't think would 'feel called upon to make the sporting offside concessions which gave the Russians their draw at Chelsea, their winning goal at Tottenham and three of their ten at Cardiff'. The *Daily Telegraph* and *Glasgow Herald* agreed that Rangers would provide the Dynamos with their stiffest test, but neither sounded too confident of the Russians' being defeated. The betting public were even more pessimistic: bookies were offering only evens on a Russian victory but there was no shortage of takers.

The Dynamos ate their usual sumptuous breakfast – porridge, tongue, minced beef, salted potatoes, Russian sardines, jam, Russian biscuits and tea – and admired the day's special edition of the *Daily Record*, which featured pictures of themselves and their stadium in Moscow alongside statements of welcome in both English and Russian. A few of the players took their usual morning stroll down Renfield and Sauchiehall Streets, and those who hadn't yet succumbed to the lure of tartan ties were given another chance. A light lunch was taken around noon, and shortly thereafter they climbed aboard their bus for the two-mile ride to Ibrox.

Ten of the players who had faced Chelsea and Cardiff would be in the team to play Rangers. Trofimov had either aggravated an old injury or sustained a new one at White Hart Lane, and Archangelski reclaimed his spot. Leonid Soloviev had badly damaged an ankle in the same match and, like Trofimov, was not expected to play again before the spring opening of the new Soviet season. His place in the starting line-up went to Boris Oreshkin, who had substituted for him against Arsenal. Oreshkin, the Soviets obligingly revealed, was twenty-nine years old, had served in the Soviet Navy during the shore defence of Leningrad, and now worked in a Moscow factory.

The Caskie row had reinvigorated the rumours of ringers in Dynamo shirts. Glasgow was buzzing with them, the *Bulletin & Scots Pictorial* reported; the Russians had refused Caskie, but they themselves would be fielding several men who had turned out for Leningrad. The paper also printed Yakushin's denial. 'One or two of our players helped Leningrad,' he said, 'but it was eight or ten years ago, and all have been members of Dynamo for many years.' Semichastny chimed in with dubious corroboration: 'I played for a village team when I was younger, but I am a real Dynamo now.'

Generally speaking, it seemed as if the Russian line was

being swallowed. In Tuesday's *Daily Express* it was pointed out that 'some writers in Russia' were claiming that Bobrov usually played for the Red Army and two unnamed others for Leningrad Dynamo. A day later the same paper was suggesting that all three of these players had in fact recently been transferred to the Moscow club.

Extra trams and buses had been put on, a special train service instituted between Glasgow Central and Ibrox, and as the morning wore on the queues around the ground steadily increased. On a stretch of waste ground at the nearby corner of Copeland Road a flourishing black market in tickets had been established, and several sellers had their wares examined by representatives of Glasgow CID, who were investigating reports of widespread forgeries. The rosette-sellers also struggled to keep up with demand. Both red and blue favours were available, but the most popular version featured a blue ring on a red background.

The gates opened at noon; first inside were two young boys clutching sandwiches and bottles of lemonade. They were followed by thousands of fellow truants from school and work: as with every Dynamo match in Britain, the number of local grandmothers who had gone to meet their maker had suddenly hit an all-time high.

Inside the ground the atmosphere was festive. The growing crowd sat on the terraces eating their lunch, listening to the records playing over the loudspeaker system, and talking about the match to come. The only serious outbreak of trouble occurred when a group of impatient spectators sustained several crush injuries in overrunning a police cordon; the only moment that evoked echoes of Stamford Bridge came when several men and women, led by a sailor, climbed to the top of the scoreboard and perched there, until the police finally succeeded in forcing them down.

Recorded music gave way to live. The Govan Burgh Band opened the proceedings, performing 'My Ain Folk', the 'Internationale' and a Russian selection before giving way to the Glasgow Police Band, which played a number of reels from its regular spot in the enclosure. By this time the Dynamos were on the pitch, going through their usual warm-up sequence, Khomich and the forwards using four balls, the rest of the team inter-passing the other two.

When it came to the presentations there were two bunches of carnations, one for trainer Arthur Dixon and one for captain Jock Shaw. Dynamo were in their usual kit, the pride of Scotland in white shirts with thin blue hoops, white shorts and their traditional red and black socks. Referee Thompson, who had handled the last pre-war English Cup Final between Wolves and Portsmouth, wore a white jacket over a white shirt. His two linesmen were Mr W. G. Livingstone, a fellow Englishman, and Bob Calder, a Scot.

Mr Thompson offered Semichastny the choice of calls, and the Dynamo captain guessed wrong. Shaw chose ends, leaving the Russians to play the first half against the stiffening breeze.

The Russian goal straight from the kick-off at Arsenal must have been on many minds as the referee blew his whistle to start the game, not least those of the Rangers players. They came out of the blocks like men on a desperate mission, flying into tackles and mercilessly harrying each Dynamo in possession until the ball was won. Swiftly dispatched down the middle, it was neatly flicked on by Smith to Gillick, but Semichastny got across to concede the corner before the inside-right could get a shot off. The crowd roared in anticipation of an early Rangers strike, but Radikorsky beat Williamson to the swinging ball and headed away.

The Scots' optimism proved short-lived. After crossing the halfway line, Radikorsky threaded the ball through a retreating Rangers defence to Kartsev, whose first-time reverse pass created a shooting chance for Beskov just outside the penalty area. The centre-forward was in the process of pulling the trigger when he was felled from behind by Symon.

Right – **GLASGOW RANGERS** – Left

DAWSON

2 GRAY 3 SHAW

4 WATKINS 5 YOUNG 6 SYMON

7 WADDELL 8 GILLICK 9 SMITH 10 WILLIAMSON 11 JOHNSTONE

Referee:
Mr T. Thompson

Linesmen:
Mr. R. Calder
Mr. W. G. Livingstone

---

11 SOLOVIEV S. 10 BOBROV 9 BESKOV 8 KARTSEV 7 ARCHANGELSKI

6 ORESHKIN 5 SEMICHASTNY 4 BLINKOV

3 STANKEVICH 2 RADIKORSKY

KHOMICH

Left – **MOSCOW DYNAMO** – Right

The free kick was no more than twenty yards from goal, but, for reasons best known to the Rangers' defence, no wall was put up. Kartsev took the kick almost casually, firing a less than powerful shot just inside Jerry Dawson's right-hand post. It crossed the line at a very savable height, but the goalkeeper was slow to get across and down. It was 'sad to see the grand veteran give away the first Russian goal by his slowness to move', L. V. Manning lamented, but the real error was the failure to protect him with a wall.

Two minutes gone: 1–0 to Dynamo.

Shaken and most definitely stirred, Rangers surged forward again. Two attacks ended weakly with long-range shots from Watkins and Symon, but the third broke through the last line of the Russian defence. Dribbling in on goal, Williamson was bundled over by Stankevich, and Rangers were awarded a rather dubious penalty. Entrusted with the task, Waddell captured Kartsev's casual approach but not his accuracy, thumping the ball straight at the top of Khomich's head. The Russian keeper's knees bent beneath him as he threw up his hands, deflecting the ball on to the crossbar, and Semichastny swept the rebound out for a corner.

This came to nothing, as did another minutes later. The Scots were still pressing, and the forwards worked an opening for Symon, who wastefully shot over from close to the penalty spot. Khomich was then violently bundled over the goal-line for a corner which came to nothing. The Rangers wing-halves were stretching the Dynamo defence with a stream of long passes, but the wingers' failure to provide a good final ball meant that the visitors rarely looked in real trouble.

During this first twenty minutes the Russians had mounted few attacks of their own, but in the twenty-first

Sergei Soloviev suddenly danced past Gray, drew in other defenders, and slipped the ball across for the incoming Archangelski to crash a fifteen-yard shot against Dawson's bar.

At the other end Smith escaped his shackles sufficiently to hit a first-time shot over, but almost immediately afterwards the Russians provided the move of the match, and perhaps of the tour. Again it started with Soloviev, but this time all five forwards were involved in a dazzling succession of interchanges. The wandering left-winger found Archangelski, who in turn found Bobrov in the inside-right position on the edge of the penalty area. He dwelt on the ball for just a couple of seconds, drawing two Rangers defenders before calmly stroking it across the area to Beskov. The centre-forward, with an elegant first-time flick of his left foot, sent the ball back to the right, slotting it between Rangers' spinning defenders and into the path of the unmarked Kartsev. He hit the ball first time, across Dawson's despairing dive and into the bottom left-hand corner.

'As perfect a goal as had ever been scored at Ibrox', Frank Coles wrote in the *Telegraph*, adding that 'the Rangers' defenders looked bewildered'. As well they might: this wasn't the sort of goal that was scored in Britain, or at least not by professionals.

It had been scored against the run of play, but for the next fifteen minutes Rangers seemed too shocked to recover their area dominance, and Dynamo enjoyed what was to prove their best spell of the match. The Russians' first-time passing delighted the Scottish crowd, even though their own team was being made to look cumbersome in comparison, especially in attack. In defence there were compensations, particularly in the sterling displays of Watkins and Young, but the number of free kicks given against the Scots was growing alarmingly, and it seemed only a matter of time before the Dynamos made it three.

And then, as at Stamford Bridge, the tide abruptly turned. Perhaps the Russians took their collective foot off the pedal just for a moment, and then found that they couldn't get it back on again. Perhaps Rangers simply tried harder, ran faster, fought more fiercely. Perhaps, after half an hour of observation, the Scots had worked out how to stop the Dynamo attacks. Perhaps they decided to kick them off the park. All four explanations have been suggested, and all four carry at least a grain of truth.

The argument for a tactical Damascus was aired in the *Western Mail* and the *Daily Record*. In the former, John Graydon thought that 'Glasgow Rangers found a way of cutting into the brilliant forward movements of the Dynamo players before they became really dangerous, and in so doing revealed holes in the visitors' defence', while in the latter, Davie Meiklejohn argued that 'Rangers denied them that open space for the through pass which is the end of all the Dynamo attacking plans. The Dynamos had no gaps to put the ball through, and as they hesitated the tackles went in.'

Proponents of the 'they-don't-like-it-up-'em' theory were found in the *Glasgow Herald* – 'when Glasgow Rangers realised that the Russians are inclined to shirk a tackle they began to take a tighter grip on the game' – and the *Daily Sketch*, but in the latter L. V. Manning also came close to accusing the Scots of over-violent play. It might have been 'stern, quick tackling' that reduced the Russian attack to slow motion, but at least some of it had been rather too 'hard and ugly' for his taste.

Whatever the reason, or combination of reasons, the balance of the game changed dramatically in the last third of the first half. Russian passes began going astray with startling frequency, and on the few occasions a forward broke through the Rangers defence he was flagged for offside. Rangers now seemed faster on the ball, while the Dynamo defenders were simply hoofing it downfield to clear their lines. Khomich was coming under intense pressure, much of it considerably more physical than he was used to. At one point he had both Smith and Gillick literally lying on top of him.

The increasingly desperate Dynamos were now resorting to measures that the Scottish players found considerably more reprehensible than the violent tackles that they themselves had been dishing out. The Russians were doing a lot of holding and pushing, particularly in the penalty area, and the crowd was becoming annoyed by what it considered the referee's leniency. When Johnstone was blatantly body-checked by Dynamo right-back Radikorsky, a storm of booing erupted on the terraces.

The pressure finally paid off in the fortieth minute, though there was more than an air of good fortune about the goal. A forward ball by Watkins, hooked on over Semichastny's head by Gillick, fell between Smith, Radikorsky and Khomich about eight yards from goal. As the converging threesome collided with one other, the ball seemed to bounce off Smith's midriff and into the empty net.

The crowd went wild, and the Rangers players responded by competing even more fiercely in the remaining five minutes of the half. When Rangers were awarded a free kick just outside the area, some aggravation occurred in the neighbourhood of the Russian wall, and Torry Gillick was given a stern lecture by referee Thompson. 'There was quite a nip in the game now,' Alan Breck wrote in his *Glasgow Evening Times* match report, erring on the side of understatement.

Bill Struth can have had no complaints about the level of commitment shown by his players in the first half, and any doubts he might have had about the violence of their tackling had doubtless been silenced by the Dynamos' less than gentlemanly response. If the Russians didn't like it up 'em, the Rangers boss must have reasoned, then his team would be foolish not to stick it up a little further.

In the other dressing room, Yakushin had more complicated equations to solve. He had seen his forwards kicked up in the air, and his goalkeeper assaulted on a regular basis, and he had heard the crowd's cheers. He had seen his defenders do what Russian defenders usually did under pressure, and he had heard the boos. Did he tell them to carry on doing just what they were doing? It was important that the Dynamos didn't lose, but they had also come to make friends, and to reflect well on their homeland. The aims of the tour would not be met if the team went home hated by the British public, no matter how successful they had been in terms of goals scored and conceded.

The second half carried on where the first had left off, with intense Rangers pressure. A Gillick header from a corner and a Symon free kick both went narrowly wide before Khomich saved spectacularly from Williamson. Rangers were winning all the fifty-fifty balls and seemed generally a yard faster than the Dynamos, though in one breakaway attack Archangelski shot just over.

The Ibrox roar was growing louder by the minute, and the Russians must have found it at least a little intimidating. There had been nothing like this at Stamford Bridge, even with 100,000 people breathing down their necks; this noise was altogether more raw and elemental.

But for all the crowd's help Rangers couldn't score. Young and Symon kept pumping the ball forward, and Gillick and Watkins worked tirelessly, but there was nothing incisive about the Scots attacks – it was all bludgeon and no rapier. Everything went down the middle, and mostly in the air. On the few occasions when sheer force proved sufficient to prise an opening, the forwards' shooting was woeful. On one occasion Khomich came for, and failed to collect, a cross. The ball was headed straight up in the air by one Rangers forward, and then completely miscued by another.

The Dynamos continued to push and hold, the Rangers to treat Khomich like a sparring partner. Both sets of players, but particularly the Scots, seemed to be having trouble holding on to their tempers.

There should have been a calming break when the Russians brought off Bobrov, but play was not stopped. In the *Glasgow Evening Citizen* Harry Young claimed there was 'no sign of a limp about him as he withdrew', and added a specious 'Well, well!' for good measure. In Friday's paper, thirty-six hours after the match, he went a lot further:

> Early in the second half, when Rangers were rising to the height of their power, the Dynamos slipped a twelfth man – Dementiev – on to the field. The substitute had been sitting on a bench at the popular side of the ground, and while the play was still proceeding he discarded his overcoat and, unknown to the referee, took his place in the line-up. Most of the 90,000 crowd did not see it happening, and one of the first to spot it was Jock Shaw, the Glasgow Rangers captain. He

> immediately protested to the referee that there were twelve men on the field, and the official seemed non-plussed as to the action he should take. It was only after that that Bobrov, the original inside-left, walked off.

The only corroboration of this story – and a partial corroboration at that – came in the following Saturday's edition of the *Glasgow Evening Times*. It quoted Jimmy Smith's account of what Torry Gillick had allegedly said to Mr Thompson: 'Hey ref, there's a fellow playing here I haven't seen before, and the fellow who was playing there is still there.'

If the two Dynamos were briefly on the field at the same time – and that does seem to have been their usual *modus operandi* when it came to making substitutions – it's not hard to imagine Gillick making such a jocular remark to the referee. It is much harder to believe that 'most of the 90,000 crowd' – not to mention the rest of the press box – failed to spot either the original substitution or twelve Dynamos on the field for any length of time. It wasn't a foggy day.

At least Dementiev had made his tour début at last, and his arrival coincided with the most even spell of the second half. At one end Archangelski again went close, at the other Khomich was forced to fall on a close-range effort from Gillick after Waddell had jinked his way past Stankevich and Oreshkin. The fouling had also evened out, and there were all-too-frequent blasts from the referee's whistle. Most were for relatively trivial offences, but every now and then someone did something outrageous enough to bring the temperature back up to boiling point. Shaw was caught badly by a flailing Dynamo boot, and two Rangers forwards found their faces in the goalmouth mud before a free kick had reached them. At the same end left-winger Johnstone was lucky not to be sent off for kicking Khomich in the ribs when the goalkeeper clearly had possession of the ball. This particular foul may even have had a bearing on the final result, because it slowed up the Dynamo goalkeeper considerably.

As the last quarter-hour approached many observers expected the Dynamos' superior fitness to show, as it had in all their other games, but these expectations proved wrong. The exertions of a long season and tour may have finally caught up with the Russians, or the Scots may have been running on heart alone, but over the last fifteen minutes Rangers seemed noticeably fitter than their opponents. The substitution of Duncanson for Smith – another international, but a much younger one – had an immediate effect: he had been on the pitch only three minutes when Rangers were awarded their second penalty.

Raymond Glendenning described it thus to his Home Service listeners:

> Johnstone, the left-winger, he's racing down now . . . he's put it back to the left-half Symon . . . Symon's going forward . . . a long pass . . . away down the field to Williamson who's racing forward . . . he's got the ball in the left-wing position . . . he's got Johnstone right up now, he's got Duncanson up . . . he's trying to get past the full-back . . . he's done it, and he's . . . [roar from crowd] . . . actually, as he tried to get past the full-back there . . . the Rangers players are appealing for a penalty . . . but the referee will have nothing of it and it's a goal kick . . . no, he's going over to consult the linesman . . . Mr Calder's waving his flag . . . I thought it was a deliberate obstruction there myself, but I can't tell you . . . it's so very different from this angle . . . and the referee's talking to Mr Calder and he's ordered a

> penalty . . . he has ordered a penalty . . . and I think quite rightly . . .

The Glasgow evening papers agreed, but majority opinion considered it a dubious decision at best. 'The ref appeared to see the incident quite clearly, and he waved play on,' the *Manchester Guardian* noted. It was not lost on many that an Englishman had allowed himself to be overruled by a Scottish linesman.

But a penalty it was. Waddell had missed the first, so who would take this one? The seconds seemed to drag by as the Rangers players looked enquiringly at each other, until George Young bravely stepped forward and took the responsibility. The Russians, meanwhile, looked crestfallen.

Young spotted the ball with great deliberation, stepped back a few paces and took a deep breath. The crowd held theirs as he ran forward and struck the ball firmly to Khomich's left, about halfway between goalkeeper and post. Khomich, who seemed poised to move in the other direction, didn't move at all. It was 2–2, with twelve minutes remaining.

During those minutes football went out of the window. Rangers threw everything at the Russians but skill, and for football's sake it was probably a blessing that they didn't score. They could hardly have come closer. Seven minutes from the end a twenty-five-yard rocket from Watkins almost broke a post, and a few minutes after that Khomich made a brilliant save from Duncanson, flying to turn a low shot for a corner.

'RANGERS NEEDED JUST A FEW MORE MINUTES' ran the headline in the *Glasgow Evening News*, and it could well have been true. But long after the result had ceased to matter, most of the 90,000 crowd would be talking about the beauty of the Dynamos' second goal, and how football had once been played like that in Scotland.

The Dynamos, of course, thought they had been robbed by a Scottish linesman, and twenty-one years later one of their own linesmen would wreak the ultimate revenge on the Scots – he would present the World Cup to the auld enemy with a decision every bit as dubious.

16

The primacy of the collective

'Three times opposing players almost came to blows . . . twice at least punches were exchanged,' claimed the *Daily Mirror* next morning, but the players who trooped wearily from the Ibrox pitch seemed to bear each other no ill-will. Perhaps if one side or the other had won it would have been different, but honour had been salvaged by both, at least in the matter of the result. Rangers had upheld British pride against the foreigner and Scottish pride against the English; Dynamo were bloodied but had maintained their unbeaten record. The Russians could have put the game beyond reach long before half-time; Rangers had looked the likeliest winners at the end. The Scots could point to a penalty missed and a post struck, Dynamo to a penalty wrongly given and a quivering bar. It had been a fair result.

After the match the two sides traded compliments. Rangers Chairman James Bowie announced himself 'amazed' by the Dynamos' positional excellence, and by how 'far advanced' they were in the theory of the game; one of his players wondered out loud how the Russians had 'learned the fundamentals of the game so quickly and so well, while boys in this football-minded country never learn them at all'. For his part, Yakushin judged the Scots both the fittest and the best footballers his side had met in Britain, and claimed he had no complaints about the manner of the match or the result.

The atmosphere was certainly friendly enough that evening when the Scottish club played host to the Soviet party at St Enoch's Hotel in central Glasgow. The usual huge dinner was consumed, the usual pledges of lasting friendship made, the usual gifts exchanged. The Dynamos, who received official badges from the SFA, framed coats-of-arms from the Lord Provost, and quaighs – ancient Scottish wooden drinking cups – from Rangers, probably needed to repack their suitcases before boarding the night train for the south.

The initial reaction from Moscow had also accentuated the positive – 'No European team playing in Great Britain has ever achieved such brilliant victories' was how Moscow Radio saluted the draw at Ibrox – but before the day was over fresh accusations of British rough play were emanating from the Soviet capital, and by Saturday *Izvestia* was indignantly listing the walking wounded: Semichastny with his bandaged head, Beskov limping, Kartsev hardly able to walk, Khomich bruised all over.

The morning after the match the British press was worrying at the fair-play issue. Opinions on the disputed penalty – which were fairly evenly split between yes, no and maybe – did not follow national lines, but when it came to apportioning blame for the violent play which had done so much to mar the game as a spectacle, the difference between the English and the Scottish papers was striking. The *Daily Mail* apportioned blame equally – 'Rangers' strong tackling and body-charging made a contrast to the subtle elbowing, and, very often, obvious pushing . . . the natural outcome was a more or less rugged fight' – but most of the English papers laid the blame squarely at the door of the Scots. L. V. Manning obliquely observed that the Dynamos 'were clearly under the impression this was not football as they believed it to be played by its inventors'; Frank Coles found himself forced to admit that some of the Rangers' tackling had been 'more robust than it need have been'. In the *Daily Express* Henry Rose, while noting the Dynamos' shirt-pulling and pushing, accepted that 'the vicious stuff came from the Rangers'.

The *Manchester Guardian* blamed the Scots more for a failure of the imagination. Most Dynamo infringements of the law had obviously been 'the result of their normal style of play and not the outcome of a deliberate intent to foul', and the Rangers players should have been grown-up enough to realise as much. Instead of which they had frequently lost their tempers and created numerous nasty incidents.

The Scottish papers – and even Scots writing in the English papers – took a very different line. 'It was only natural that Glasgow Rangers should take exception to the holding methods of the Russians,' wrote Tommy Muirhead. 'There were moments of retaliation that should not have taken place. I'll leave it at that.'

And so did the rest of the Scottish press. The Dynamos were blamed in a variety of ways – 'Soviet man-to-man marking led to incidents,' as the *Bulletin & Scots Pictorial* quaintly put it – but no one dared criticise the Rangers players for either their tactics or their brutish behaviour. On the contrary, the tendency was to feel almost aggrieved, as if Rangers had somehow been tricked into looking worse than they were. 'Nobody minds good, honest robustness,' 'Waverley' wrote in the *Daily Record*.

> Rangers took a lot and gave something back, but there was more than robustness from certain of the Dynamos.

> If you ask Jock Shaw, he'll tell you, if he feels like it. When he was lying on the ground in pain it wasn't any ordinary mishap. It was something you don't put in print. Had the Dynamos been satisfied to play the game as we are accustomed to seeing it played, Rangers would have done the same. As it was, Rangers would have been No. 1 fools to take it like lambs, and not give it back.

As a clinching argument he cited the Dynamo goalkeeper. 'Flying through the air as he did . . . and finishing up among the legs of oncoming forwards', Khomich was 'only asking for trouble'. How could he complain about being kicked in the ribs if he was so determined to throw himself on to forwards' boots?

It was not a good morning for the Scottish sense of fair play, but a few shafts of illumination somehow managed to break through. The *Glasgow Herald* noted reluctantly that 'from the spectator's point of view the Russian play is more attractive', the *Glasgow Evening News* that the Dynamos' football in the first half was 'easily the best in the whole game'. Further afield, the *Western Mail* pointedly observed that 'all the typically Scottish football we hear so much about came from the Dynamo team'; and in the *Sketch* L. V. Manning admitted to fearing that Rangers' success would 'speed up the Scottish changeover from its traditional classic style to something less good to look on'.

The goals might have been shared, but when it came to points scored for artistic expression there had hardly been a contest.

As late as the previous Friday a game between Dynamo and a representative XI in Birmingham on 5 December had seemed likely, and on the following Monday, as the Russians argued with the SFA over Caskie, it had still seemed enough of a probability for the FA to pick a provisional team (see Appendix 3) and for the Aston Villa authorities to order the printing of 70,000 tickets. Since no one was sure just who Dynamo would be playing – an FA XI, a Midlands XI or just Aston Villa – a blank space was left where the opposing team was usually named.

Then, on the evening of the St Enoch's Hotel dinner, Moscow Radio had announced that the Dynamos had played their last match in Britain. Even the tourists had apparently been taken by surprise, and on Thursday morning no one seemed too sure if the tour really was over. Another news agency claimed that the Russians were considering playing Racing Club de Paris on their way home, but the FA was not officially informed that they had played their last game in Britain until the Thursday evening, when Dynamo representatives attended a meeting at Lancaster Gate. Even then, Rous seemed reluctant to accept the Russians' decision as final. 'There is little prospect of Moscow Dynamo playing a further match,' he told journalists after the meeting, whereas in fact there was absolutely none. Yakushin's players had looked tired at Ibrox, and the Soviets had nothing to gain from sending them out against either a strong English club or an even stronger representative team. A Russian version of 'quit while you're ahead' must have been the Dynamos' motto at this point.

So, as Villa officials began dreaming up creative ways of recycling 70,000 worthless tickets, the Dynamos settled down to a week's holiday. Moscow Radio had provisionally named Wednesday 5 December as their date of departure, which gave them plenty of time for sightseeing, shopping, giving interviews, watching football and attending farewell bashes. It was even announced that they would be joining British football players and experts for a round-table conference on the following Monday. The games might be over but the Dynamos were still news.

They figured in a second Commons debate on the Thursday. During discussion of a proposed new clause to the finance bill reducing entertainment duty on sport, one MP pointed out that the Dynamos had paid £6,600 to the Treasury out of their shares of the gate money. Since they were handing over all their takings to the Stalingrad Fund, wouldn't it be a nice gesture, he asked, to refund their tax? And wouldn't Anglo-Russian friendship be strengthened? The House was unmoved, and the proposed clause was defeated.

On Friday the *Daily Worker* celebrated the end of the Dynamo playing programme by pointing out the political moral. The Russians might not have been a 'wonder side', but they had certainly been a very good one. How could it be, the paper asked, 'that a country which has engaged in so little international competition or friendly football can produce players of this high calibre?' The explanation was simple.

> Anyone with the slightest knowledge of the Soviet constitution could supply it. The answer is that the Soviet Government and the Soviet people believe that every citizen is by right entitled to full facilities for engaging in sporting activities. And by full facilities they mean, not as we mean here, the right of lads to kick a ball around on the recreation ground or in the streets until they are turned off as being a menace to other folk, but proper physical training and technical and practical instruction in the game. Those who wish to play soccer are supplied, through their clubs, with the

> equipment, playing space, trainers, coaches, masseurs, doctors and referees necessary for them to engage in this very wholesome pursuit.

The *Worker* had seen the future, and it played better football. After an exhausting season back home the Dynamos, most of whom had never played abroad before, had come to England, where 'they were handicapped by ground conditions, a heavier ball and several of our rules, particularly those applying to shoulder-charging, charging the goalkeeper and tackling', and still emerged undefeated. They had taken some 'severe buffetings', and the fact that they'd come through them, both physically and mentally, 'speaks volumes for their early training'. After all this, the *Worker* concluded, who could fail to recognise 'the important and far-reaching effect that the policy of the Soviet Government has had'. State socialism was the future, on the pitch and off.

But if socialism couldn't yet be built in England's green and pleasant land, perhaps the English could import its footballing offspring from elsewhere. On Saturday it was reported that an unnamed north-country manager had offered Vsevolod Bobrov an amateur contract, and on Sunday the story moved even further into the realms of tabloid fantasy. The still unnamed manager had apparently managed to break through the ring of bodyguards which protected the Dynamos, and to sequester himself with Bobrov for a discussion of terms. The Russian – who was soon to become one of the most famous sportsmen in the Soviet Union – allegedly said that he would stay in England if a wife was provided for him.

This wasn't the end of the matter. On returning to Moscow, Konstantin Beskov would claim that a British club director had offered £10,000 for himself and Bobrov.

The club in question was later identified, by persons unknown, as Arsenal, but the following day George Allison described the whole business as 'manifestly absurd'. The story probably had very little foundation in reality, but if any British club could have secured the services of the two Russians for the price mentioned it would have been more of a steal than an absurdity.

On the same day this story took off, another came to a rather embarrassing close. It had already been revealed – on the day of the Rangers match – that Torry Gillick was still officially on Everton's books, and it now transpired that the controversial Caskie's registration would be going through only on Saturday, three days after the game. Neither of them had been eligible to play against the Dynamos.

Yakushin could have been forgiven an 'I told you so', but he restrained himself admirably when talking to journalists that day. With the playing programme so successfully negotiated he was obviously in a relaxed frame of mind, and was more than happy to talk football.

According to one British journalist he admitted to using a blackboard to illustrate moves, but only the British would have regarded it as a guilty secret. Yakushin obviously believed in coaching, and he thought he had learned a few things from his hosts. 'I do not mean charging especially,' he added with a smile. Personally, he considered the British more adept when it came to ball-handling, technical skills and tricks, but thought the Soviets were superior when it came to teamwork. 'The principle of collective play is the guiding one in Soviet soccer,' he said. 'A player must not only be good in general; he must be good for the particular team.'

In his team there might be no place for a Stanley Matthews, though Yakushin hastened to add that he was going on only what little he had seen through the fog at White Hart Lane. 'His individual qualities are high, but we put collective football first and individualism second, so we do not favour his style as we think the teamwork would suffer.' Someone like Kartsev, by contrast, an apparently ordinary player for Lokomotiv, had fitted in perfectly at Dynamo, and had become a better player because of it. In Soviet soccer each player felt responsible for the whole team.

Off the subject of football, Yakushin was having trouble finding a nice doll in Scottish Highland dress for his younger daughter. He said he had enjoyed the attitude of the young English ladies and found a lot left to be desired in the English weather – it would have been better if they had come in spring. Asked whether Stalin had seen the Dynamos play, Yakushin replied 'evidently he has', adding, with a perfectly straight face, that the big man was 'interested in everything, in all our lives and in all our ways'.

The round-table conference on Monday 3 December was billed as the perfect opportunity for 'an interchange of experiences, opinions and hints'. Charles Buchan certainly welcomed it: 'Unlike a lot of our experts,' he noted acerbically, 'the Russians are quite willing to learn from experience.' Others in attendance at Paddington's GWR Hotel included the managers of Charlton, Chelsea and QPR, and the assistant manager of Arsenal. George Allison was conspicuous by his absence, as were all the players who had faced Dynamo in the twin battles of White Hart Lane and Ibrox, but Tommy Lawton was there, happily sipping ginger beer with his old sparring partner Mikhail Semichastny.

Elliseyeva had been banished for the evening, her place

taken by the more football-minded Evgarov, and for two and a half hours the two sides discussed a wide range of football-related topics. The Russians were eager to know more about British training methods – they obviously couldn't bring themselves to believe that running round a pitch was the only one – and shamelessly enquired about players' private lives. In return the British learned several things about Soviet football. It turned out that Soviet linesmen's flags were bigger, and varied in colour according to the conditions. Players with bad disciplinary records could be 'relegated' to a lower division for a season or more. Central House were the best team in the Soviet Union, Grigory Fedotov the best player.

A little more light was thrown on the professional status of the Soviet players. It was now claimed that they underwent several weeks of pre-season training in the Caucasus, and that during the season they worked only in the mornings, all without losing a kopek of their supposed full-time wage. In matter of fact, the jobs were largely fictional and the financial rewards were all for playing football, but at least the priority was finally clear – these were not players who took time off to train in their lunch hours.

On the question of rules, the Dynamos' admission that obstruction was a legitimate tactic in Soviet football – as it was in ice hockey – provoked an interesting discussion between the two sides. The Russians agreed that shoulder-charging, as understood in Britain, was allowed in the Soviet Union, but not against the goalkeeper. Tackling generally was much more restrained, but beyond noting that the sliding tackle was outlawed, the Russians found it difficult to define what constituted too hard a tackle. On the other hand, standing in someone's way, impeding them with hand or body, or simply pushing them, were all considered more or less legitimate tactics.

Both sides were in a grey area here, although you would never have known it from the British press comments over the previous few weeks. The laws of the game were one thing, their interpretation something else again, and the British, having originally laid the laws down, were particularly fond of confusing the two. When it came to obstruction they were actually on very dubious ground. In Britain it had always been considered illegal, but had not been codified as such in the 1863 laws, and wide global divergences had developed as a result. In the *FA Referee's Chart and Player's Guide to the Laws of the Game* issued in 1939, obstruction had been mentioned only as justification for the charge from behind, not as a foul meriting a free kick, and this remained the position until 1953, when the new FIFA *Universal Guide for Referees* both confirmed obstruction as an offence and laid down an indirect free kick as the penalty for transgression.

For the moment the two sides amicably agreed to differ. No doubt the Dynamos privately considered British tackling thuggish, while the British felt Russian tactics were underhand and unsporting. Both were right, but it would be several decades before significant action was taken to outlaw the tackle from behind and the so-called professional foul.

In other respects, though, the future was already present. The FA had produced its new toy, a board marked out as a pitch with magnetic players, and it seemed that everyone wanted a turn moving the figures around.

Tommy Lawton thought that all those present learned a lot, and Charles Buchan also seemed pleased at the time, though in later years he would claim it had been a one-sided affair. 'All they wanted was our training methods, our technique, our plans in general,' he wrote in 1955, as if the Cold War had already been under way in 1945, and they had all been discussing military secrets rather than football.

The following day the Soviet view was put to the public in the usual roundabout way. An interview with Mikhail Semichastny was first broadcast on Moscow Radio, then released to the press in the form of an English-language transcript, and finally printed in full in the London-based *Soviet Weekly*.

All the matches had been difficult, the Dynamo captain began, but the one against Chelsea had been especially so. Cold weather in Moscow had inhibited their training programme after the Soviet season ended in mid-October, and the prospect of meeting an unknown team on foreign soil had engendered 'a certain nervous strain'. Once that first game was behind them, and they had acquired a better idea of British tactics and overall strengths, they had been able to play with 'considerably more calm'.

Semichastny was probably more complimentary about British football than he need have been. He rightly praised the local heading and shooting skills, but his admiration for 'the extraordinary technical skill with which they control the ball, pass it and trap it' was somewhat mystifying. Yakushin, too, had praised British ball skills, so this was more than just the case of a stopper centre-half being bowled over by the odd trick. But what were these opinions based on? That very weekend Stanley Matthews, in his Sunday newspaper column, had been lamenting the decline in individual ball control among British players, and how they could 'learn a thing or two' from the Dynamos. Was he talking about something else? It's tempting to imagine two completely different sets of skills, both of which could be called ball control, but which flourished in different environments, one in the hurly-burly of British league football, one in the more generous time and space allowed by the slower Continental game.

Semichastny was not so complimentary about British tactics, which he found 'elementary'. Attacks were too predictable, defenders played too deep, and the overlapping system of covering was too easily undone by a sudden switch of play. Soviet tactics, which maximised the possible combinations in attack and featured more flexible man-marking in defence, were clearly more advanced. Turning to the rules of the game, the Dynamo captain repeated Soviet opposition to British charging in general and charging of the goalkeeper in particular. He was also unhappy about referees consulting their linesmen, as had happened at Ibrox. There should be 'only one decisive voice on the field'.

Apart from that, he had mostly nice things to say. The pitches had been wonderful and most of the terraces covered, but they had been 'surprised by the poor equipment of the service rooms in the stadiums, dressing rooms, showers, and so on'. Of course, British football was 'on a money basis', and everything was done at the stadiums 'to accommodate as many people as possible and consequently make more money'.

He had been gratified by the warm welcomes they had received in Wales and Scotland, but saved his highest praise for the British evening sports editions. 'Immediately after the match,' he said, with the air of someone savouring some wonderful mystery, 'as you leave the stadium, you can buy special extra editions with the results not only of the match you have just seen, but with the results of all the matches that took place in Britain's towns that day.'

Those were the days.

* * *

The social whirl accelerated as the departure date – now set for Thursday 6 December – approached. They had been invited to dine with the Lord Mayor at the Mansion House some days before, but had hesitated about accepting, apparently unsure what sort of politics they were being asked to endorse. The Soviet Ambassador had then obviously decided that a good dinner was a good dinner, and the invitation had been accepted on two conditions: the ambassador's wife should not be the only woman present, and there should be no ostentation. On hearing the latter the Lord Mayor was said to have exclaimed that they had got the gold plate out in the Russians' honour, and if they didn't like it they could eat off the floor.

The evening was a huge success regardless. Besides the Mayor and Mayoress, Ambassador and Ambassadress, the FA had rounded up many of those who had spent the previous evening chatting with the Dynamos at the GWR Hotel. The candles flickered prettily, the gold plate glowed, and the Russians insisted on standing for each toast even though they had been told it wasn't necessary. 'In Russia we stand,' Radikorsky said, proudly showing off his newly-acquired English, while further down the table Oreshkin simply muttered 'souvenir' when one of the newsmen noticed him pocketing a cigar. A player named V. I. Lemeshev made his sole media appearance of the tour, getting snapped by the *News Chronicle* photographer as he bowed before the Lady Mayoress, and several other Russians were treated to a poem by one of the councillors:

> Caviare's the roe of a virgin sturgeon,
> The sturgeon's a very rare fish.
> Not every sturgeon's a virgin sturgeon,
> So caviare's a very rare dish.

The following morning the tourists did penance for dining off the gold plate, visiting the grave of Karl Marx in Highgate Cemetery and a house in Finsbury Park's Holford Square which Lenin had once graced with his presence. After this brief Marxist-theme excursion they returned to the Imperial to prepare for the final farewell reception at the Scala Theatre.

Eight hundred guests attended that evening's entertainment, and it made for an impressive send-off. After Andreanov had offered his mostly British audience what sounded like a compliment, assuring them the Soviet people were bound to respect British football because Britain had given birth to the sport, gifts were exchanged in great profusion. The Moscow Dynamo club was given a blue and gold banner by the FA, the individual players a wallet and a badge each. The Dynamos responded by presenting the FA with a red football which had been signed by all the players. Sir Godfrey Ince, who had captained the first British XI to play in Russia some thirty-one years earlier, then presented the Russians with a signed photograph of that team. Finally, there was a fountain pen and leather-bound autograph book for Elliseyeva, who seemed genuinely surprised at the accompanying cheers of appreciation. She had known nothing about football when she left, she said, and now she knew too much. She hoped never to see another game.

The Dynamo players were lined up on stage, and each was given a cheer in turn, before two films on Soviet sport were screened. These greatly impressed some of the viewers. 'It is obvious we know little or nothing about Russia as a sporting nation,' Tom Morgan wrote in the *People*, while the ubiquitous Tommy Lawton thought them 'magnificent examples of the supreme physical fitness demanded of sportsmen in the Soviet Union'.

By the time the films were shown much alcohol had been consumed, and a mood of semi-hysteria seems to have overtaken the gathering. The Dynamos gave three loud cheers for Britain, and the Brits cheered whenever Stalin put in a cinematic appearance. The Russians said how impressed they were by tartan ties and London Transport, and how deeply touched they had been by the British public's warm reception. Their Ambassador expressed his conviction that the tour had 'helped in creating a better understanding between us, and the furtherance of our common cause', and if anyone was left wondering what the common cause was he had the decency not to ask.

The only man missing, as semi-hysteria shaded into sentimentality, was Vassili Kartsev. 'He just did not feel like a party,' one journalist was told, a statement that was happily taken at face value, even though such a display of individualistic licence ran counter to just about everything else that had happened on the tour. Ten years later the same journalist would have drawn very different conclusions from the inside-right's absence. Then the most obvious explanation would have been that the Soviet authorities were afraid Kartsev would misbehave – an outburst of frankness at best, a defection at worst – and had arranged to keep him on ice until the plane left. In 1945 it was possible that Kartsev was ill – or, even, perhaps, that he was related to one of Beria's cronies, and therefore a law unto himself – but it beggared belief that an ordinary player could refuse to attend an important occasion just because he didn't feel like it. This ran contrary to everything the British press had been told about the primacy of the collective, and to everything they should have learned during the previous four weeks about how the Soviets operated. But no one tried to dig deeper.

The realities of Soviet sport and the Soviet Union, like the moribund state of British football and the British Empire, were best viewed with the traditional blind eye.

A strong whiff of farce pervaded the Dynamos' departure, just as it had their arrival. They were scheduled to leave from Northolt aerodrome at 9 a.m. on the Thursday morning, but Berlin, their fuelling stop, was enveloped in fog, and the party was told that the flight would be delayed for twenty-four hours. Unfortunately, no one bothered to tell the crowd waiting to wish them goodbye, so while the Dynamos were enjoying their extra lie-in at the Imperial, Stanley Rous, assorted dignitaries, a clutch of Red Army officers and most of the nation's football press were shivering in the cold morning air at Northolt. When news of the postponement eventually reached the waiting crowd, one of the Soviet Embassy officials was cheekily approached by a British squadron-leader eager to set up a game for that afternoon between the Dynamos and the local RAF station team.

The following morning the Berlin fog had cleared, and the three waiting Dakotas were given clearance to depart. Yakushin was all smiles, having finally selected a doll from all those that had been sent in by well-wishers; Elliseyeva had tears in her eyes as she said goodbye to friends. The war received its obligatory mention: the players were reported to be delighted that several of the Dakota crewmen had helped drop supplies to Soviet partisans during the war.

The racing bikes were loaded aboard one of the planes, and almost two tons of other baggage, much of it in the form of small paper-wrapped parcels tied with string, was spread between them. The tartan-tie industry had rarely had it so good.

Then, one by one, their wings white with frost, the three planes taxied out towards the misty runway, their passengers waving and shouting goodbyes from the open cabin windows. A few minutes more and they were rumbling up into the eastern sky, heading home to a heroes' welcome.

17

The ghosts of football past

Only seven months had passed since Hitler's death, only four since the atom bombing of Hiroshima and Nagasaki. The war was over, but it still cast a huge shadow over everything from international politics to the average British supper. At one end of the spectrum a terrible catalogue of Japanese atrocities was slowly coming to light; at the other came announcements of the puddings to come: date and treacle first, soon to be followed by marmalade and Christmas. During November Canadian furniture had been promised for 150,000 homes, along with more nylons, more golf balls, more oranges, lemons and grapefruits. Newlyweds were to be allowed first pick of the 240,000 blankets soon to be released, and children were given back their circuses when the wartime ban on dangerous animal acts was revoked. There would even be sardines in the spring.

The wartime shortages would eventually disappear, but other consequences of the conflict would run and run. Those imperial possessions of the warring nations that had endured Japanese occupation had been given a glimpse of the future which didn't include perpetual submission to the whims of the white races, and the germs of rebellion already seemed to be multiplying across wide stretches of the planet. In Indochina and China the war had not so much stopped as shifted gear; in the Near East a series of race riots in Cairo and Tel Aviv offered more than a hint of what was to come. Throughout the month, editorials in *The Times* reflected on this sad state of affairs in tones of bewilderment and sorrow. The World War was over, but where was the world peace?

Nor was violence unknown at home. Crime was said to be running at double the pre-war rate in Britain, with murder an almost daily occurrence. Soldiers who returned home and killed their wives' lovers tended to receive sympathy – several were simply acquitted – but the 20,000 or so deserters still roaming Britain with no obvious means of support were considered just a menace. The pernicious influence of Hollywood was one easy scapegoat, but frustration with the continuing shortages was a more obvious explanation. On the day the Dynamos played Rangers one young woman was held up at knife-point by three women she was accompanying to a dance at an American base. They were still wearing her coat, frock and sandals when the police caught up with them. They were 'desperately short of clothes', they told the judge, who sent them all to prison.

Increasing violence wasn't all the future had to offer. The development of Paludrine – an anti-malarial drug ten times more powerful than quinine – seemed to offer striking proof of how science could still change the world for the better. The appointment of an ex-GWR porter as the new Governor of Bengal offered the hope of a less class-bound Britain in the not-too-distant future. Martha Gelhorn's decision to pursue her work as a war correspondent against husband Ernest Hemingway's wishes set a fine precedent for the gender conflicts to come.

And then there was Dr John Wilson's atomic car, which ran at three times the speed of ordinary cars for a cost of only 8d per 1,000 miles. It was powered by a combination of uranium, heavy water and another secret ingredient which the good doctor was reluctant to disclose; it needed no petrol, oil or carburettor. The Government was naturally interested, and Wilson agreed to take Minister of Fuel and Power Emmanuel Shinwell for a trial spin on 29 November. But, alas, on the eve of the demonstration the car was sabotaged by persons unknown. Dr Wilson muttered darkly about 'vested interests' and 'certain industries', and pledged to rebuild the car, but for the moment Britain would have to do without it. The seventy-two-year-old inventor was pictured in the *Mirror*, head twisted to one side, cigarette hanging limply out from beneath his luxuriant moustache. The hardware in his hands looked suspiciously like a pair of radiator valves, but was apparently the vandalised remains of his atomic generator.

Wilson was an early example of governmental gullibility in all matters nuclear, a semi-comic figure from the past with frightening implications for the future. In fact, he had more than one thing in common with the Dynamos: they too had played on British ignorance; they too had offered a vision of the future.

Back in Moscow, the architects of this exercise in sports diplomacy were experiencing mixed feelings. In football terms the tour had been a total success: all Soviet fans – with the possible exception of a few Spartak die-hards – were rejoicing in this proof of the country's footballing vitality, and Dynamo supporters like Lavrenti Beria were over the proverbial moon. In the more complex world of sports diplomacy, however, matters were not quite as clear-cut.

The returning Dynamos certainly had a heroes' welcome: both team and individuals were honoured by the state, and cheques of various denominations were handed out to everyone who had taken part. But the Soviet authorities were also well aware that the incessant *bonhomie* of the team's last few days in London had failed to erase the impression of rampant hostility which had marred the preceding fortnight. For a team that had come to make friends, the Dynamos had stirred up a lot of anger.

George Orwell, writing in *Tribune* on 14 December, was not surprised. Sport, he thought, was 'an unfailing cause of ill-will', and if the Dynamo tour had had any effect on Anglo-Soviet relations, it could only have been for the worse. How, he asked, could it have been otherwise? Most sports were competitive to start with, and the moment the stakes were raised to include national prestige 'the most savage combative instincts' were likely to be aroused. This was true of most sports, but football – 'a game in which everyone gets hurt and every nation has its own style of play which seems unfair to foreigners' – was the worst offender.

Orwell's conclusion – that a reciprocal tour of the Soviet Union would probably do more harm than good – was bad news for Soviet sports diplomacy, but most of the other feedback reaching the Kremlin was more ambivalent. The practice of sports diplomacy, it now appeared, was very much a two-edged sword. The Dynamos had shown that Soviet football, and by implication the Soviet system, had to be taken seriously, but a system worthy of emulation was also, in a world of competing ideologies and economies, a system to be feared. One nation's demonstration of vitality could easily become the perfect fuel for another nation's paranoia.

On the individual level, it's more than possible that the Soviet presentation of the Dynamo players as just a bunch of ordinary lads – an image that was actually reinforced in the tour's few unguarded moments – helped to erode the British tendency to view Russians as creatures from another planet. And that, in all those mysterious ways beloved of chaos theorists, may have had some slight ameliorating effect during the four decades of the Cold War. If a Moscow Dynamo baseball team had returned unbeaten from a tour of the USA, then perhaps Ronald Reagan would have had a harder job selling the Soviet Union as an 'evil empire', even if there had been a dugout-clearing brawl at Yankee Stadium.

In Moscow it must have been hard to forget the genuine warmth of the British people's welcome, and early in 1946 an indication was given as to how much the Soviet authorities still wished to preserve the goodwill engendered by the tour. In an article published in the Soviet children's magazine *Pioneer*, Vadim Sinyavsky, for reasons best known to himself, chose to rewrite the history of the Arsenal game. George Allison, he claimed, had first insisted on the match being played because bets had been placed, and had then tried to get it called off after the Dynamos equalised. 'When the Arsenal goalkeeper took the fourth ball out of the net,' the radio commentator concluded, 'Allison fainted. He had bet a large sum on the match and had lost.' These allegations produced an uproar in London, and the Soviet authorities, keen not to lose all the ground they believed they had won, promptly apologised. Sinyavsky and the magazine editor were sacked, and Allison was invited on to the Soviet airwaves to put the record straight.

The tour might have proved that Russians could share a joke like anyone else, but in its prime political purpose the exercise had to be considered a failure. Promoted as a means of extending the wartime alliance into the subsequent peace, it ended up as nothing more than a footballing postscript.

In all probability it could never have been anything more. Centrally planned state socialism and free enterprise capitalism were like matter and anti-matter – they could not coexist in the same space – and so the post-war world was doomed to a prolonged argument over the border between the two systems. The countries of Eastern Europe liberated by the Red Army were bound to fall on the state socialism side of that border – Soviet security required as much – but the Americans would not accept that the dollar be for ever locked out of Poland, Czechoslovakia and the rest: their vision of a flourishing American-led world economy required no less.

There was no third way for the third member of the Big Three to espouse. The Soviets hoped the British would play the honest broker in disputes between themselves and the Americans, and among the British people there were certainly many who sympathised with the idea that the atomic bomb should be somehow internationalised, but there were no decent cards left in the British hand. There might be a socialist government in Whitehall, but the British economy remained an important part of the global free enterprise system, with all that that implied.

On the day the Dynamos left for home the terms of the American loan to Britain were announced. In return for immediate solvency, Her Majesty's Government had agreed to give up the system of tariff preferences which made the Empire a paying proposition. For the rest of the century the dollar would rule, and the British would be junior partners of the big firm in Washington, clinging somewhat desperately to phrases like 'special relationship', and echoing the anti-Communist rhetoric which turned the Russians once more into hostile aliens.

In the process, as has already been mentioned, the British came to see the tour through a lens coloured by the Cold War, and the same was true of the Soviets. After bending over backwards to be nice in 1946, the latter bent over backwards to be nasty in 1947. A musical comedy called *19–9* – the goals scored for and against on the tour – was produced in Moscow; it featured a bunch of incorruptible socialist heroes in a decadent land, bravely fighting off everything from bribes to fist-throwing forwards in their pursuit of sporting excellence.

In purely sporting terms the tour had lived up to the highest Soviet expectations, and its immediate impact on both Soviet sport in general and Soviet football in particular was overwhelmingly positive. In December huge audiences flocked to see filmed recordings of the matches at cinemas throughout the country; the tour, according to *Red Sport*, had 'set Russian sports enthusiasm aflame', and Soviet athletes were 'getting ready to enter the international field on a scale never equalled before'.

A golden age beckoned for Soviet football. The dramatic increase in the size of domestic crowds – averaging 45,000 in 1946 – could partly be ascribed to post-war euphoria, but the Dynamos' success in 'the home of football' had certainly increased the appeal of the product on offer.

What had Soviet soccer coaches learned from the British tour? Winners usually learn less than losers, and the Dynamos don't seem to have introduced any radical changes in style or tactics on their return. It had, after all, been Yakushin's innovative tactics that had brought them such success in both Britain and the Soviet Union, so there was no reason to do more than tinker. Years later,

Konstantin Beskov would rightly claim that the team's fluid formation anticipated the Brazilian 4–2–4 of the late fifties, but anticipate was all they did.

Soviet clubs undertook more tours in 1946 and 1947, but none to so demanding a venue as Britain. Having apparently established that Soviet football was among the world's best, the authorities seemed reluctant to risk disillusion, and the Dynamo tour of Scandinavia in 1947 represented the furthest they were prepared to venture beyond their East European backyard. In that same year the Soviet football authorities took a retrograde step, changing the rules governing the domestic game to allow charges on the goalkeeper.

The sudden deepening of the Cold War thrust both the country and its footballers into isolation, and for several years it seemed like the 1930s once again. The enormous popularity of the domestic game was not missed by the Party leadership, and strenuous efforts were once more made to hijack football for socio-political ends. The Soviet game's obvious failures – crowd hooliganism, violent play, the 'star syndrome' among players – were put down to a lack of sufficient political-ideological education, the successes to the magic ingredient of collectivism. 'What is the basis of the Soviet style?' *Soviet Sport* asked itself. 'The answer lies in collectivism, in close interaction; in the absence of me-ism.'

When, in 1952, the country emerged from its years of isolation, the boasts of pre-eminence proved impossible to live up to. The first Soviet national team for a quarter of a century – one that included ageing Dynamo tourists Bobrov, Beskov and Trofimov – was knocked out of the Helsinki Olympic tournament by Yugoslavia, and in the resulting scramble for scapegoats back home the Central House of the Red Army team was temporarily disbanded. In 1958 the Soviets entered their first World Cup, but in this competition they were doomed to be perpetual underachievers, only once, in 1966, reaching the semi-final stage. The national team's only trophy, in forty years of trying, would be the 1960 European Nations Cup, a competition severely weakened by the absence of the top Western European nations. On the club front the record would be almost as bad: the only Soviet-era team to win European trophies would be Dynamo Kiev, who took the Cup Winners Cup in 1975 and 1986. 'I thought they'd have gone from strength to strength,' Cardiff's Buller Lever said, 'but they haven't . . . they never went anywhere.'

In the domestic league the same teams dominated the early post-war years. Moscow Dynamo started badly in 1946, but eventually finished second behind Central House, an ordering that would be repeated in three of the next four years. Dynamo won the title in 1949, and then five times between 1954 and 1963, but in the thirty years between the Cuban missile crisis and the break-up of the Soviet Union they managed only one more league triumph, and that in the truncated half-season of 1976. As the years went by, the team's identification with the security forces became ever less acceptable, the crowds grew thinner, and the team had little but past glories to recommend it.

Of the players who came to Britain in 1945, many went on to greater things. Konstantin Beskov managed the team in the sixties, and, like Mikhail Yakushin, had more than one spell as national team coach. Vsevolod Bobrov starred in the Central House team which won the league in three consecutive seasons, and also won Olympic gold as an ice hockey player. Evgeny Archangelski joined Dynamo on a more permanent basis at the beginning of the 1947 season;

Sergei Soloviev went on to take the all-time Dynamo scoring record with 127 goals. Alexei Khomich enjoyed a highly successful second career as a sports photographer after handing on the Dynamo gloves to the legendary Lev Yashin. All of them became Soviet celebrities. They were the men who had given football a second motherland.

The Russian tour, according to Buller Lever, 'lifted everybody' in war-weary Britain. But what was its long-term impact on the evolution of British football? The Dynamos had offered a tactical revolution in their style of play, but they had also come up with a whole series of related surprises: pre-match warm-ups, substitutions, a different system of refereeing, an emphasis on diet and scientific preparation, coaching by blackboard. Not surprisingly, the British found a pick-and-mix approach to the latter easier to adopt than the fundamental changes suggested by the former.

The Dynamos were still in England when QPR became the first British team to try a pre-match warm-up. On 24 November they came out twenty minutes early and stayed out until the kick-off, thus establishing a British pattern which lasted for around forty years. It wasn't until the eighties that British clubs finally adopted the Dynamo habit of returning to the dressing room ten minutes before the kick-off.

On 25 November Chelsea's John Harris used his column in *Reynolds News* to argue for a British adoption of the Continental substitute rules. It seemed to him that the refusal to allow substitutes for injured players 'struck at the very root' of British fair-play instincts, but such arguments would go unheeded for another twenty years.

Those who favoured a radically more scientific approach to players' health and fitness would wait just as long – in the matter of diet, considerably longer – but those who believed in the importance of coaching were at last securing a foothold in the British game. Men like Walter Winterbottom, appointed England's first manager in 1946, believed that skills and tactics often needed to be taught, and such men were ready to employ whatever means seemed necessary, even if these included Yakushin's blackboard.

The Dynamo tour certainly seems to have convinced Stanley Rous that further insularity would be fatal to British football. He had talked about rejoining FIFA on the day after the Chelsea match, and in 1946 the four home countries did just that. The FA was also now doing its best to encourage English clubs to travel abroad in the off-season.

Adopting the Dynamos' non-playing habits and becoming more open to foreign influences was one thing, learning to play like them was something else again. One British team – Stoke City under manager Bob McGrory – actually tried for several matches in early 1946 to adopt the Dynamo style of play, but the results were not encouraging. Over the next few years no other team announced its intention of following the Russian example, but the push-and-run style developed at Tottenham was strikingly similar. To the best of my knowledge, Arthur Rowe, that style's principal architect, never recognised any debt to the Russians, but it's possible that he first saw the light on one of those dramatic afternoons in November 1945.

Perhaps not. Generally speaking, it has to be said, the Dynamos' wake-up call to British football went unheeded. The progressive excellence of their football was plain to see, but few chose to accept the evidence of their own eyes. The list of caveats and excuses was endless. The Russians' football was beautiful, yes, but their opponents had been badly chosen. British football had been affected so much by the war, and of course the Russians had cheated: they had used their elbows, had twelve men on the pitch, been allowed offside goals. And with their special diets and their months of training in the Caucasus they had been so much fitter. British players were undoubtedly the best in the world, so how else could the litany of lucky draws and losses be explained?

British superiority had been challenged, and most of the nation went into denial. 'They left these shores and were forgotten,' Ralph Finn wrote in his history of Chelsea. 'Nothing of their teamwork and their integrated play was left for us to ponder over. They had been played down so much that they were not considered worth bothering about. It was the greatest travesty of football fairness I ever met; the most biased insularity I have ever encountered in the field of sport.'

It was a loss that didn't show up in the club accounts. Football attendances kept on rising through the early post-war years, reaching a peak of 41,270,000 in 1948–9, and this boom, like the wider economic growth of the 1950s, served to mask an underlying decline. Visiting foreign teams provided regular reminders that British football lacked tactical ingenuity and basic skills, but it was not until the Hungarians won 6–3 at Wembley in 1953 that the warning was finally heeded, and then only in the most superficial sense. After Puskas, Hidegkuti and the rest had humiliated England twice – they won the return in Budapest 7–1 – British defenders finally stopped assuming the number on a player's shirt limited him to a particular section of the pitch, but there was still no widespread adoption of a game rooted less in strength and speed than in skill and finesse.

There is something in the British character – or whatever you wish to call the ingrained prejudices which have taken root on this island over several thousand years – that has, over decades, steadfastly resented anything that threatened to dilute the vision of football as a hard physical struggle between consenting males. And that has included everything from blackboards to ball skills. British football has always had room for the runners and the tacklers and the workers, but the divinely gifted have all too often been denied what should be their rightful place at the heart of the team. Britain has concentrated on breeding football conformists, players who can be relied upon when relegation threatens, who can be trusted to batter grimly away at the most unyielding defences in the service of the nation. There has been little nurturing of nonconformists, of players who might pick the lock of foreign defences; artistic success, unlike effort, cannot be produced on demand with such satisfying regularity.

More than fifty years on from the Dynamo tour, not much has changed. Michael Owen and David Beckham are skilful players, but the men who have truly lit up the opening years of the Premiership – Eric Cantona, David Ginola, Dennis Bergkamp, Gianfranco Zola – have all been foreigners. Britain has produced its nonconformists – Glenn Hoddle and Alan Hudson spring to mind – but up until now such talents have always been strangers at the gate of British football. All too often British coaches have considered footballing magicians an unaffordable luxury, when magic, more even than winning, is what generates the golden memories. Glory, of course, is when the two go hand in hand.

The Dynamos offered proof of this: they won only two of their four games, but their style of play left a scent of magic in the air.

It wasn't just the exotic quality of the football that captured the imagination. There were also the political undertones, the controversies about the rules, the air of uncertainty which hung over everything from the date of their arrival to the composition of their team.

None of it could happen now. The world has been shrunk by telecommunications, homogenised by constant contact. Football, like much else, has been stripped of its surprises: a wonder player might suddenly emerge, probably aged about fourteen, from some remote African country, but a whole team? If the Dynamo tour of 1945 was to be re-enacted in the next millennium the visitors would have to come from outer space.

APPENDICES

1

English league tables – 4 November 1945

(These two leagues were re-formed into Divisions One and Two for the 1946–7 season)

League South

	Pl	W	D	L	GF	GA	Pts
Charlton Athletic	13	10	2	1	36	13	22
Birmingham City	13	9	1	3	37	14	19
Aston Villa	14	8	3	3	42	21	19
Wolverhampton W.	13	7	3	3	22	15	17
Derby County	13	7	2	4	28	18	16
West Bromwich Albion	14	7	2	5	40	30	16
West Ham United	13	6	4	3	21	18	16
Millwall	12	6	3	3	25	15	15
Brentford	13	6	3	4	19	11	15
Fulham	13	6	3	4	27	24	15
Chelsea	**13**	**7**	**1**	**5**	**26**	**28**	**15**
Portsmouth	13	6	2	5	28	22	14
Coventry City	12	4	5	3	17	14	13
Nottingham Forest	13	3	6	4	20	16	12
Southampton	12	4	2	6	29	28	10
Leicester City	13	3	4	6	17	25	10
Tottenham Hotspur	12	4	1	7	22	35	9
Arsenal	**13**	**2**	**3**	**8**	**18**	**33**	**7**
Newport County	13	3	1	9	14	37	7
Luton Town	13	1	4	8	15	34	6
Swansea Town	13	3	0	10	23	53	6
Plymouth Argyle	13	0	5	8	14	36	5

League North

	Pl	W	D	L	GF	GA	Pts
Chesterfield	13	8	3	2	31	11	19
Blackpool	14	7	4	3	37	27	18
Liverpool	13	7	2	4	29	17	16
Sheffield Wednesday	12	8	0	4	26	20	16
Stoke City	14	8	0	6	32	25	16
Sheffield United	12	6	3	3	28	18	15
Huddersfield Town	12	7	1	4	39	29	15
Bradford Park Avenue	13	7	1	5	23	19	15
Everton	12	6	2	4	22	16	14
Barnsley	12	5	4	3	26	25	14
Bury	13	6	2	5	21	29	14
Newcastle United	12	5	3	4	34	17	13
Bolton Wanderers	13	4	5	4	23	16	13
Preston North End	14	4	3	7	32	27	11
Manchester United	13	3	5	5	20	21	11
Manchester City	12	5	1	6	21	24	11
Grimsby Town	11	5	0	6	20	25	9
Burnley	12	3	2	7	14	26	7
Sunderland	13	4	0	9	13	38	7
Blackburn Rovers	12	3	1	8	19	37	6
Leeds United	12	3	0	9	17	34	6
Middlesbrough	12	2	2	8	13	39	5

Third North (West)

	Pl	W	D	L	GF	GA	Pts
Wrexham	11	7	2	2	21	12	16
Accrington Stanley	11	6	3	2	20	9	15
Crewe Alexandra	11	6	3	2	32	15	15
Rochdale	11	7	1	3	29	23	15
Chester City	11	5	2	4	27	25	12
Tranmere Rovers	11	5	1	5	20	22	11
Oldham Athletic	11	3	4	4	16	17	10
Stockport County	11	3	1	7	24	27	7
Barrow	11	1	3	7	12	29	5
Southport	11	1	2	8	14	35	4

Third North (East)

	Pl	W	D	L	GF	GA	Pts
Gateshead	11	8	1	3	35	17	17
Rotherham United	11	7	1	3	33	16	15
Darlington	11	7	0	4	32	26	14
York City	11	5	3	3	22	17	13
Halifax Town	11	5	3	3	28	27	13
Bradford City	11	4	2	5	24	24	10
Doncaster Rovers	11	4	2	5	20	24	10
Hartlepool United	11	3	1	7	13	24	7
Carlisle United	11	3	1	7	21	34	7
Lincoln City	11	1	2	8	18	37	4

Third South (North)

	Pl	W	D	L	GF	GA	Pts
Queens Park Rangers	14	11	2	1	41	9	24
Norwich City	12	7	2	3	42	20	16
Port Vale	13	5	5	3	21	19	15
Watford	13	7	1	5	25	31	15
Notts County	12	6	2	4	27	28	14
Northampton Town	14	4	3	7	16	26	11
Clapton Orient	14	3	5	6	15	27	11
Ipswich Town	12	4	2	6	18	22	10
Southend United	12	3	3	6	24	31	9
Walsall	12	3	2	7	15	25	8
Mansfield Town	12	2	3	7	21	27	7

Third South (South)

	Pl	W	D	L	GF	GA	Pts
Crystal Palace	12	8	2	2	30	19	18
Bristol City	14	8	1	5	35	30	17
Cardiff City	12	8	0	4	49	21	16
Bristol Rovers	12	6	2	4	27	25	14
Brighton and Hove Albion	14	7	0	7	35	38	14
Bournem'th & Boscombe Ath.	12	5	2	5	37	30	12
Swindon Town	11	5	2	4	20	19	12
Exeter City	13	4	3	6	25	26	11
Aldershot	14	3	4	7	25	44	10
Reading	12	2	3	7	24	29	7
Torquay United	12	2	3	7	14	40	7

2

Scottish league tables – 25 November 1945

First Division

	Pl	W	D	L	GF	GA	Pts
Rangers	**15**	**10**	**3**	**2**	**44**	**21**	**23**
Hibernian	16	8	5	3	35	19	21
Celtic	16	7	6	3	30	21	20
Aberdeen	15	8	3	4	36	19	19
Third Lanark	16	9	1	6	40	36	19
Heart of Midlothian	16	6	6	4	38	28	18
Motherwell	16	7	4	5	28	25	18
Falkirk	16	7	3	6	33	26	17
Partick Thistle	16	7	3	6	33	28	17
Queens Park	15	4	5	6	29	34	13
Queen of the South	16	5	3	8	30	43	13
Morton	16	3	6	7	34	39	12
Clyde	15	3	6	6	27	31	12
St Mirren	16	4	4	8	28	40	12
Kilmarnock	16	4	4	8	35	55	12
Hamilton Academicals	16	1	4	11	26	60	6

Second Division

	Pl	W	D	L	GF	GA	Pts
Dundee	16	14	1	1	58	14	29
Airdrieonians	16	9	3	4	47	31	21
East Fife	16	9	2	5	39	24	20
Ayr United	16	8	2	6	40	30	18
St Johnstone	16	7	4	5	49	45	18
Dunfermline Athletic	16	7	3	6	42	30	17
Albion Rovers	16	8	1	7	26	30	17
Dumbarton	16	7	2	7	36	32	16
Alloa Athletic	16	7	2	7	37	35	16
Arbroath	16	6	1	9	29	55	13
Raith Rovers	16	5	1	10	33	38	11
Cowdenbeath	16	4	2	10	28	46	10
Stenhousemuir	16	4	2	10	20	56	10
Dundee United	16	4	0	12	31	49	8

3

The FA's provisional selection for the representative game planned for 5 December at Villa Park

Goalkeeper:
  Frank Swift (Manchester City)

Full-backs:
  Laurie Scott (Arsenal)
  George Hardwick (Middlesbrough)

Half-backs:
  Frank Soo (Leicester City)
  Neil Franklin (Stoke City)
  Joe Mercer (Everton)

Forwards (from):
  Stanley Matthews (Stoke City)
  Raich Carter (Sunderland)
  Jesse Pye (Notts County)
  Tommy Lawton (Chelsea)
  Len Shackleton (Bradford City)
  Leslie Smith (Aston Villa)

4

The forty-five players who faced Dynamo

Joe Bacuzzi (Fulham, guesting for Chelsea and Arsenal)
Jimmy Bain (Chelsea)
Cliff Bastin (Arsenal)
Harry Brown (QPR, guesting for Arsenal)
Peter Buchanan (Chelsea)
Eric Carless (Cardiff City)
Roy Clarke (Cardiff City)
Horace Cumner (Arsenal)
Jerry Dawson (Glasgow Rangers)
George Drury (Arsenal)
Jimmy Duncanson (Glasgow Rangers)
Colin Gibson (Cardiff City)
Torry Gillick (Glasgow Rangers)
Len Goulden (Chelsea)
Jock Gray (Glasgow Rangers)
Wyn Griffiths (Cardiff City, guesting for Arsenal)
Reg Halton (Bury, guesting for Arsenal)
John Harris (Chelsea)
Ken Hollyman (Cardiff City)
Charlie Johnstone (Glasgow Rangers)
Bernard Joy (Arsenal)
Tommy Lawton (Chelsea)
Danny Lester (Cardiff City)
Arthur Lever (Cardiff City)
Kevin McLoughlin (Cardiff City)
Stanley Matthews (Stoke City, guesting for Arsenal)
Beriah Moore (Cardiff City)
Stanley Mortensen (Blackpool, guesting for Arsenal)
Marsh Raybould (Cardiff City)
Ronnie Rooke (Fulham, guesting for Arsenal)
Bobby Russell (Chelsea)

Laurie Scott (Arsenal)
Davie Shaw (Glasgow Rangers)
Jimmy Smith (Glasgow Rangers)
Fred Stansfield (Cardiff City)
Scot Symon (Glasgow Rangers)
Jimmy Taylor (Fulham, guesting for Chelsea)
Albert Tennant (Chelsea)
Willie Waddell (Glasgow Rangers)
Charlie Watkins (Glasgow Rangers)
Reg Williams (Chelsea)
Billy Williamson (Glasgow Rangers)
Terry Wood (Cardiff City)
Vic Woodley (Chelsea)
George Young (Glasgow Rangers)

5

The tour record

Tuesday 13 November
(Stamford Bridge: 85,000)

Chelsea	(2)3
Goulden, Williams, Lawton	
Moscow Dynamo	(0)3
Kartsev, Archangelski, Bobrov	

Saturday 17 November
(Ninian Park: 40,000)

Cardiff City	(0)1
Moore	
Moscow Dynamo	(3)10
Bobrov 3, Beskov 4, Archangelski 3	

Wednesday 21 November
(White Hart Lane: 54,600)

Arsenal	(3)3
Rooke, Mortensen 2	
Moscow Dynamo	(2)4
Bobrov 2, Beskov, Kartsev	

Wednesday 28 November
(Ibrox Park: 90,000)

Glasgow Rangers	(2)2
Smith, Young (pen)	
Dynamo Moscow	(0)2
Kartsev 2	

Overall aggregate: 19–9.
Dynamo goal-scorers: Bobrov 6, Beskov 5, Kartsev 4, Archangelski 4.
Overall attendance: 269,600.

Select bibliography

Allison, George *Allison Calling* (1948) Staples Press

Allison, William *Rangers, The New Era 1873–1966* (1966) Glasgow Rangers FC

Barrett, Norman *World Soccer from A to Z* (1973) Pan

Bastin, Cliff *Cliff Bastin Remembers* (1950) Ettrick Press

Batchelor, Denzil *Soccer: A History of Association Football* (1954) Batsford

Buchan, Charles *A Lifetime in Football* (1955) Phoenix House

Butler, Frank *The Art of Modern Football* (1956) Faber

Crooks, John *Cardiff City Football Club: The Official History of the Bluebirds* (1992) The author

Docherty, David *The Rangers Football Companion* (1986) John Donald

Edelman, Robert *Serious Fun: A History of Spectator Sport in the USSR* (1993) Oxford University Press

Fairgrieve, J. *The Rangers* (1964) Hale

Fishwick, Nicholas *English Football and Society* (1989) Manchester University Press

Glanville, Brian *Arsenal Football Club* (1952) Convoy

Glanville, Brian *Soccer Nemesis* (1955) Secker & Warburg

Golesworthy, M. and Macdonald, R. *The AB-Z of World Football* (1966) Pelham

Gray, Andy *Flat Back Four* (1998) Boxtree

Henshaw, R. and LaBlanc, M. *World Encyclopaedia of Soccer* (1994) Gale Research

Hugman, B. J. (ed.) *Football League Players* (1988) Arena

Jeffs, P. *The Golden Age of Football 1946–53* (1991) Breedon Books

Joy, Bernard *Forward Arsenal* (1952) Phoenix House

Joy, Bernard *Soccer Tactics* (1957) Phoenix Sports Books

Lawton, Tommy *Football Is My Business* (1946) Sporting Handbooks

Logos *Dynamo and All That* (1946) Valiant
Matthews, Stanley *Feet First* (1948) Ewen & Dale
Meisl, Willy *Soccer Revolution* (1957) Phoenix Sports Books
Mortensen, Stanley *Football Is My Game* (1949) Sampson Low, Marston
Morton, Henry *Soviet Sport* (1963) Collier-Macmillan
Oliver, Guy *The Guinness Record of World Soccer* (1992) Guinness
Riordan, J. *Sport in Soviet Society* (1977) Cambridge University Press
Riordan, J. and Peppard, V. *Playing Politics: Soviet Sports Diplomacy to 1992* (1993) JAI
Rollin, Jack *Soccer at War* (1985) Collins
Rous, Stanley *Football Worlds* (1978) Faber
Russell, Dave *Football and the English* (1997) Carnegie
Sewell, Albert (ed.) *The Chelsea Football Book No. 2* (1971) Stanley Paul
Sharpe, Ivan *40 Years in Football* (1952) Hutchinson
Sinfield, George *Soviet Sport* (1945) Russia Today Society
Taylor, R. and Jamrich, K. *Puskas on Puskas* (1997) Robson
Walvin, J. *The People's Game* (1994) Mainstream
Whitcher, Alec *Soccer Calling* (1946) Southern
Whittaker, Tom *Tom Whittaker's Arsenal Story* (1957) Sporting Handbooks
Young, Percy Marshall *Football Through the Ages* (1957) Methuen

A NOTE ON THE AUTHOR

David Downing is the author of several acclaimed works on twentieth-century history, biographies, and of fiction. The holder of a Master's degree in international relations, he has travelled extensively, particularly in Eastern Europe and the former Soviet Union. He currently divides his time between Britain and the US.

Index